FINGERPRINT

FINGERPRINT

John Sack

Random House New York

to my mother

Library of Congress Cataloging in Publication Data

Sack, John.
Fingerprint.

1. Civilization, Modern—20th century.   2. Conformity.
3. Social values.   4. Sack, John.   5. United States—
Biography.   I. Title.
CB430.S22   1983   306′.0904   82-40117
ISBN 0-394-50197-7

Manufactured in the United States of America

2 4 6 8 9 7 5 3

FIRST EDITION

Contents

1 / Happy Birthday, Dear Me

Or, The Great Dictatorship

THE moon in June. And little eels of moonlight in the Hudson River. On the left bank, my mother and father are in bed, cuddling, turning the lamp with the crewel-worked cotton shade off, the radio with the yellow celluloid dial on. To the music of

> Whispering, while you cuddle near me,
> Whispering, so no one will hear me,

a crooner on the Blue Network of NBC.

"I don't know where it is," my father whispers.

"Oh, this has to happen to *me*," my nice mother doesn't whis-per. But thinks it.

"I don't know how," my father whispers.

Far below, the newlyweds hear the horns of the river tugboats. *Shh*, let us tiptoe out to look in six hours later, when, in the motionless bed, in the right (or is it the left? my source doesn't know)—in a murky fallopian tube in Manhattan my autobiogra-phy begins. A tenth of a millimeter long and a microgram in weight—*hello*, my self at sunrise was a wet white caviar egg in whose yolk were forty-four chromosomes (a mouse has forty, a skunk has fifty, and I had forty-four chromosomes) and an *x* sex chromosome and a *y* sex chromosome: the algebra for a snip, a snail, and a puppy's tail or the raw material that a little boy's made of. And nothing else—no, there wasn't even an umbilical cord to connect me to Mommy. At this young age, I was perhaps hasty to try to do God's own miracle: to create a baby boy of this unpromising goo. Consider: I was without instructions in that lonely abdomen in Manhattan. I had none of the leaflets like in erector sets to illustrate where to put all the wing nuts, and I couldn't read one if I had one. I didn't have a headphone set on which pediatricians at mission control could tell me, "Sack, at o6oo hours commence mitosis."

"Holoblastically, sir?"

"Holoblastically."

A babe in the ever-loving woods, that was me. An innocent in that broad forest of fimbriae—a zygote, though, who understood that a trip of ten thousand miles commences with a single step. So squeezing myself like a toothpaste tube, I got those chromosomes to my mitotic equator and I put their centromeres along it. A helix inside of a helix, my deoxyribonucleic acid was a spool of wool which kittens had gotten into, but I used polymerase to unwind it at—would you believe it? ten thousand r.p.m. A yo heave ho, to the centrosomes went the chromatids of the chromosomes, and zap: I succeeded and I was two little cells. Yet even today what can I say when someone says, "You little bugger! How did you know how to *do* it?" Is it honest to answer, "It was beginner's luck" or "I had this system, see?" No, I simply *knew* it, a birdie told me—and twelve hours more and I was four little cells, and twelve more and I was eight: sixteen: a month later and I was taller, fatter, heavier by eight thousand fold. A quarter inch high, I had already made me four little thumblike limbs—a pair of arms with hands and a pair of legs with feet, which (yes, I knew in- tuitively that my feet were for walking on) had extra layers of skin on their soles like the calluses on an embryo camel's knees and the ones on an embryo warthog's wrists to kneel upon in their ex- trauterine life. I had already made me a nose which could, in time, smell vanilla in ten million parts of air, two ears whose range from the softest to the loudest sound would be one trillion times, and two eyes whose range would be one hundred trillion times: to look at the sun and to see a lit match at fifty miles. I had made myself gills in the loving memory of my ancestry: ontogeny recapitulates phylogeny and I knew it at minus nine months old. Hooray for me, I tell you! I had made me a heart that beat.

Is it presumptuous to compare myself to Coleridge, the English poet? In his *sleep* he wrote two to three hundred lines of marvel- ous poetry, though when he awoke he remembered only,

Alph, the sacred river, ran
Through caverns measureless to man,

and fifty more. Asleep, Voltaire wrote much of *La Henriade,*
Stevenson *The Strange Case of Dr. Jekyll and Mr. Hyde,* and
Dorothy Parker

> *Hoggimous, higgimous,*
> *Men are polygamous,*
> *Higgimous, hoggimous,*
> *Women monogamous.*

Tartini was fast asleep when he dreamt that the Devil was playing
a violin sonata that he—Tartini, on waking up—scribbled down
as *The Devil's Sonata.* Shall we go on? While catching some z's,
Howe was attacked by a cannibal with a spear shaped like a,
eureka, sewing-machine needle, and Kekulé was approached by a
snake shaped like a ("Suddenly, what was this?" Kekulé tells us.
"The snake took hold of its tail") a benzene molecule. A golfer,
Nicklaus, was sound asleep when he dreamt that his thumb should
go so and thereupon won the U.S. Open. All very well, I say, but I
wasn't simply asleep, I was totally zonko when I created a blessed
human being. A miracle—why, to make one little fingernail is a
job requiring a thousand words in Patten's *Human Embryology*
("The nail develops from the undertucked epithelium and the
proximal part of—")

In my ninth month, I decided (I did, though except for Hip-
pocrates the doctors had not yet acknowledged it)—I decided to
become born. Accordingly, my adrenals created a *millionth* of one
microgram of estrogen or, perhaps, cortisol—I forget, "I regret
that I was not as wise as the day I was born," Thoreau. As it
passed into my mother's womb, the white estrogen—as I had
intended—or the cortisol labilized her decidual lysosomes, which,
in their astonishment, released some of their prostaglandin syn-
thase, which, is everyone with me? converted her arachidonic acid
to prostaglandin f-two-alpha, and her contractions began. "Jack,
I'm beginning to feel it," she reported to Daddy, who, putting the
radio with the yellow celluloid dial in his 1922 sedan, was soon
driving us to Fifth Avenue Hospital in Manhattan. But the hospital room was on DC and the radio was on AC or else vice versa:

my source remembereth not, and as the doctor came up the hospital elevator my father was running to and fro, looking saucereyed. My mother's sister accosted him.

"What's wrong, Jack?"

"I'm looking for the electrician!"

"She doesn't need the electrician!"

"But the radio doesn't—"

"She doesn't need the radio!"

The doctor, Leon Loizeaux, had now taken off his black frock coat, his red-piped vest, his red bow tie, his wing collar, his shirt, his pants, and, having put on a gown, already was in his seventh minute of washing up. His very efficiency is what recommended him to my Mommy. A nurse at this very hospital, my mother used to assist at the doctors' deliveries—or tried to but fainted at the first blessed event. "*Help her*," the obstetrician cried, and the other nurses carried her to the nearest room: the labor room. My mother lay in the bed there thinking, Oh, goodness gracious, out of that little hole—a baby boy, and tears rolled down my mother's cheeks. And then the doctor hurried in, "You thought that the stork would bring it?"

"Oh no," she sobbed, embarrassed at not conversing with him as she had been taught to: arms behind her, thumbs interlocked. "It was just so *emotional!*"

At any rate, my mother knew that no other obstetrician was as intently efficient as Loizeaux, from scrubbing himself three times to thanking each of the nurses afterwards, patting each on the shoulder once. No nonsense for Leon Loizeaux! He didn't goose anyone or, like some other doctors, accompany a mother's moans with a popular song like

> *Horses, horses, horses,*
> *Crazy about horses, horses, horses,*

no: there wouldn't be horseplay in the delivery room for Mommy, who paid three hundred dollars for Doctor L.

Now, Loizeaux, who had delivered babies in Iowa in the nineteenth century, driving by horse and buggy to the farmhouses there, and who had delivered ten thousand since then (and who,

God bless him, is still alive: to your good health, doctor)—can be forgiven for thinking that he, rather than I, was creating me. In his misapprehension, he laid my mother out on a flat contraption that the *docteur* devised for Louis XIV—for Louis, a seventeenth-century peeping tom, had wanted to watch through a curtain crack, that is the honest truth. To see better too, my mother's doctor used one of these delivery tables—to lie underneath a birthing stool as I came plopping like out of a gumball machine might seem to Loizcaux inefficient as well as infra dig. And though, unlike in some other cultures, he didn't do apache dances around the delivery room or gallop in on an appaloosa to frighten the dumb little embryo out, he followed the SOP and strapped down my mother's legs, set an anesthesia mask on her face, administered ether and, as she slept unawares, cried, "Scissors!" "Sponge!" "Her blood pressure, nurse!" In the absence of air conditioning, the lights sent the temperature to one hundred degrees, and the sweat stood out on Loizeaux's brow. A nurse with a washcloth wiped it, but the sweat trickled down his legs right into his shoes until the unprecedented moment when—*waaa*, the author of this very paragraph appeared.

Oh reader! If you were only there! To see this fruit of my nine months' work—of my single-handed labor in my mother's womb! Oh, you would see me, and tossing your hat to the heavens would say, "Glory be! Two eyes! Two ears! A nose with nostrils, a mouth with lips! Ten fingers! Ten toes! He did it! He did it! He did it!"

O<small>N</small> being born in a meadow pipit's nest, a cuckoo reacts like a jumping jack and it ungratefully throws the meadow pipits out. A sea turtle crawls from its ruined eggshell, creeps to the sea beyond the horizon, inches in, and swims to Brazil a thousand miles away, and a dolphin is born underwater and at once surfaces for air. A kangaroo crawls to its mother's pouch, a possum crawls to its mother's pouch in one second flat, and a dog crawls to its mother's breast—or, at times, intuiting that it's a dog's world outdoors, tries to crawl right back in. Please credit me with puppy intelligence, reader: it was coded into my chromosomes to desire my mother too. Not only would her yellow colostrum be a perfect diet but to suck it would signal her I was out, and the afterbirth would come out too. A few seconds old and I felt, *I want my Mommy.*

Fat chance. My mother was a case etherized on the operating table: dead, I supposed. My eyes emerged from a nine months' night to startle at one thousand watts: the overhead lights, so traumatic that it still elicits tears to see sunrises in *Sunseed* or in *Orfeo Negro* or in Disney's *So Dear to My Heart* (the Atlantic, and Columbus pushing west like a sea turtle, and the sun finally shining down) or to listen to Melanie, "I couldn't see the sun 'cause the sun was in my eye," or even, sometimes, to see sun-kissed oranges. To be born under searchlights like at a world première is efficiency become idiocy—why, a *horse* has horse sense enough to foal in the barn's darkest corner. In this modern room, my ears didn't hear the lullaby of my mother's heart but the officer's voice of Loizeaux saying, *"Clamp,"* at least he wasn't like one of the hospital obstetricians and he didn't burst into

> *Yes sir, that's my baby,*
> *No sir, I don't mean maybe,*
> *Yes sir—*

thank God for small favors. His gorilla's hand grasping me, I was held upside down and—I didn't deserve it, doctor, but I was spanked and the cord which worked as my air hose, my water tube, my food funnel for practically all my life was, *aiiiii*, was sliced by the man's machete like a rock climber's rope and I thought I'd die. A solution of silver nitrate into my little eyes, a rubber catheter into my little nose, a cold clamp around the remains of my umbilical cord—oh Lord, oh Lord, one minute old and I was already a battered child. In the seventeenth century, the nurses used to use swaddled children for playing catch: that's how I felt on March 24, 1930, the sun in Aries, the moon in Aquarius, the day the honeymoon ended.

Montesquieu said, "We should weep at a person's birth, not at his death," and I know I was wailing like a professional mourner at an Irish wake. I seemed overemotional to Loizeaux, who shot some morphine into my mother's bottom, aware it would wear away by breakfast, but (the callousness of it) who never reported this to *me* as he reassigned her to her hospital room. I had been born to the only species that is immediately wheeled away, and, as her replacement, my eyes opened and I saw, *curses,* they're already there: the Authorities. All wearing white. All versed in *Williams Obstetrics.* All coming on with their scissors, sponges, stethoscopes, the essentials (in their philosophy) of all sublunary life—no, I wasn't born that day, I was drafted! *"Fall in,"* Loizeaux should have said, *"and hut, two, three, four,*

> *Jody was there when you left, you're right,*
> *Johnnie is very bereft, you're right,*

sound off, sound off!"

"*Waaa! I want my Mommy! Lemme go!"*

Objectivity. A while ago (be patient, reader, in a few minutes my sad story resumes)—a while ago, I went to Manhattan to pay another call on Fifth Avenue Hospital, or, as it's known now, to Flower and Fifth Avenue Hospitals, by strolling there on a warm morning in June. In front was its semicircular drive—I recognized it, not from my own real birthday but my sister's, three years later. The drive seemed smaller today, and the stone walls turned out to these adult's eyes to be mere concrete replicas. Alas, to think the construction crews for my little hospital were the great-great-*twenty*-grandchildren of the masons of Europe, who without any SOP not only built the cathedral walls but who chiseled the high reliefs of people collecting wood, as at Paris, or warming their feet, as at Amiens, or working their fields, as at Florence. And did the gargoyles, too.

I went inside. It was dim there except for a red neon light for a gift shop—off—a gift shop—off—a gift shop off of the lobby displaying plastic dolls for $1.98. Of the other visitors, one in red pants attracted my eye by hurling himself at a pay telephone to call the New York City Police. "Listen," he shouted into the spit-stained receiver, "I'm at Flower Fifth! I've been waiting for a patrol car all day!" His father, he shouted, was up on the seventh floor with a $55-daily nurse that he couldn't even tell, "I want an enema, please," for the nurse's native language was Hindi. So the man had gone straight to the hospital administrator.

"I want an English-speaking nurse."

"You're creating a racist issue."

"I'm not that kind of guy, really."

"I'll have you locked up!"

Or so the man in red pants shouted to NYPD, shouting that he was still waiting for an armed escort to the seventh floor and his dying father.

As for me, I rode the wide elevator to the sixth floor. And putting a yellow robe on, I went to the room where the blessed sunlight (well, the light, anyhow, and its reflections in stainless steel) first shone upon me. To be honest about it, I didn't have a sense of déjà vu. Under glaring lights, a red-bearded obstetrician was at a table, sweating, his mustache a sweat-soaked sponge, his glasses two sea-sprayed portholes, his fingers practically spastic while he filled in the hospital forms in triplicate—he had just delivered a baby, apparently. His writing, that of a doctor, was, of course, incomprehensible, but I at least read the seven hundred questions on the printed forms. For the mother,

Episiotomy: *yes* □ *no* □
Laceration: *yes* □ *no* □
Sulcus tear: *yes* □ *no* □
Cervix tear: *yes* □ *no* □
Cervix repair: *yes* □ *no* □
Anesthesia: *yes* □ *no* □

etcetera, and for her pride and joy,

Name
Number
Apgar score

etcetera, an Apgar score being like a report card for a newborn baby: a zero equaling dead, a seven satisfactory, a ten almost qualifying him for Harvard Law.

A baby itself went by me. Nude, supine in a plastic isolette, the isolette on a baby carriage of stainless steel—a ham in a supermarket cart, it was rolled to a nursery where it was *everything* except nursed, a nomenclatural mystery. It was weighed, measured, diapered, attached at its nipples to two electrical wires to a green oscilloscope and a red digital display all for, I'm sure, unassailable medical reasons, and in the oscilloscope's moon-landing light and the digital display's 98.6's the baby cried softly—for the doctors didn't have a twentieth-century pacifier, a tape of its mother's heartbeat. On its back, the baby groped like in blind man's bluff at its sterilized air: no, at its oscilloscope wires: no, at its clear plexiglass. no no no. Its arms swayed like a seaweed on the ocean floor, and its eyes stared as though it were looking for something lost: it couldn't remember where and it couldn't remember what.

I felt I remembered, though. And watching it, I was soon thinking of Goethe's song,

> *Know you the land where the lemon trees bloom,*
> *Where the oranges glow in the old orchard's gloom,*
> *Where the wind ever soft—*

It is sung by Mignon in *Wilhelm Meister's Apprenticeship*. A sad-eyed child in Germany, Mignon alludes to a utopia where even the marble statues say, "Oh, what have they done to you, poor little child?"

"Know you the land?" Mignon says to Wilhelm Meister.

"It must be Italy!" Wilhelm answers.

Not very cleverly, it seemed to me at Fifth Avenue Hospital. For even if we haven't been to Italy (or to be contemporary, to California), we know we have tarried under the lemon trees—we have basked in the breezes there. In her autobiography an American writes,

> *Where had I known it? A land of idyllic meadows, a land of melting music, a land where one's sweetest impulses broke into dancing and singing. What is the source of such preoccupations?*

The womb, the heart whispers back. "We cannot be certain what happens when we die, but," says the Freudian analyst Nandor

Fodor, "we may safely say that at one point we have been with the Infinite: at the time within the womb." Of all of the pirs, sris, lamas, swamis, roshis, rishis, yogis, and gurus whose practices lead to (quote, unquote) a new consciousness, a few understand that the consciousness is anything except new. Ram Dass in *Be Here Now*,

But way away back is a memory, as if you have tasted of something, somewhere, that's been so high that nothing you can experience can be enough.

And lest someone think it's a baby's first chocolate malted, there is an illustration, too, of an embryo in a lotus leaf—the jewel in the lotus, amen, the Buddhists would say.

Amen. In the hospital's sterile room, the child in its dry aquarium reached like a lonely anemone for its paradise lost. Of course, as I watched it I didn't infer that it had departed a rock-candy mountain where it had nothing to do—no, let all its phenomenal fingernails testify no. That isn't heaven, that's hell, as the man in the story discovered when he found himself dead and in a king's castle, a paradise where he had foot washers, shoe shiners, pants pullers, shirt putter-onners, tie tiers, tooth brushers, nose blowers, eye washers, ear waxers, hair brushers, every valet he had ever wanted, and three shifts of back scratchers, too. "Well, thanks, but I want to do something myself," the man in the story complained.

"But that's the one thing you cannot do."

"Well, I'd rather be in hell, then."

"And where do you think you are?"

No, I didn't think that a mother's womb is a sound stage for *La Dolce Vita*. It's simply the one retreat on our well-planned planet where a man is a rose that unfolds to its own imperatives: to its natural bents. The one whose law is, what's right is whatever's after a man's constitution, what's wrong is whatever's against it: Emerson, the one where a fat vernix caseosa gives a man sanctuary from what he will later call the System. The womb is the last place left on the earth where we're free.

"The one whose grace overflows: the perfect one, the newborn child," said Lao Tse. In its nursery room, I said goodbye to the perfect one in its $2,000 astronaut's suit and its plastic-protected capsule and I left Fifth Avenue Hospital. In front underneath the American flag, I was witness to a brouhaha between the red-pants-wearing man and the New York City Police. "Well, what does that mean," the man shouted as the pedestrians ran the gamut between them. "What does that mean, I caused problems?"

"I don't know," the policeman shouted. "It's something that you and him—"

"Well, why," the man shouted. "Well, why—"

"—as an individual ought to work out," the policeman shouted. "He's a gentleman and—"

"He's not a gentleman," the man shouted.

"Well, he said the same about you," the policeman shouted.

"He's not a gentleman," the man shouted, and I toddled away.

I'M writing about efficiency—oh, you didn't know? in this cunning guise of autobiography, and I must digress to Dr. Frederick Leboyer. An obstetrician in Paris, he did deliveries in the forties, fifties, and sixties at a hospital close to the Parc Monceau, the hospital on occasion phoning at two, three-thirty, and five in the morning to say there's another *bébé* due and Leboyer, ten minutes later, his pajamas off, his pressed pants on, gunning into the deserted streets in an Alfa, a knight in red armor, a twentieth-century hero. At the hospital, his bedside manner was "Who knows better? You or me?" He used anesthesia: ether, and if his patient protested he lectured her, "*Ce sont des boniments,*" "You're mad." But then one day—

And one day, Leboyer was born again: literally, at his therapist's he remembered and he *relived* the thirty intolerable hours of his ostracism from Eden. It's too much, I'll never make it, Leboyer thought. "*Que de cauchemars sont—*"

*How many nightmares came to me! I wasn't asleep, but I dreamt
I crawled in a low narrow tunnel,*

the words aren't those of Leboyer. No: they were written by Zola in *Springtime: A Convalescent's Diary*, Zola had typhoid fever then and Leboyer is seldom without a copy of *Springtime*,

> *my knees slipping into the quicksand, my forehead hitting the stone. At times, I suffered horribly and I despaired of the sand and the stones confronting me: the amount seemed immeasurable and I told myself, It will take me a thousand years—*

"The child suffers too," the therapist said to Leboyer. "What?" Leboyer said. "The child suffers too," the therapist reasserted. "Buddha said, To be born is to suffer."

A revelation for Dr. Leboyer. In astonishment, he inspected a postpartum photograph of a newborn baby. To look at, it could be coming out of a cauldron of boiling oil—of napalm in Asia, and Leboyer thought, *C'est impossible! C'est ça le Vietnam!* "His closed eyes," he has written since, "his open mouth, the head that turns, the hands that implore. Is it possible he suffers immense pain?" It is possible—yes, and Leboyer now does deliveries in a room with little light, little sound, he settles the newborn baby on its mother's stomach and he does nothing. "Do what consists of doing nothing. And order prevails," said Lao Tse. And within minutes (as against months) the joy of just being itself in a free world shows and the child smiles.

Ah, good Dr. Leboyer! I sit alone, sometimes, an old videotape in my hippocampus commences and an old anxiety seizes me—my cells themselves seem to have twisted ninety degrees and I am afraid without knowing why. If only the stars could circle east—if only the 1930's could start anew and I had your gentle hands to deliver me, Dr. Leboyer. Or if on that afternoon in March my mother simply said, "It is come," if she then made dinner, went to her bedroom, had me, and peeled an old bamboo to cut our umbilical cord, as the young mother does in *The Good Earth*. It isn't an unsound procedure—as one obstetrician says, in nineteen out of twenty cases the baby would still fall out if the mother's tied to a tree in Central Park. Alas, the moving finger writes and so, to return to the 1930's and my true adventure story at Fifth Avenue Hospital, in Manhattan, my mother was held incommunicado and I was rolled to the, *ahem*, nursery, to be measured, measured, weighed, to be found wanting, probably, to be given a serial number as a starter set in a world where my social security number would be in the millions and my driver's license (I kid you not) the quadrillions, and to be allowed to cry and cry until kingdom come. And hallelujah, the kingdom came at six o'clock in the morning as I was brought to my mother—*my mother's alive*—and as she kissed me and caressed my arms, my hands, and (oh ye of little faith) my fingers, to assure herself that I had ten. All organs accounted for—a small segment, though, of an ear wasn't there, and my mother's father danced at our bedside, saying, in Yiddish, "*Oi, mein mutters oier!*" My mother's ear!

"Bubby's ear? I never saw it."

"She wore a *sheitl*, that's why," my mother's ecstatic father said. A dark brown wig—I was one day old, and I'm translating this for *you?*

A few weeks later, I was driven to our apartment over the Hudson, was undressed, undiapered, and tenderly washed in a Bathinette (a white rubber tub on X-shaped legs) as my mother, still in her midi maternity dress, kept on cooing at me, "So who is a sweet little baby? Who is an ussy pussy? Who—" tickling me as she washed me—"Who loves you? Mommy loves you!"

"Goo!" I suppose I said. Ah, those were the days, mother mine!

I was bottle-fed. Now although breasts had sufficed for the genus *homo* for three million years, at five every morning my mother woke up, selected a half-dozen bottles, turned them on a soap-sudded bottle brush like a prayer wheel in Tibet, dipped them into a bottle sterilizer and, in fifteen minutes, extracted them by bottle tongs to replenish them with a contented cow's milk and Mead Johnson's Dextri-Maltose, and I got the holy bottles at six o'clock, ten o'clock, two o'clock, six o'clock, and ten o'clock to the vertical minute every day. Oh, those bottles came at me as precisely as passenger trains in Mussolini's Italy. I could be starving, really, my eyes rolling, my tongue lolling, my hands dragging on the blue blanket like a couple of stranded crabs in my desperate search for a morsel: a nail, a diaper pin, it just didn't matter, if I was *screaming* it didn't help if I didn't scream at six o'clock, ten o'clock, two o'clock, six o'clock, or ten o'clock as defined by the Standard Time Act of March, 1918, and as determined by Captain Freeman, the then superintendent of the U.S. Naval Observatory in Washington, D.C. And conversely: my mother had a conniption fit if fate ever intercepted her and she wasn't at her laboratory at the appointed hour. One morning, we two were delayed at the pediatrician's—we hurried out at five minutes after the magic hour as shown by the doctor's clock, the banker's clock, and the watchmaker's clock, my mother eyeing them all as we hurried to Broadway. We missed the bus, and Mommy did what she hadn't ever done in the Great Depression. Her body trembling, she waved down a yellow cab—a cab! twenty cents! why, she went to the opera itself via IRT—and bolting into it shouted out, "Riverside Drive!" Ten minutes late!

Oh merciful God! The dear sweet woman—the nurse with the liquid eyes who if someone cried in her nursery cried in concert with him. What possessed her to be like one

> *Who, blessed with tumid bosoms, hear*
> *His wailings with unfeeling ear,*

a poem by Erasmus Darwin, Charles's grandfather, and what possessed her to operate a bottling plant as a cottage industry and to put ten-cent rubber nipples into me at six o'clock, ten o'clock, two o'clock, six o'clock, and ten o'etcetera, as though her son and ussy pussy were a parking meter that is guaranteed not to turn red until all four hours are up? All right, the answer is she was possessed by Luther Emmett Holt, a doctor at Babies Hospital in Manhattan.

Now, Holt, a descendant of Ebenezers, would get to his office at eight-thirty every day and, not even saying hello, would start to work—never laughing, never smiling, never talking to a toddler except as a justice sentencing him to thirty teaspoons of castor oil or thirty days in the Tombs. On one occasion (so I've read recently) a little girl on a diet wanted just one, *uno, un*—a piece of candy for Christmas, and her mother wrote and Holt answered,

> *My dear Mrs. McIntosh,*
> *Why you should wish to make your daughter ill on Christmas rather than on any other day I fail to understand.*
> *Yours faithfully,*

Mr. McNasty. An acquaintance called him a highly efficient machine—someone, I bet, who buttered his bread with the second hand of a ship's chronometer at six o'clock every day. And biting a cubic centimeter off, he probably chewed it fifty, precisely, fifty times like the slave-state characters of Zamiatin's *We* ("Fifty is the number of chewing movements required by the law") and then swallowed it at 6:01, reporting this in his bloated diary. He himself wasn't my baby doctor—he was known to my mother for his *Care and Feeding of Children*, for Holt was a best-selling author and the 1930 equivalent to Dr. Spock. His little green book is what taught everyone in the tens, twenties, and thirties to use arithmetical tables (well, at least it didn't stipulate slide rules, as some doctors did in Boston, or concentric discs on a circular spoke as in Philadelphia) to compute the constituents of my morning milk, and to feed me these chemicals whenever the sun went through sixty degrees of its heavenly orbit—the scientific method, the doctor contended. "A child trained to eat properly can be trained to do anything else."

Or efficiency *über alles*. I do not love you, Dr. Holt, you didn't even say, "Say ahh, John," yet you profess to know more than my own miraculous organs by having annexed to your signature the first and last letters of the word mud. In fact, in his little green book the man admitted that the mortality rate is three times higher for a bottle baby than for a breast baby. The cold rate is four times higher, the skin disease rate is eight times higher, the diarrhea rate is twenty times higher. And although his inventory of what little children mustn't eat is like something out of Leviticus —no bread, biscuits, pastry, pies, bananas, raisins, prunes, celery, cabbages, cucumbers, radishes, onions, cauliflowers, tomatoes, corn, sausages, bacon, livers, kidneys, ducks, geese, pork, ham, corned beef, venison (oh Jesus, he left out the *chateaubriand*), tea, coffee, beer, wine, or candy—although he proscribed these, there are Hopis a hundred years old who as infants ate bread, biscuits, whatever, who weren't scolded as long as they didn't try to toast anything in the family fire. And

Methuselah ate what he found on his plate,
And never, as people do now,

Did he note the amount of the calory count,
He ate it because it was chow,

and lived for nine hundred years, as unknown writes in *The Best Loved Poems of the American People*.

In *fact*—as I was growing up not eating bread, a thousand miles west in Winnetka, Illinois, a doctor at a children's hospital had a really revolutionary formula. Her theory was, if infant gorillas do not need dieticians, it might be that infants of *homo sapiens* don't. On her dinner table were all the cuisines known to man, apples, oranges, pineapples, peaches, pomegranates—oh, I've lied about pomegranates but she had thirty-three dishes in all, including crackers and calves brains. At this farmers market, each of her infants (beginning at six months old) ate and ate without interference. At first, it might gnaw on a napkin, perhaps, or a teaspoon till it had learned that a spoon didn't dissolve in saliva, sampling till it had selected, say, a menu of peas, carrots, and bone marrow. To her satisfaction, the calory count of her mad hatter's banquet came to eight hundred to sixteen hundred—or precisely right, and the percent of protein ten to twenty, which is also precisely right. In six years and 36,000 meals, the babies had no diseases except for an epidemic of glandular fever but, by helping themselves to some seconds of beef, recovered fast. In fact, there was a baby there whose peculiar choice of cod liver oil at breakfast, dinner, or supper continued until the x-rays showed it had overcome a critical case of rickets—oh, you don't believe it? See the *Canadian Medical Association Journal* for September, 1939.

Myself, I believe it. While growing up, I was the house eccentric in my insistence on no sugar, thanks, on my corn flakes, and I was whispered about in dark corners of our apartment in Manhattan. My mother wondered what is it? Some sort of Jewish law? Thou shalt not eat Cuban cane? No, I just didn't *like* it—and forty years later a doctor looked at a six-hour laboratory test, and if I'd been there with a whole box of Domino he couldn't have been more alarmed. "*Do not eat sugar. Do not eat sugar,*" the doctor practically screamed at me. "*It's toxic for you!*"

I told him yes, I had known it for quite some time. A baby's a perfect being, says Oscar Ichazo. "Every person is perfect and in unity with the entire cosmos. And then something happens—"

Now where was I? Oh—one month after being born, I was one month old, or old enough for my toilet training according to Holt (and according to no other culture on earth: in fact, in practically all it wouldn't start till my second or third or fourth—*year*), and my mother consulted the little green book on the bedroom shelf. It didn't stipulate that all the tots in America do their number two at six o'clock, specifically (the simultaneity would be hell on the city water departments), simply that any Jack or Jill's bowel movements be at *exactly* the same minute every day—if six o'clock on Monday, the book insisted on six o'clock on Tuesday, Wednesday, Thursday, Friday, Saturday, and Sunday. "At first," it continued, "there may be necessary some irritation by tickling the anus or introducing inside of the rectum a small cone of oiled paper or—"

Enough! To know about the forgotten art of wax-paper pederasty, enroll in *origami* in Tokyo but don't interrogate me— I'm just a Joe who's trying to write a G-rated autobiography. So: it was spring, 1930, and I didn't know if I'd been born in America, AMERICA, AMERIKV, or some satellite of Antares or if the authorities (the stones on my little chest like the witch killing presses) led, at the capital, to Coo or Hoo or Roo, I just didn't know but I *knew* I had been delivered into a great dictatorship or, as the kids in the 1960's would say, a fascist state. A state with an a priori assumption that we are just idiot savants to be bossed, bullied, bludgeoned, to use just three of the sixty sizzling words of Proudhon, and, one more, betrayed, or we won't work correctly and in which dictators (dressed, not in black shirts but in white laboratory coats)—the great dictators wouldn't just let us be. According to Jacques Ellul, the French philosopher, I had been born in the harshest dictatorship there is: "In comparison, Hitler's was really a trifling affair."

One month old and I was the slave of Efficiency. My space and time were circumscribed by the crib's wooden bars and the clock's anchor escapement. My legs were useless: sure, but I was also handcuffed to keep me from tasting my own delicious thumbs (though my elbows weren't in plaster casts as recommended by Dr. Holt) and my mouth was a sewer sump for the A&P's ammonium phosphate, potassium sulfate, salt, and sugar worst of all. "Waaa!" I cried as my mother sought to force-feed me with spoonfuls of Junket.

"No, this is *good* for you," she cooed on the doctor's authority.

"Waaa!" I cried, convinced she was Borgia attempting to poison me.

Even today, I'll wince at the red-dyed sugar in a hummingbird's diet. Now understand: I don't disagree if I'm told there is One Best Way to do everything ("If it be to boil an egg," said Emerson) or that everyone ought to, *must*, do everything by the One Best Way. To be thrifty of all four dimensions (as well as of dimes and dollars) was our ideology even in the seventeenth century: the time of the Pilgrims. In the eighteenth century, we were exhorted to "lose no time" by Benjamin Franklin, in the nineteenth to "give account to God for all the time afforded us" by the older sister of Harriet Beecher Stowe. "Christianity," she declared, "teaches that we have no right to waste a single hour," and in the twentieth century we are still wheedled to waste not, want not, by Exxon, Incorporated. Very well, I'll grant that a sort of imperative inheres in efficiency and, by rights, that the One Best Way is really the One and Only Way. Myself, I've never boiled an egg except by immersing it in boiling water: to immerse it in boiling sauvignon is one other option that no one would recommend even in France.

But this is just common sense. It announces itself to the same intuition that, in my mother's womb, instilled me with blood instead of cold carrot juice, and in spite of its classic efficiency it doesn't derive from the Table of Chemical Elements. And that's where I do disagree with the doctors, lawyers, etcetera, who don't apprehend that we were efficient (and are efficient, still) from the time of our first mitosis. As they define it, efficiency is not inherent within us but must perpetually be imposed upon us. They insist that a man (unlike an orangutan, say) is nothing without a tough exoskeleton of locks, clocks, pocket computers, top-secret clearances, coffee, milk of magnesia, martinis, the FBI, marines, umbrellas, electric eyes, law, life insurance, cigarettes, supermarkets, superhighways, fingernail polish, pills, diplomas, telephone poles, plans, passports, aspirins, air-raid sirens, timetables, enemas, diets, air conditioners, aircraft carriers, institutions, tennis rules, the TV, table manners, missiles, signs that say do not touch, corsets, coffins—that a man cannot get to midnight without strangling on his cravat if he isn't recorded, reformed, regulated (to use some more seething words by Proudhon) and, one more, robbed, by a superstructure of principals, provosts, and university presidents, by managers, directors, and company presidents, by mayors, governors, and the president of the United States. In their philosophy, we either suffer them or deteriorate into the, quote, unquote, the dissolute condition of masterless men, a seventeenth-century phrase by Thomas Hobbes.

At one month old, I wasn't in any society but a system with the one raison d'etre, efficiency: a society is organic, a system is organized, a society is inherent, a system is imposed upon us, a society is instinctual, a system is intellectual, a society (as I use the word society) is the gemeinschaft, a system is the gesellschaft, a society's culture and a system's civilization. A society is the sum of the free encounters of the souls comprising it: a society's alive and the System of my mother country (my planet, actually) was a dead thing encrusted upon me. A callus, a cancer, that was to keep me for one half century from the sweet serenity that was my condition to March 24, 1930—to keep me from freedom, if freedom is something more than do I want A for the Anacin or B for the Bufferin. In my mother's womb, I'd been practically in a samadhi tank,

> *I within did flow*
> *With seas of life, like wine,*
> *I nothing in the world did know*
> *But 'twas divine,*

Thomas Traherne, but I now succumbed to our epidemic disease: tension, for the System had its choke holds around the life, the *prana*, the *mana mana*, the *tumo*, the *tch'i*, the me within me (the *quintessence* of me: Paracelsus) and had stoppled them up, the pus in about-to-burst boils.

It was torture, but I at least didn't die as one or two babies do—for causes unknown, according to doctors—every hour, or as the baby whose autobiography ran in *The Tatler*, in London, three hundred years ago did. On being born to this sudden efficiency,

> *I found myself in the hands of a sorceress. I cried out, but the, witch, for no provocation, takes me and makes me swallow an horrid mixture. I thought it a harsh entrance into life to begin with physic,*

but the eye-opener then was a spoonful of almond oil. Nor was the baby breast-fed, for

> *the wives of this age, for fear of their shape, forbear suckling their own. I pined away, and [I] should never have been relieved had it not been that on the thirtieth day a fellow came to visit me,*

a man who thought that the cure-all for coughs, vomits, insomnias, pimples, and (in time) impotence was an ice-cold shower,

> *upon which he soused me head and ears into a pail of water, where I had the good fortune to be drowned and so escaped being married to an ill-natured wife.*

Well, hooray for *The Tatler*, I say. It saw, at its very inception, that the quest of efficiency would end in extermination, that its one great god would be Shiva.

THE subtitle of that little green book was *A Catechism for Mothers*. In other words, questions and answers, for Holt had addressed himself to three hundred questions that in three million years no known mothers had had to ask about babies. Is it all right to sleep with them? "Never," Holt answered, having asked it. "There is the temptation to frequent nursing, which is injurious." Is it all right to rock them? "By no means," Holt answered. "It is a habit easily acquired, but a very useless and sometimes injurious one." Is it all right to kiss them? "No," Holt answered. "Tuberculosis, diphtheria, syphilis, and many other grave diseases may be communicated this way." Is it all right to play with them? "Never," Holt answered. "They are made nervous and—"

Jesus! Was there ever a Hitler audacious enough to rant against the unanimous sense of one hundred thousand generations of man? To cuddle a pink little baby is a compulsion of all woolly animals but the Frankenstein monster. And pink little babies demand it or (as the saying is) their spines shrivel up or their blood becomes bile: or they become violent in their adult life. We know that the Arapesh cuddle their babies, who, as adults, do not become violent, and the Ashanti do not cuddle babies, who, as adults, do become violent, even to throwing their spears and "*Oseye oseye oseye*"'s at horrified tourists. And though in certain societies the end result is the opposite, there only is one society where the babies cuddle, the children couple, and the adults become violent—the Jivaros, of Ecuador. And *personally*, I don't think that the Jivaros are cuddled enough—why, all day the mother is out doing weeding while the sisters sing in Jivaro,

The baby will cry, the baby will cry,
And without milk the baby will die,

or, more often, it will become a head-hunter and a head-shrinker in Ecuador. God—*gorillas* all cuddle and no gorilla in Africa was ever observed to hurt another gorilla (though it may stare daggers at one, sometimes) and gibbons cuddle, baboons cuddle, howlers—

Waaa, I say unto you! Untouched, uncuddled, what was I to say except *waaa*—in all human history, a signal to every awake (and even asleep) mother that was a sinking ship's SOS. A lament that a diaper's wet or a pin's sticking in or the complainant's alone—do something soon. As late as the early seventeenth century, all of the baby doctors said to do anything, *anything*, cuddle it, dandle it, tickle it, or Jesus, or give it Arpège if a baby should cry. Dr. Jacques Guillemeau, the surgeon to three kings of France,

> *If by chance he doth weep, endeavor by all means to still him [by] observing what may be the cause thereof: that, as Galen saith, he may have that he desireth or be rid of that which troubleth him.*

Do what comes naturally, the doctor said. Go nurse him or rock him or sing to him, *something*, or he might get a headache or even burst, the good doctor said and England agreed,

> *Hush thee, my babby, lie still with thy daddy,*
> *Thy mammy has gone to the mill,*
> *To grind thee some wheat to make thee some meat,*
> *And so, my dear babby, lie still,*

a lullaby of the early seventeenth century.

But soon there came Science and its philosophy that the earth— its rocks, its flora, its fauna—needs to be kicked until it has yielded to the One Best Way. So by the late seventeenth century, we had advice that we hadn't heard in all of our days since *australopithecus:* a book by Dr. John Locke (Locke was a doctor too),

> *Crying requires severity to silence it, and where a command will not do it, blows must, for the will must be bent by a rigor sufficient to master it. If,*

continued the great philosopher (a man who also suggested that we cut apertures in our children's shoes to let water in)—continued the great philosopher of, er, democracy,

> *if it were done without passion, soberly, laying on the blows slowly, stopping when it had made them pliant, penitent, and yielding, they would seldom need the like punishment again.*

So do it, the doctor ordered, or there will be disconcerting noise in your residence: there will be cries, screams, caterwauls, though he didn't suggest like the Duchess in *Alice* to beat every baby when he sneezes (because he knows it teases) or when he just laughs. The system of Locke, the doctors prescribed until, in a subtler form, it appeared in Holt's little catechism. A book my well-meaning mother bought for a dollar (a *dollar*, a few months after the Crash) to learn there's a cry of "indulgence" that

> *is heard even in infants, who cry to be rocked, to be carried, to suck, or for any other bad habit. How is such a habit broken? By never giving a child what he cries for.*

Waaa! Waaa! I was lying (to continue my choppy autobiography) in my $50 crib in Manhattan, no, in my $49.95 crib if I know my father well—I was lying in solitary confinement on Riverside Drive. Too uncoordinated to use my diapers as semaphore flags or my rattles as tap transmitters (in international code it's *dit dit dit dit* and *dah dah dah* and—in other words, *hold me*), I could just *waaa* as I clawed at the atmosphere full of Not-Mommy. A few years more, and I'd have been as articulate as the boy in *The Musical Box*, by Genesis, and I'd have cried out, "Touch me, touch me, touch me,"

> *Now now now now now!*
> *Now now now now now!*
> *Now now now—*

until someone understood. In the song, after twelve more *nows* the governess tosses the musical box at Henry's head, destroying him. Not quite destroying me, my mother sat as I squalled—sat at her orange basket, took out a silver needle, needed a silken thread, threaded the silver needle, needed to simply thread the (oh, my mother couldn't manage it, in her own eyes were tears, it was torture to listen to me and know on the most august authority no, I shouldn't hold him, I'll spoil him)—to thread it and sewed, sewed, sewed, until the timer reported that the potatoes were done. The steel spring, the steel wheel, the steel alarm of the timer reported, "*Waaa*," my mother jumped up to attend to it, I concluded that I alone couldn't communicate with her and I fell asleep, defeated. And after that day I didn't cry—I didn't ever.

"See, the book's right," my mother's sister told her. "He doesn't cry if he knows it won't tempt you to pick him up."

"Mm," my wet-eyed mother answered.

So (to get ahead of our story again)—so I didn't cry for forty years. To dam up those tears, my body built a white wall of intellect, my muscles pulled like a wet suit around me, my smile became a tight rubber band and my laugh the reaction to all life's occasions—dammit, it all succeeded and I was without the resource to process pain. My only recourse if pain appeared was to run away: from women, especially. Oh, Mary, Marie, Monique, Loi, Lois, Linda, Lorelle, Annie, Janet, Jackie, Joanie, Joanie, Kristi, Kristin, Kristina, Karin, Kalista, Pamela (Pam, especially you)—it was the cowardly way and I'm sorry. A life without pain is a life without pleasure, too—a life, according to Gibran,

in the seasonless world where you laugh but not all of your laughter, and weep but not all of your tears,

but I was the Dutchman caulking the cracking walls and I never cried. No doubt, I'd have died without having cried and I'd be accosted by one million dewdrops just as Peer Gynt ("We are the tears which weren't shed"), but the dam at last burst at forty years old.

I was living with a golden-haired girl in California. We had just rented a cottage (oh, sentimental me: we had rented a house but I called it our honeymoon cottage) to whose windows the raccoons would come to snatch up our loving offerings while we sat in bed and whispered like St. Francis, "Hello, raccoons, hello." In the morning, I'd wake up and stand staring down (and asking myself is this mine, is this mine) at that spiral of golden hair, and I'd wake up Nolene by carrying the stereo speakers in and putting on Melanie, quietly,

Take you an apple and take you a song,
Watch a baby day be born,

instead of letting the lady awake to a dream-destroying alarm. We had lived for a month together when the telephone rang for Nolene, her mother had cancer in Portland, Oregon, her mother had six more months and Nolene, of course, went to Oregon for the six long months.

Now, I looked at our cottage and all I saw was Not-Nolene. In the garden was Nolene not lying nude in a red net hammock, in the living room was Nolene not making an olive bargello belt, in the bedroom was Nolene not dancing with me to *Daniel* or—I just couldn't bear it, I turned the stereo off. On her dresser were a few pins, hairpins, pennies—the relics of our one month together, the residue of her earthly existence, the toe bones of St. Cecilia. I couldn't live with them and I couldn't without them, "My lady," I wrote to Oregon or tried to and suddenly burst into tears—oh, my *lady* should be beside me, I thought, I shouldn't have to correspond with her. I remembered how we had passed a movie marquee a few evenings earlier and I'd climbed up a wobbly ladder with a half-dozen letters of fire-engine red: NOLENE, the marquee was shouting soon, *Nolene*, I was sobbing now in our half-empty bed as I reached as far as my two arms could to Oregon.

For weeks after that, I kept sniffling, snuffling, or ultimately (the warm water that my eyeballs were in uncontrollably running over)—or sobbing at popular songs, "Lord, I let her slip away," or at popular movies like 1776, George Washington in his letter to Congress, "Is anybody there? Does anybody care?" It seemed to old moist-eyed me, Nolene had been someone who cared, *cared*, who had left little love-notes (photos of golden-haired lovers or gulls in the yellow sunset) or pebbles painted with an *"I care"* everywhere: and I had cared too, I cared that she was in Oregon, her mother dying and no one around to comfort her. And sobbing about it, a metaphor came to my inward eye, and I saw myself as a little boy in whose arms was an awful burden of *care:* a ton of crumpled brown paper (I had been writing to Oregon on brown stationery) for my Nolene. It was ten stories high, and I just staggered under it. Oh, take this mountain from me, Nolene!

The image changed. In my tortured thoughts, in my aching arms was a big, big, yellow bouquet that was not for Nolene but for my indelible mother, for Mommy. We, too, had met every night to hug good night, a portrait above us, a girl in whose bursting arms was a big, big, yellow bouquet for her own—*Mommy*, I cried although forty years old. *I care for you.* No, that wasn't it, *I need you, Mommy!* And zap: there was no bouquet in my now empty arms as they reached: reached: *reached* for her, and I was again in my little hermitic crib in Manhattan and, the image changing again, in my hot delivery room, for I had now abreacted (as Zola, tortured by typhoid, had) to no years old on March 24, 1930. A soggy dough, I felt I was tugged, twisted, wrested, wrenched, rammed, crammed, crushed, crashed, crunched, clobbered, batted, battered, buffeted, bashed, beaten, eaten alive (a number of words omitted by Proudhon) and processed as a prisoner was by the Spanish Inquisition. In my mind's eye, a dagger materialized to slash my umbilical cord, and as I doubled up I shouted out, *Mommy! I need you! Now now now now now!*

No response. At that coming-out in Manhattan, my source of all life, love, elation was a stiff on the hospital table: a statue of candle wax, a victim of ethyl ether, a sacrifice to the One Best Way, and I supposed I was dying too. And now once more, the horror of death congested me as I cried and I cried, as some of those forty years of tension dissolved—*tension* being the desperate effort not to let oneself cry. "And," said Philip Wylie,

> *the idea that the world's filled with big children, running businesses, driving armies, who have used their days to bury infancy within themselves, alive and screaming, is so monstrous that, were it true, societies would fly to pieces.*
> *Well?*

Well, I told my real living mother what I thought of those cocky authorities and of their cursed efficiency now—of Holt, who said a baby should cry for thirty minutes each day ("It is the baby's exercise"), of Spock, who said thirty minutes is nothing to worry about ("It doesn't hurt"), and, yes, even of Salk, who said he agrees with the early seventeenth century ("If my baby is crying, should I pick him up? Certainly. Studies have shown that if—") Who shall decide when the pediatricians disagree? The answer, oh my loving mother and all mothers, everywhere, is no one need decide anything, is you yourself know in your heart—is you yourself always knew. You never needed efficiency.

2 / Life With Father

Or, Is Efficiency Inefficient?

CLOSE to Christmas, 1930, the frost on our windows, the water on our radiator cocks, my mother crouched in our living room in Manhattan and reached out her reassuring arms, "You can do it, John," my mother said. "You can walk!" She didn't use her expertise as a white-hatted nurse by instructing me, "Now tense the left iliacus as you relax the left gluteus maximus and as you balance yourself on the opposite planta like the Hermes of da Bologna." If she had, I think I'd have *crashed* into one of her whatnots and its copper-luster cups and its other treasures of Tut—either that, or fallen flat on the floor like the noted centipede, the one that fell, confounded, in the ditch at "Pray, which leg comes after which?" I was, after all, not one year old (and was just propped up by a pair of white shoes, white socks) as I used intuition to do what other *hominidae* couldn't do with their shaggy legs for ten million years: to let my feet toddle to Mommy. "How did you manage them?" I hear someone say, and I must answer as another centipede did in another poem, by Chuang Tsu,

> *I do not manage them.*
> *They land everywhere*
> *Like drops of spit,*

but they landed accurately, and I went straight to my mother's much-wanted arms. "Wonderful! Wonderful! He *walked* today," my proud parent said as my father came home.

"How far?" Daddy asked her.

"I don't know, Jack," Mommy answered him. "From there to, oh, about there."

"Six feet six," Daddy said after setting a spring-driven steel tape on the rug and scribbling this on a square-ruled yellow pad.

My father was an efficiency expert. His fate (and the cause of his fatal flaw) was his coming of age in the early 1910's in the course of a fad, furor, madness, what will I call it? a real religious revival for efficiency. But even then with trolley cars on Broadway, the philosophy that we were dismally inefficient if left to our own devices was a couple of centuries old. In the late seventeenth in Paris, de la Hire had used mathematics to demonstrate that a gondolier ought to *pull* not *push* on his oar in Venice: if, for instance, a gondolier were to lean at seventy degrees,

the sine of seventy degrees is to the sine of its complement as three is to one, approximately, and all of his strength is reduced to just twenty-seven pounds,

de la Hire explained in a monograph (ignored by most gondoliers) in the *Memoirs of Mathematics of the Académie Royale des Sciences*. That long ago, he had intimated that we are reeds, indeed, that we are made out of matches which must be glued and be guy-wired or we will topple over.

A little history now. Coulomb, in the eighteenth century, computed that we ought to go upstairs with a load of 116 pounds—a pound less (or a pound more) would be the second best way, and by nighttime we ought to have carried a total of 864 foot-tons of watermelons, whatever, though to carry the same melons *down* is the second best way to just dropping them. The mid-eighteenth century had the first efficiency expert, too, in Paris. A watch in his manicured hand, he calculated that to make twelve thousand pins a man needed twenty-four hours—or two for the pinpoints, ten for the pinstems, twelve for the pinheads, or (*tick tick tick tick tick tick, ouch*) seven seconds per pin. Or efficient enough, though we can assemble pins in one sixteenth of a second today by replacing a two-thumbed man by an F. W. Buendgens Machine.

The first person on an assembly line (a line, rather, for the *disassembly* of slaughtered hogs) was in the mid-nineteenth century in Cincinnati. Once every thirty seconds, he hit a hammer on a hog's head to render it more compliant to the head chopper, the heart chopper, and his other confederates. In everyone's ear in that blood-splattered room was an incessant chop-chop-chop,

"One feared that the walls must give way or the ceiling crack," said Sinclair in *The Jungle*. "It was too much!" At the very least, it was more clamorous than the kitchen (according, again, to Chuang Tsu) of China's Prince Wan,

> *The cleaver sighed*
> *Like mild winds.*
> *Rhythm! Rhythm!*
> *Like ancient tunes.*
> *The ox fell apart*
> *With whispers.*

But there, the oxen chopper followed the Tao and his own six senses, not the One Best Way.

By the twentieth century—by my father's day, we had practically no senses left, and the efficiency experts took it upon themselves to tell us when, where, and *how* to do all the two-handed deeds in God's creation. A bricklayer boss in Boston was cornered once by Gilbreth, the efficiency expert who is portrayed in the Late Late *Cheaper by the Dozen*. "Notice," Gilbreth said. "No two men use the same way of laying bricks."

"If you open your mouth, I'll lay a brick in it," the boss retorted according to Gilbreth's biographer.

"It's important," Gilbreth said. "If one bricklayer is right, then all the others are wrong."

"Stop bothering me," the boss continued. "Or this brick goes in your mouth, edgewise."

Far from deterred, Gilbreth for three more years was a bricklayer-watcher until he could lay in not eighteen but in four and a half efficient steps, and he listed them in a book whose forthright title was *Bricklaying System*. *One*, he seized the nearest brick in his one left hand and the mortar—in the metal trowel—in his other hand, *two*, he pivoted like a T-formation quarterback as, *splat*, without stopping, he threw the wet mortar at the wall, *three*, he didn't spread it, stupid, he threw it just perfectly and he clapped on the breathless brick in one half second, *four*. In time, Gilbreth was laying in ten not thirty seconds (in his haste, he fell from a scaffold and he broke both of his ankle bones) and was telling his own construction crews to lay by the one, two, three, metronome, or they were fired.

Now talk about slave labor! No one, not even the pharaoh, commanded the four thousand masons at Giza to pivot counter-clockwise ("𓈖𓏤𓂋𓂝𓏏𓏲𓏏𓏥𓏏" or "You aren't serious," the masons would have said) and the king didn't tell the masons at York to *throw* the wet mortar at the cathedral there or, indeed, to do much more than to stay awake ("It es ordayned yt ye masonns sall be at yaire werke and yai sall noght slepe") except for a half hour every day in June and July. Until the twentieth century, we had been bricking our *domos, domus,* and home sweet home as a method of self-expression, sort of like sewing samplers, until we were strung up like puppets by Gilbreth's *Bricklaying System,*

If tapping is necessary, tap one tap instead of several light taps.
This reduces the operation to one half second,

and the buildings went up like beanstalks when a bricklayer's work was as choreographed as a man's first lesson at Arthur Murray's.

"If a man won't do what is right, *make* him," said Frederick Winslow Taylor. The greatest of our efficiency experts, in the early twentieth century he went around saying, "No, *this* is the way to do it, no back talk now!" His philosophy was, the one best way to do anything—to go and shovel coal, say—is a rule that reveals itself to the stopwatches of the diligent engineer. One winter day, he did retain one at M.I.T. to shovel coal in the cellar—in the engineer's cellar—until the man calculated that the coal soared into the bin at six m.p.h. and, accordingly, that he had shoveled it at 212 foot-tons per day. Taylor had other questions, though, and the assiduous man at M.I.T. was still digging like the seven dwarfs (and was timing himself with a $20 stopwatch, penning in the split seconds on square-ruled pads) in April. "Have been overworked lately," he wrote to Taylor in May. "My hair turning gray," he wrote to Taylor in June. "I have been thinking matters over, and," he wrote to Taylor in February of the following year,

in justice there ought to be some conclusion to our undertaking.
I have felt that I have been going to the limit of my nerve,

and the man underlined it, the *limit* of my *nerve*. No matter: for Taylor had other shovelers in Pennsylvania and had computed that a shovel's proper load is twenty-one and a half pounds, not a half pound more or a half pound less of anthracite or bituminous coal.

In time, Taylor was called to the marble halls: to Congress, to testify on (among other things) the science of shoveling coal. His starched shirt a Carcassonne and his celluloid collar a battlement, he sat down before the special committee of the House of Representatives. "Now gentlemen, shoveling is a great science," he said under oath.

"Ha ha," the committee laughed.

"You may laugh," Taylor continued. "But gentlemen, the one right way is to press the forearm against the upper part of the right leg, and," he testified as his invisible shovel dug in the crimson carpet, "to *throw* your body on the shovel like this. Any of you who don't know this, try it."

"I am interested in your forearm," the committee chairman said.

"Yes sir," Taylor said.

"I wonder whether you had any consideration in your investigation to the direct application of—"

The questions ended at ten in the evening, and Taylor left for his ornate room at the New Willard Hotel. There, he pulled out the dresser drawers, he stacked them at the bed's headboard, he added on one dozen pillows from the wide-eyed maids and, his pajamas on, he crawled into the new improved bed to fall asleep like a dead indian, sitting up—the one best way to guard against his incessant nightmares. At the hospital three years later, he would wake up, wind up his watch at four-thirty in the morning and die, the greatest efficiency expert in America.

"**E**FFICIENCY," said the committee to the go-go author of *Bricklaying System*, Gilbreth, "has become sort of religion with you."

"Yes sir," Gilbreth testified.

And truly, it was the new religion of the early 1910's: a fad, furor, madness for its total implementation in the home, school, church (and yes, the baby doctor's office) as well as the coal company. A woman's home is one more factory, we were informed in magazines like the *Independent:* "To lose ten minutes is to reduce the day from par to ninety-eight percent." To string a string bean in two swift seconds, we were directed to sing some song in two-four time, like *Rufus Rastus Johnson Brown*, or four-four time, like *Ida, Sweet As Apple Cider*, "The shelling of peas, on the other hand, could be to a count of three-four time." The meal must be at exactly, *exactly*, the same minute on Monday, Tuesday, Wednesday, Thursday, Friday, Saturday, and Sunday, and the one best way to scrape the plates afterwards is to

have a paper napkin, daintily crumpled [in] the right hand, lift the plate with the first and second fingers of the left hand, and—

And this should be *booked* on a square-ruled pad as many as five years ahead and in fifteen, five, or (I kid you not) one-minute intervals, we were instructed by Mrs. Gilbreth. Her husband, Gilbreth, had already died of a heart attack, saying, "I had an idea for Lever Brothers."

In school, too, we must capitulate to the One Best Way, a superintendent told the National Education Association in Philadelphia. In language classes, he had computed that it had cost four dollars (and three and a third cents) for Greek for every dollar for French. "I know nothing," the man admitted, "about the absolute value of Greek compared with French: however, the price must go down or we shall invest in something else." As for church, it was business too, a man of the cut-rate cloth said in Chicago, and the jesting editors of the *Nation* ran the square-ruled calendar of a new-age clergyman,

9.30. *Visited the fatherless.*
10.27. *Bound up the brokenhearted.*
11.03. *Spoke to ten patients. Offered three prayers.*
12.15. *Lunch,*

as the man of God computed that he had been ninety-seven percent efficient.

In these early 1910's, the Vatican of the new religion was the Efficiency Society of Manhattan, and its fanatic president was Dewey (or Dui, he sometimes spelled it with sixty percent of the printer's ink)—not the admiral, the philosopher, or the governor but the inventor of the Dewey Decimal System. If you ever wondered, he had invented it while listening to a sermon at Amherst, explaining, "I came near shouting eureka. The proverb said simple as *abc* but simpler than that was 123." And not just for literature: on his square-ruled pads, he listed the thirty constituents of his own routine,

> *rise early*
> *breathe deeply*
> *eat slowly*

up to his ten thirty bedtime: then, he scored himself in each category on a scale from zero to nine, quite like the Apgar score at the Fifth Avenue Hospital. For instance: in indian summer he had resolved to sing every day *(Rufus Rastus,* I suppose) and he scored a nine every day in that happy category. He resolved to go riding and, in one yellow-leafed week, did it and scored a nine every day but Friday and also resolved to make love to Annie, his wife, scoring a nine on Monday and, for a reason that's lost in history's mists, an eight on Thursday. On the weekend, he worked out the averages (for his *rise early*: nine) for his seven days. In the 1910's, there was no one except for Himmler (who would enter the day, hour, and *minute* on all his correspondence, even on birthday cards) as efficient as Dewey, who, however, scored a four in his *commit to writing* category.

And *meanwhile,* my father (no, I haven't forgotten him) was age eighteen in Manhattan. One day there, he woke, washed, and dressed in his father and mother's tenement in the most crowded community in existence: the Lower East Side, in second place was Bombay, in third was Calcutta. On the fire escape, his brother was still asleep while he rolled up his left shirt sleeve like a heroin addict to attach a black leather box (in which on a white kosher scroll was a snippet of Deuteronomy) to his left upper arm. As ordered, he didn't fart or fall asleep while he wrapped the black leather strap into the שׁ -shape, the ר -shape, and the י -shape—

the three leather letters of God's quite cumbersome name, and, Prometheus bound, his cap, his shawl, and his thing like a third eye on his balding head, he looked like a man in a straitjacket when (for the two thousandth time) he turned to his mandatory prayers. "ברוך אתה ה אלקינו מלך העולם —oh, the hell with it," he shouted, or something, and I say hooray for my Daddy for catching the first ship to Panama.

To that half-built monument, the Canal. A few years before, our target date was the twenty-second century, and the head engineer was a man whose effects included a coffin to return to America in. But now, we shoveled up one hundred thousand cubic yards every day—a pharaoh's pyramid every month, and at sunset over the Caribbean, *sic*, the only topic was "How many cubic yards today?" It was even reported there, the captain of the dirt-digging ship the *Gopher* had slipped on a line, fallen overboard, knocked himself out on a clappet (a clapper? a crapper? it isn't in my *Webster's*) and, upon coming to one week later, said, "How many cubic yards today?" To my father, to escape from the black leather box (and the other do's and dont's of his sunless dungeon) to the wide, wide, efficient world was to participate in a second exodus: in freedom, or so he hoped.

He was at sea eight days to Panama. In his gray felt hat (he hadn't taken his yarmulke) he got off at Colón and went straight to the admin building, saying, "I want a job down here."

"Bully! Go get yourself a shovel and—"

"Thank you, sir!"

"And shovel up twenty-one and a half pounds at Miraflores."

Well, I wasn't there and I made that up. My father, though, was a canal-maker in Colón, a brick-builder in Boston, an I-wonder-what in Vienna, and, all through my childhood, an efficiency expert at Davega's, an outlet for golf, tennis, table tennis, billiard, and bowling balls in Manhattan. In that capacity, he didn't dress in a sweat suit: he dressed in a gray woolen suit (and in gray-rimmed glasses) to sit at a well-chipped warehouse desk and, by the pallor of one gray fluorescent light, to put thousands of little 123456789 and o's—to put these larvae on square-ruled pads to calculate that to get bowling balls, say, to Manhattan, the most efficient way was via sea. From dockside, he had them delivered by trucks with a timer (*tick*, it registered that it had stopped at a coffee shop) and had them displayed under a gray fluorescent light, the most efficient light. And *most* efficient if it just wasn't on—

> *When not in use,*
> *Turn off the juice,*

he insisted, though the most efficient way of turning on a fluorescent light is not ever turning the damn thing off. He worked until six and, stepping out to a crowded coffee shop for a 25-cent tuna, a 10-cent roll, a 5-cent coffee (the food coming out of a narrow hole in the kitchen wall) and a 40-cent check, he ate in ten quick minutes to return to his chip-chopped desk to write *forty cents* on a square-ruled pad and to calculate till it was ten on the dust-covered clock.

Another day. And turning off the fluorescent light, he went outside to his old 1922 jalopy. The odor of toasted dust was in his upholstery as *arrrrr*, as *arrrrr*, as he started to put-put-put to a new four-bedroom home in Larchmont, the moon an old faded button as seen through his yellowed windshield. At the gas station, a pale gray nebula, he bought just a dollar's worth while he scratched the day, time, mileage, and *one dollar* onto a square-ruled pad—a few more lightless miles and he scratched in *ten cents* while tendering this to the faceless man at the bridge going out of Manhattan. Go, for five seconds he would accelerate, *slow*, and for five seconds he would coast to use fifty percent of the gasoline that a man whose foot was a lead weight on the accelerator would: a fallacy, actually. My father was (and I must admit it) a quite inefficient expert, and it wasn't efficient to go, slow, go, slow, go to Larchmont at a hop-frog's gait in the lonely night. On reaching our unlighted home (unlighted, as I was asleep with my panda, my sister with her betsy-wetsy doll, my mother with no doll whatsoever)—on reaching home, the head of our sound-asleep household went to the "sunroom" though the ink-black night was a drape of funeral crepe over the six French windows. He pressed a red button and, *zzz*, like gnats in the night the fluorescent light on his leather-topped desk went on as, sitting down, he tiredly took out a square-ruled pad. In his 123's like wriggling things on a microscope slide, he put every cent he had spent that day,

Times.....05
Tribune.....05,

he added up these microbes and subtracted their total from the balance the day before. And counting his pocket money out, he muttered *dammit* when he discovered that he had less (or more, sometimes) than he mathematically ought to. So once more he added—anyhow, it would be two in the morning when he fell asleep in the sunroom, sitting up. Efficiency.

He awoke with a start at seven, generally. Now, Gilbreth had shaved like a two-gun gunner with a shaving brush in his right hand and a shaving brush in his left, saving seventeen seconds, he had dressed in a three-piece suit and had buttoned his vest up—buttoned it *up*, not down, saving a total of four seconds every day or one eight-hour day in his indefatigable life. My father shaved with a one-handed, two-bladed razor—he patted his talcum on, and, though he was almost bald, he also arrayed a few gray hairs like the pale blue lines on his writing pad. He dressed in a three-piece suit and ate at seven-thirty, telling us, "Dammit, I'm late."

"Daddy," I'd say, perhaps, for I was now six years old. "Do you know what this is? Ilh flsthrp?"

"Dammit, where is the butter dish? I'm late!"

"They told it to us on *Tom Mix*, Daddy," I'd say.

"Jack? It ought to be somewhere there," my mother would say.

"It isn't here, dammit! Oh, here it is!" And pulling the butter dish out of the melon ballers, the grapefruit cutters, the cherry pitters, the time-savers like the kachina dolls at some indian altar, he started to butter his Wonder Bread.

"I'm glad you've got it, Jack."

"I figured it out with my Tom Mix Decoder, Daddy. It's—"

"I don't have time! I'm late!"

Oh Daddy! Dear Daddy! In retrospect, I doubt if I'd say that your threescore years and ten constituted the Good Life. Nor would my Daddy say so, nor even concede that he could attain it at that stage of man's ascent. In his eyes, he was still in his hated tenement: no television, technicolor, credit cards, and it befell him (his whole philosophy went) to persevere on his inhospitable orb so as to bestow on his children and on his children's children a world which works.

Now, I don't know about that. It sometimes seems that the world which works is God's old obsolete one, not the efficient one of the *après*-seventeenth centuries. For instance, let us consider my father's daily bread. For six thousand years (we still have some scraps of bread from the stone age) it had served as our staff of life: in pyramid times, the people of Egypt were *"bread-eaters"* because of their eating nothing but, and the grain goddess of Greece, I'm told, was the sister of Zeus. Nor was that bread an embarrassment to the epicures then—no, not according to Petronius ("It is good for my bowel movements, too," he wrote in *Satyricon*) or Pliny, who wrote of such variations as oyster bread. No one, though, wrote of *efficient* bread, for it took more time to concoct than a newborn baby: to begin with, it took nine months for the flour in its flour barrels to age and turn white. For according to Shakespeare in *Troilus and Cressida,*

> *"He that will have a cake must tarry the grinding."*
> *"Have I not tarried?"*
> *"Ay, the grinding, but you must tarry the bolting."*
> *"Have I not tarried?"*
> *"Ay, the bolting, but you must tarry the leavening—"*

and (according to Shakespeare) you must tarry the kneading, the oven-heating, the cake-baking, and

> *"—nay, you must stay the cooling, too, or you may chance to burn your lips."*

In the seventeenth century, though, we learned that a loaf of bread is a six-sided polyhedron of carbohydrate and we got faster at making it.

We got efficient. We didn't wait (or sit rolling butter balls) as the flour turned white—no, we just whitened it with plaster, an ingredient that a man wouldn't add in Egypt or he'd have been nailed up by his ears, quite literally, or in Europe in the middle ages or he'd have been hung in a baker's gallows: a basket that he had to jump from into the mud. In the eighteenth century, we added plaster and also chalk, copper sulfate, potassium aluminum sulfate—an emetic, unfortunately—quicklime, lead, and can you believe it? the bones of the dear departed or, as an English pamphlet called it, *Poison*,

> The charnel houses are raked to add filth to the food of the living,

an act that anticipated the food in *Soylent Green*. To be sure, another pamphlet rebutted that to bake bone-bread is an English tradition,

> Fe, fa, fum,
> I smell the breath of an Englishman,
> Be he alive or be he dead,
> I'll grind his bones to make me bread,

but nobody called it traditional to add embalming fluid to milk, another procedure of the efficient eighteenth century.

For six thousand years, the second step at the baker man's was to add milk, yeast, sugar, salt, and shortening and to slowly, *slowly*, as if we were masseurs, to create a cream-colored dough, until in the nineteenth century we were efficient at kneading, too. No hands, Mommy: we set a devoted team of dogs (chowchows, perhaps) on a treadmill until the snow-white flour and the milk, yeast, sugar, salt, and shortening couldn't tell up from down and a dog whistle blew. For six thousand years, it was step three to wait overnight as the dough rose, but in the nineteenth century we used soda water instead of yeast and pff! the dough rose in one moment like an automobile's inner tube. But baked, the stuff used to bounce on a man's lower molars ("It isn't bread at all," someone wrote) and to taste no more agreeable than a foam-rubber sponge, so we supplanted the soda water with carbonated wine.

And now it's the twentieth century! All aboard, everyone, for a cook's tour to a one-block bakery of Wonder Bread! A warm aroma that's redolent of the side streets of Paris accosts us, but don't anticipate anyone in a mushroom hat or a child at the oven, caroling,

> *Pattycake, pattycake, baker man,*
> *Bake me a—*

No! To go through the steel-sheeted door is to see wet-with-sweat employees in *helmets* (a pan can plummet off the conveyor belt and can brain someone) and in those earmuffs of airport personnel as, *ring*, the ring of the bells spells trouble, *honk*, the honk of the horns implores the repairman, and *clank, clank, clank*, the staff of life clanks on its crazy conveyor belts at 150 loaves every minute. My friends, I've been to Detroit: to River Rouge, and I've heard nothing there as loud as at Wonder Bread.

I said Wonder Bread! In the midst of this 1812 overture are the pneumatic tubes for the three tons of flour every hour. It's white as white sugar after its chlorine rinse (in the thirties, we used trichloride until we learned that it causes hysteria) and the removal of its brown wheat germ, an act that could call for the baker's gallows in the retarded middle ages. The germ (with ninety percent of the vitamins) is too much alive not to suffer here—to spoil, and the manufacturers use it for hog food, instead, or unload it on Mr. Kretschmer. "Kretsch!" I can almost hear them cry. "Hey, whattya want the wheat germ for?"

"To market as Kretschmer Wheat Germ."

"No one'll buy it, Kretsch! It's brown as a horse's manure!"

"Well, brown is beautiful, man."

At that factory, the wheat and the milk, yeast, sugar, salt, and shortening go through so many rounds in a 110-volt kneader that a sixth ingredient has to be frantically added—a bromo (well, a potassium bromide pill) so the dough won't collapse in the baking pans, an instant victim of KO. No matter: the slaphappy stuff has a hot hour in the dough-rising oven, a hot twenty minutes in the bread-baking oven, an R&R in the cooling room, a ride on the crazy conveyor belt (oh goodness, a red alarm: a traffic jam, and it advances to full speed ahead) and the end result of this *sturm und drang* is sliced and is wrapped in the friendly ▐▌ ▐▌ ▐▐▐▐▌▐▌ ▐▌▐▌s and the red and blue polka dots that we can identify from the other end of the A&P. Pale, white, pallid, and, in words of one syllable, dead, the bread is a triumph of total efficiency that (oh, the paradox of it) is inefficiency, really, for it's without redeeming value to our intestinal tracts. We buy it on Monday and it's still factory fresh on Friday. It isn't moldy—no, for even the germs wouldn't eat it. Wonder Bread.

Which (to continue) my father the earnest efficiency expert was buttering up in our breakfast room in Larchmont. Or, perhaps, was it Bond Bread?

"I'm late, dammit, where's the jam?"

"I'm just about to get it, Jack," my mother said on this characteristic day. "Do you want the strawberry jam or—"

"I don't care, dammit, either one!"

"I think you'll like the strawberry jam," my mother assured him. And came from the kitchen bringing a jar, unscrewing the top.

"I haven't all day to wait around for the jam! I think if I chiseled a hole in the kitchen wall—"

"Oh Jack. Not another hole."

"Now dammit, you're always against me! If there were a hole, there wouldn't be a lousy one-hour wait for the jam! You just could push it through—"

"Oh Jack."

"Oh Jack! Oh Jack! I won't listen to your nagging me, I'm going to do it on Sunday!" And saying this, my father tossed down a coffee as though he were splashing on after-shave and he dashed to his dusty automobile and Davega's.

I had been eating my corn flakes. To have eaten the box, instead, as every sensible mouse will do (and why not? the box is the higher-priced part)—to have eaten the red letters KELLOGG's would be more nutritious but I was eating the flakes, instead, thinking, Oh, one more hole! I hope I won't have to help him! I wasn't happy—no, I was scared when my father summoned me on Saturday or Sunday, "John! Where are you, John!" It never meant get a catcher's mitt (a mitt would be two dollars wholesale, but I was never offered one)—it never meant get a softball, son, it meant get a flashlight and be some statue of liberty for ten, for twenty, for ("Dammit—don't move it") thirty whole minutes while the ambitious head of our household tried to embed a few more percents of efficiency into us. A hammer (oh, please don't hit me, Daddy, I thought) in his right hand and a chisel in his other hand, he always started (and often finished) by cutting a horrid-looking hole in some innocent wall. A hole for fluorescent lights in whose pallor we practically lived in a shirtwaist factory— a hole for the light switches and for the red-eyed reminders that the attic or cellar lights were on ("*Turn out that light*," my father would call like the father in *Long Day's Journey*). A hole for the plumbing pipes or—holy cow, it seemed that he wouldn't be content until he had sacrificed every wall of our well-loved home to camp in a whole quarter-acre hole. A hollow where he would sit in the sun (under a quilt umbrella, perhaps) in the assurance that he could commence construction at Go.

And truly, I don't remember when we didn't live in a setting of horrid-looking holes. Our home practically merited a purple heart because of my father's and Murphy's Law: *Anything that can go wrong, will*, like the hole in the kitchen wall for my mother's strawberry jam. On the weekend, my ill-starred father and I did indeed chisel a hole wide enough for a pizza pie—we chiseled it and found that it framed the drainpipe of the toilet bowl on the second floor. "Oh dammit, I need some elbow joints," my father said, he obtained them at Sears and rerouted the meddlesome pipe on the weekend after. And double dammit—it clogged, the out-flow didn't get by the right-angled elbows, on the second floor the bowl overflowed, the dirt dripped into the breakfast room and my breakfast cereal, and I died from hepatitis—no, I exaggerate. My father bandaged the kitchen wall (in his term, temporarily) with a few hairy squares of Celotex and returned to a long-forgotten hole in that tortured room. For fluorescent lights.

"God dammit! Who has the BX cable?"

"I don't have it, Daddy," I cried.

"Why not? You know where it is!"

"I looked—"

"It's down on the ping-pong table!"

"I looked and I didn't find it, Daddy," I cried.

"You didn't look!" And shouting this, the hammer-holder went to the cellar (or as he called it, the rumpus room) to root in the rubbish heap on the ping-pong table—the wires, water pipes, rubber hoses, clotheslines, wooden slats, and the last several years of the *New York Sun* and its cherished column on *First Aid to the Ailing House*, an obstacle course for a ping-pong ball but a void of BX cable. His saliva showed as he shouted, "It isn't here!"

"I told you so, Daddy!"

"So dammit! What did you do with it?"

But bless him, I say, for the man was a dreamer of the impossible dream, a Quixote on whose silver chisel were the words: erase inefficiency everywhere. It wasn't enough for my father to tap-tap-tap on the aching walls and to gouge out a two-floor model home on one maple-shaded lot in Larchmont—no, his daydream ran to the water's edge in Manhattan and even beyond it to Washington *und morgen die Welt*. In this kingdom come, he wanted to wake up at seven on Monday, Tuesday, Wednesday, Thursday, and Friday and, his appetite satisfied by the strawberry jam, to hurry out to a tear-shaped car and, *presto*, to press on the red DAVEGA switch and to whoosh away like an invoice in a pneumatic tube. He would read the *Times* as this bullet brought him to the big glass bubble over the snowproof, rainproof, dewproof island of Manhattan and, *whoosh*, to his lobby, popping him as a toaster would to his swivel chair on the forty-fourth floor. And there he would sit in ultimate bliss as his 123456789 and o's danced on his calculator in white fluorescent lights—ah, this was paradise enow. A promised land he was lucky enough to see (in a miniature model) at the 1940 world's fair in Queens.

The Futurama! I was ten years old, but I can remember the hot afternoon that my brow-mopping father put his old hammer away to drive to it. One hour's wait with a chocolate cone and we plopped on some armchairs for a sort of sidewinder's slide into an air-cooled tunnel of love—whatever. "Now," called a voice from the armchair wings, "we have arrived in this wonder world of

1960. Sunshine, flowers, flowing streams, the things wrought by God are unchanging. But what wondrous improvements—" And going into a U-turn suddenly, there was a light and we peered at a wondrous thing: an apple orchard of that faraway year, 1960, a bell jar on every apple tree to insulate it from apple aphids and apple worms.

"John! Oh, look at those apple trees!"

"I'm looking, Daddy," I said, but I wasn't thrilled with them. I don't know why—I may have heard an old popular song in my inner ear,

> *Playmate! Come out and play with me!*
> *Climb up my apple tree!*

I never played when I was ten (I looked for the BX cable, instead)—I hadn't time to climb but I still didn't like the paraboloids over the many-limbed apple trees. I didn't know it, but analogous thoughts came to E. B. White of *The New Yorker*, who, upon seeing the off-limits orchard, asked where will the little children climb? And where will the little birds nest? Two hard questions that we were asked in the real living 1960's by Cat Stevens, "Where do the children play," and Joni Mitchell, "Leave me the birds and the bees, please."

And slither: at our serpent's pace, we went by those shrouded trees to a tall-towered city ("The city of 1960 has abundant sunshine, fresh air, and—") and I still wasn't carried away. In the absence of hopscotch squares, it appeared no more frolicsome to inhabit than to chisel out on a Saturday or Sunday. It wasn't especially apt to ring to the laughter of little children—oh, well, there was a roller coaster full of (the voice in the armchair alleged) of boys and girls shrieking with glee. But somehow a one-minute ride on a roller coaster (as against roller skates) was so—*foreseeable*, as scornful of our sudden urges as a car that catapults us to the forty-fourth floor. In this miniature model, we had built us a world like a grandfather's clock, and it ticked and it tocked sixty times a minute, indifferent to showers, sunshine, sorrows and joy. A world that's without surprises is one without laughter, too—a man who can re-create creation is a god after that, and (as we're reminded by Archibald MacLeish) the God of our testaments is not susceptible to surprises and he never laughs,

If God should laugh,
The mare would calf,
The cow would foal—
Diddle my soul,

no, in our wonder world we were as grim-visaged as Jehovah. But that world itself—it was immaculate of all imperfection or, in the words of our armchair wings, was "Strange? Fantastic? Unbelievable? Remember, this is the world of 1960! Here is—"

"Just twenty more years," my lip-licking father said. "Just twenty more years."

He didn't make it. Six months before the millennium came, he was constructing a hole between the breakfast room and the living room (for the TV: the set would sit in the pantry next to the corn flakes to cast situation comedies at us)—he was chiseling this and he suffered a heart attack. "Oh, I've got this pain," he cried, and was driven down to Manhattan in the hot old jalopy. In the hospital room (a few corridors from my own delivery room) he was put underneath an oxygen tent and a no-smoking sign—it was very efficient, though prior to this century we were efficient at not having heart attacks at all. He was given a Demerol, and after some sleep he obtained the tools of his trade, somehow, and was soon sitting up in his cellophane wrapper—in his oxygen tent—as he scribbled his 123's on a square-ruled yellow pad. And seeing him, I almost wept (oh Daddy, I thought, thirty years of those prison-window pads and no idle minute to throw me a football, baseball, basketball, a forty-percent-discounted ball from Davega's)—oh, I almost wept and the doctor shouted, "What in the hell?"

"I need an electric calculator, dammit," my father said.

H₁E died after three more heart attacks. And hearing this, the rabbi came up to Larchmont to our one-holed living room (and our one-holed breakfast room, for the old jam-jamming hole to the kitchen still had its Celotex after twenty troublesome years, and, by the way, those fluorescent lights did a flick-flick-flick like in old nickelodeons)—the rabbi came to our porous house to inquire what to say on Sunday. We just didn't know. My dry-eyed mother and I—we sat on the white silken sofa, we looked at each other impotently, we couldn't recollect what my father tried to do and actually did. So what could we say of this inefficient expert, of John Jacob Sack? A boy who was taught to look at God's good green earth as one hundred thousand cubic yards to evacuate every day, he matured to a man whose eulogy might be by Butler, who wrote about those who

> *In vain strive nature to suborn*
> *And, for their pains, are paid with scorn,*

but I couldn't tell the rabbi that. So the rabbi looked up *Sack* in the college classbook (oh, the tragedy of it: my father once was at Harvard, a magna cum laude and the man most likely to succeed) and in those incunabula he found that my father was on the Harvard rifle team. On the qui vive, the rabbi rose at the crematorium's chapel on Sunday to praise my late father for his marksmanship. "And Jack Sack. His aim was true, and he hit the mark every time. יתגדל ויתקדש," the hard-working rabbi said, "שמה רבא בעלמא די־ברא כרעותה, וימליך מלכותה בחייכון וביומיכון ובחיי דכל־בית ישראל, בעגלא ובזמן קריב, ואמרו: אמן."

The very next day, we descended to our inflammable rumpus room to start carting away the *Suns* and the yellow papers (no—the yellow confetti and a few dozen generations of bloated worms) to the county dump. We sold the old pockmarked home to a man who didn't give a pin for efficiency, a man who redid the "sunroom" in avocado and (in place of the leather-topped desk) in an avocado plant, an asparagus plant, an umbrella plant, a crown-of-thorns, and a Sony stereo set for his children's music,

> *Our house*
> *Is a very very very fine house*
> *With two cats in the yard,*
> *Life used to be so hard.*

The wan fluorescent lights, he supplanted with so many yellow bulbs in Finnish shades that he seemed to have honey-coated walls like on old honey jars. The half-built hole in the living room, he hid with a Navaho rug whose spirit (the indians supposed) could come and go via one white thread, and the half-built hole in the kitchen—well, he had the wall pulled down to be closer to his life-loving wife ("How about if I use the Szechuan peppers?" "Yeah! But don't use the dill." "No?" "It would clash with the Szechuan, I think"). In this happy-go-lucky cottage, the only trace of my paterfamilias (and the irony was, he had never touched it)—the only memorial was a sunroom shelf with the *Harvard Classics*. He himself or his ashes, rather, weren't in a marble urn ("I don't want to think about him," my mother said) but in a mass grave at the crematorium like the ashes of Germany's Jews.

And yet! I can swear that the poor ghost of Daddy is still invisibly with us. He died, if I'm not deceived, with the old hammer in his hand, and I can still hear him *("God dammit")* as he forges more of a fad, furor, madness for the total attainment of e̶f̶f̶i̶—*sorry*—efficiency. I'm writing this up in Larchmont on the six thousandth day of our wonder world: of the 1960's and 70's, but our whole world is a hole in the wall that still doesn't work. No, I'm in this breakfast room and I can't get the salad dressing from the new wasp-waisted bottle or the grated cheese from the can or (yo heave ho) the little white strip from the Minute Maid Orange Juice. To get from here to Manhattan is fraught with so many perils that all the steering wheels must be in Daddy's inadequate hands. Not long ago, a hundred automobiles were in one earth-ending accident—a person died (and a person was born) and, in Manhattan, the one-horse carts in 1910 were faster than the automobiles now. *Giddiup*, Davega's is now defunct but I can see Daddy's thumbs at ten thousand companies, even at General Motors on Fifth Avenue: Chevrolet has recalled a half million cars and Cadillac four thousand ambulances because of the wheels falling off. Barton's has recalled four thousand fruitcakes because of the moth-infested nuts, and Clairol one hundred thousand hair-spray cans because of their causing cancer. Is madam wearing a Dalkon Shield? I'm sorry, but it has been recalled.

No, we may inhabit a wonder world—a wired world, but I can sense who is wiring it ("God dammit! Where is the BX cable?"). One day, the lights in Manhattan all petered out: the traffic lights, too, and one other day the phones pooped out, "I might as well be

dead," people said. The radar reports two Russian atomic attacks
every week, the teletypes sent a red alert—an atomic attack—to
our radio stations, and a buoy escaped from a nuclear sub to
signal to Washington, *Sunk.* A disc jockey played a popular song
in New Jersey,

> *My heart knows what the wild goose knows,*
> *And I—*

or whatever, and it ignited the two 40,000-horsepower jets of a
nuclear missile in Trenton: up, up, and away, except that the crew
careered from the mess hall to disconnect the *wanderlüstige* thing.
A false alarm—a burglar alarm is a false alarm on forty-nine
out of fifty occasions, and I'm getting a buzz, *zzzzzz*, from my
automobile with the belt law-abidingly on.

Oh Daddy, I don't think I'll get through the next twenty years
of our mad arcadia. We have fifty thousand dangerous chemicals
in America—it rains nitric acid in San Francisco and sulfuric acid
in Washington, rotting the Washington Monument, and the river
caught fire in Cleveland, burning the bridges there. The nitric
oxide in SSTs, the freon (a million annual tons) in hair sprays,
etcetera, the methane (a hundred million annual tons) in the farts
of domestic cows—the contents of our cloud-cuckoo-land turn the
O_3 to O_2 and the ultraviolet light to an Angel of Death. The sulfur
dioxide kills the trees sixty miles out of Los Angeles and the
chlorine cripples the cows outside of Tampa—the critters fall to
their knees, the sea around us is fifty percent destroyed by DDT,
and sludge worms are the only living things in Lake Erie. Oh help,
there's an ocean monster off of Manhattan: the product of three
million toilets, its twenty square miles of polio, hepatitis, and
encephalitis viruses is—stop it, Daddy—is *moving*, is slouching
ashore at our summer resorts on Long Island. Its hour come
round, as the poet would say.

Oh Daddy! Oh Daddy! Atomic bombs are dropping on me,
Daddy! In one bad year there were five—a jettison in Georgia, an
accidental jettison in Georgia, a couple of crashes in Texas, a fire
on the flight line in Iowa. All except one of six safeties were on *go*
on one accidental bomb on North Carolina, and another atomic

bomb is *still* in some swamp in North Carolina. Ten years ago on the shore of Spain—the Costa del Sol, there was a big long thing in the sand, silver-colored, around it a one-inch band of olive drab and a few white words (CAUTION: HAZARDOUS TO YOUR HEALTH, perhaps) in English. It was one meter high, and Roberto was walking, walking, up to—*caramba! es la bomba! scrambarito!*— the hydrogen bomb we had jettisoned, the boom-boom-boom on the Spanish shore. We have some thirty thousand more—for a start, outside of Albuquerque we have enough to kill every man, woman, and daffodil on this irreplaceable earth if, Daddy, the bombs aren't lost. A plant in Apollo, Pennsylvania, has lost enough uranium for four atomic bombs or hasn't detected it on the ping-pong table or Jesus Christ! Or did you deliver it to the Israelis, Daddy? Or—

No! No! I must pinch myself! I am not ten anymore, and I can't continue to see that bald-headed man in my every nightmare. So *requiescat in pace, pater,* the truth is that every efficiency expert is a Mr. Sad Sack, a man who according to Lao Tse,

> *Seizes the earth to reshape it*
> *And, I notice, never succeeds,*

a man who doesn't direct us to utopia but to its opposite: a world in which nylon panties destroy a man's computers and in which sulfur dioxide destroys a woman's panties. The trip to efficiency must be a hyperbola—the higher we go, the steeper it is, until after three hundred years on this snow-covered matterhorn we are digging in with our fingernails and to chin ourselves an inch higher is (*aiiiii*) to fall twelve inches back. So help me Hillary—if the engineers ever get us to 99-hundredths efficiency, in one split second a nail will have pulled from a climber's boot and we will have skidded to base camp again. The paradox is: the more "efficient" the world becomes, the more inefficient it really becomes, until, as we climb on monomaniacally, it replies to our hubris in the one ultimate inefficiency, the annihilation of man.

Oh, don't believe it, the experts tell us: *trust,* and in twenty years we will place every particle of dust in our recalcitrant world ("The world, when every particle of dust breathes forth its joy,"

Blake)—we will commit every mote to its own official bin. And then we'll extend our *tausendjährige reich* to each obstinate one of the ten thousand million million million million million million million million million million million million atoms in the known universe so that meteors, comets, and UFOs won't threaten us and our clockwork world. Ah, we will enjoy the "mathematically faultless happiness" of Zamiatin's *We*—of *2001*, of *Zardoz*, of *Futureworld* and the Futurama, we will make crazy love to some rubber robots, we will make thermos bottles up on the moon, we will rocket to Mars to see ballerinas do ten-yard grand jetés—to cite three sober predictions by Alvin Toffler, Adrian Berry, and Arthur Clarke. Ah, just twenty more years and we will have ironed the termites out—we will enjoy efficiency on earth. And everyone say, Amen.

But our own eyes report that we cannot see it. We cannot forget that of one million civilizations in our little galaxy, there may be 999,999 where the people pipe in the valleys wild but, to be honest, none is efficient enough to have visited us (oh, go away, close-encounter fans) or to have sent some regards to our radiotelescope on its extinct volcano in Puerto Rico. No, our dream of total efficiency is, *according to Mrs. Gilbreth*, the idle dream of an El Dorado. Oh Daddy! Poor Daddy! Oh bald-headed ghost with the gray glasses on! You gave up the buttercups, butterflies—the pleasures of stepping into a world that is truly charged with the grandeur of God. Oh Daddy! You gave up the very pleasure of being a little boy's dad. And for what? For what never was and will never be.

3 / School Days, School Days

Or, The Study of Solid Geometry

ONE late night in 1940, thereabouts, my father brought home the Times, the Tribune, the Sun and something new: the volume one, number one, of a paper with the consistency of pink paper towels and the title of Hits Hits Hits. Eight ragged pages long, it violated the copyright code (and was sold, accordingly, in the gloomiest parts of subway stations) by printing, in ink like automobile oil, the titles, verses, and choruses of the hit parade. "Oh Daddy! Thank you," I cried the following day and I thank him now. If it weren't for his surreptitious procurement of Hits Hits Hits, I'd still be singing inaccurately,

> My dear Mr. Shane,
> Please let me explain,
> My dear Mr. Shane—

to the music of Bei Mir Bist du Schön, and I'd be making gobbledygook of the boop boop dittem dattem whattems of The Three Little Fishes.

Soon, I knew all the top forty songs. At home there was no piano but I'd stand outside (in the snow, sometimes, like a Christmas caroler) to sing along to a piano in the stone house around the corner: to such smashes as Jeepers Creepers. Nor did I limit myself to pop, for I'd go alone to Manhattan to listen to Toscanini and Beethoven's Third and I'd even conduct the overture to Rossini's William Tell by jumping up at our dinner table and by swinging my soup spoon passionately to The Lone Ranger on NBC. "Careful. Careful. The chandelier," my mother would tell

me as Tonto grunted, "Gettem up, Scout," and as I did the segue
to Liszt's Symphonic Poem. Once, I was given the Kuder Test,
and I was apprised that I wanted to be a musician most (and a
clerk like my weary father, least) when and if I grew up, and I can
believe it. A characteristic question was *What would you rather
do?"*

> *Compose a symphony*
> *Write a best seller*
> *Discover—*

My God! No bout adoubt it, as the song in the forties went, I'd
prefer to make music, wouldn't you?

So why do I sit with this pad in my lap, writing, "So why do I
sit with this pad in my lap, writing?" The answer, alas, was my
music class at half past eight on Mondays to Fridays at my old
grammar school in Larchmont. I was ten years old, and our
teacher there was a hawk-eyed, hawk-nosed woman with a pitch
pipe like an iron oreo cookie in her ten dreaded talons. On opening day, we sat in our four-bolted seats (in rows like on square-
ruled pads) as she nibbled on one solid edge of it. *Mmmmm*, the
oreo cookie announced, and our fearsome teacher told us, "That
was *do*. Now children, try to sing it."

"*Do*," we sang at our pigeonholes in Larchmont.

"*Do*," our teacher sang.

"*Do*," we sang at our posts in the British square.

"*Do*," our teacher sang.

"*Do*."

It was boring! It was like drilling the two-times-twos into the
Quiz Kids! Why, didn't the old crone know that we didn't miss a
note of

> *Honikodoke with an alikazon,*
> *Sing this song with your Uncle Don*

on the radio every afternoon? We were goddam prodigies, but she
wasted a week apiece on *do, re, mi,* before turning to *The Blue
Book of Songs:* to the quite uninspired words of Mozart's *Alphabet.* "A-b-c-d-e," she sang at her old piano, going up the musical

scale. "F-g-h-i-k," she continued, going down and up and down again.

"Miss Rofinot," I interrupted her.

"L-m-n—"

"Oh Miss Rofinot," I said to our nemesis, whose name on other occasions was Miss Rough Nuts. "Why isn't there a J?"

In hindsight, I guess that the Austrians of the late eighteenth century had no J in their alphabet and, as they clicked their heels, said to their white-wigged superiors, "*Ia, mein herr.*" At ten, though, I didn't know this—nor did our Miss Rofinot. She turned around on her stool, snarling, "What did you say?"

"Why isn't there a J, Miss Rofinot?"

"Because! Mozart thought it was funny without it."

"Oh."

"P-q-r-s-t," the witch continued, rotating to the old eighty-eights for the more or less predictable coda of Mozart's *Alphabet.* "U v w-x-ypsilon-z."

"Miss Rofinot," I said.

"*Well, what now?*" The ogre shouted this, and her two claws curled (as though on my eyeballs) like the golden ones on the glass balls on the stool's legs. Oh God, I'm thinking now, I'm lucky I'm not in grammar school now, I'd surely be diagnosed as hyperkinetic and (as 250,000 to 750,000 children are in America) be obliged to go to my red schoolhouse on Ritalin. Or worse, a doctor would send a few watts to a pea-sized part of my thalamus, as one doctor does to the hyperkinetics (half of them *under* ten) in Mississippi. "Attends school," "More manageable," "Died three weeks after operation," he reports in the *Proceedings of the Second International Conference on Psychosurgery in Copenhagen, Denmark.*

"Miss Rofinot," I said bravely. "Why isn't there a Y, Miss Rofinot? Why's there a yippie there?"

"I told you! Mozart thought it was funny!"

"Oh."

So we sang all of Mozart's *Alphabet.* The following day, our hot-tempered teacher put a hiatus to singing songs to instill into us the principles of, I quote, diatonic notation. And drawing in spine-chilling chalk a staff, a clef, a sharp, and a quarter note like a

lollipop, the termagant told us, "Now children, this is the first note
of Mozart's *Alphabet*. The note for A is known as G."

"Miss Rofinot, I don't understand," I admitted. "Which note is
do?"

"The same note is *do*," she said irritatedly. "Oh, you and your
questions!"

"Why isn't it on the bottom line?"

"It *is* on the bottom line in the key of E! But then there
wouldn't be a sharp on the top line—no, there *would* be a sharp
on the top line and on this line and—" She drew these sharps as
hysterically as Vincent van Gogh did the big black crows (a moment before he shot himself) in the movie version of *Lust for
Life*. "But we're in the key of G major!"

Holy mother of Mozart! I was still in my corduroy knickers and
I didn't know G major from Asia Minor. "Oh," I said softly, but I
had gagged on that alphabet soup: it didn't digest and I got a big
red seventy in music. And after that, I didn't actually hate the
soother of savage beasts, as Babbage, in England, the greatest
efficiency expert of a century earlier, did, and I don't write today,

*Every noisy instrument, whether organ or harp or trumpet or
penny whistle, should be seized by the police,*

as Babbage did in *The Life of a Philosopher*. I still sang in the
shower, but I did conclude that the eighty-eight notes of black,
white, black, white (like on a tower of ten stacked staffs) would
be beyond my modest comprehension, and I still haven't written
my First Symphony in G. In grammar school, I forgot what I'd
learned from the one-two pulse in my mother's womb, and I'd
have done better as a diller, a dollar, a ten o'clock scholar, a boy
who just stood in the snow by the log-lighted house to sing along
to *Jeepers Creepers*.

It was ironic. Long after that, I'd learn that the pop piano
player around the corner was: our own Miss Rofinot. At night,
our tormentor turned on the *A&P Gipsies* and, after that, sat at
the high upright to hammer out the top forties as her sister, a
fiddler, accompanied her, and as our geography teacher, our assistant principal, and the landlady sang,

Gosh all git up,
How'd they get so lit up,

etcetera, until eleven o'clock. And after sleeping, our hep teacher
went to her other piano to bore us with *lieder* (which really
weren't by Mozart)—for her instructions were that we sing in four-
part harmony, though there were no basses or tenors at grammar
school nor, for that matter, sopranos, for the sexes were segre-
gated there. She didn't *educate* us (to *educe* what is already
there), for the school supposed we were empty kettles, to be filled
to our sagittals with the facts, facts, facts: a sharp for G, a second
sharp for D, a third sharp for A, and the red seventy if we didn't
understand.

So that was music, which ended at ix o'clock by our school-
room clock on Mondays to Fridays. Then, we lined up like
mourners to plod through the yellow corridors *(swish, swish,* the
only sounds allowed were the knees of our corduroy knickers) to
our second class: art, to paint maple leaves. We each carried a
crib: a fallen maple leaf, and we twirled it empty-headedly as our
teacher (a different bird: a wren, as cheerful as *chirp*) passed out
her watercolor trays and her watercolor papers. On these we each
pressed a maple leaf, a finger on every delicate lobe, as our pencil
described a line around it. And setting the leaf aside, in ten more
minutes we matched up the watercolors correctly (as if we were
patching the leaf at a tree surgeon's shop) and did the dirty
dishes: the watercolor trays, prior to returning them to Miss Win-
ters, as clean as Spode. I *tell* you: the class wasn't art, it was
draftsmanship, and I did worse than in music, placing last out of
thirty instead of second from last.

Alas alas. Our teacher had her instructions, but she herself
couldn't care if we painted the maple leaf in red, orange, yellow,
or heliotrope (or painted a fig leaf on an Adonis, instead) as long
as it suited us. Her choice would be to let one thousand flowers
bloom—to let us paint rainbow-colored worlds as the little boy
did in the ballad by Harry Chapin,

> *There are so many colors in the rainbow!*
> *So many colors in the morning sun!*
> *So many colors in a flower,*
> *And I see every one!*

Of course, it was recently that the teacher, retired, happened to tune to that ballad on a *Today* show. It came on as she teased her gray-colored hair in Larchmont, and she went interestedly to her credenza with the Zenith and the two porcelain dogs from China, the ebony masks from Zaïre. She heard how the little boy's teacher said, *"You're sassy,"*

> *Flowers are red, young man,*
> *And green leaves are green,*

and how she restricted him to these colors: to the wavelengths of 650 and 550 millimicrons, and my art teacher almost wept. "Oh," she said silently, "I could twist out the teacher's tongue!" And turning the Zenith off, she went out and painted a vase of purple instead of lavender wisteria.

But that was art at our grammar school. At half past nine, the art teacher watched that we didn't insert the chalk in her felt erasers as we departed at funeral-parlor pace to our penmanship class: there, to write with an arm that reciprocated like a motor's connecting rod. For one half hour, *ooooooo.*

AT midday, we did our mourners march to the cafeteria for our sandwiches (the white bread cemented by wet peanut butter) and our milk in its odd-odored thermoses, and at one o'clock to arithmetic class while we licked the last peanut butter out of our diastemata before it had ossified there. At first (the first month of school) it seemed that the class would continue the midday meal, for our teacher held up two white comestibles, telling us, "Children? You know what *these* are."

"*Marshmallows,*" we all chortled.

"Yes," our teacher concurred.

We loved them! But marshmallows went at twenty cents a pound those days: the same as ground round, and we could afford them just at Thanksgiving. At which time, my mother deposited them on the sweet-potato casserole, offering it with those suddenly languorous marshmallows (and the hot mandarin oranges, too) to my father, my sister, and me at five o'clock sharp. The spare marshmallows, we toasted in the brick fireplace, eyeing them like an Escoffier to rescue them if a wart appeared on their golden skins. To be honest, I didn't really relish the gooey things, just the old ritual: the two logs, the two-tined forks, the smell as we twisted them in the fire, and my mother telling us, "Mmmm!"

"Mommy? Do they grow like cotton bolls?"

"No, they're from the candy factory."

"Oh."

By grammar school, a score of ardent emotions united me and the marshmallow, which, if you think, is the only food in our civilization that we wouldn't eat alone. But this didn't interest our old arithmetic teacher, an arrow-eyed woman who said to us, "Children? How many marshmallows have I here?"

"*Two*," we shouted.

She held up her other hand. "And how many marshmallows here?"

"*Two*," we repeated—the more the merrier, whoopee!

"How many marshmallows all and all?"

"*Four! Four! Mmmm!*"

"Correct. Two marshmallows and two marshmallows come to four marshmallows," she announced, and she recommitted them to the red-and-blue box.

Huh? We felt cheated, and not just because we had virtually whittled the spit-sticks when we were delivered to Tantalus's torture. No, it was also because we had been introduced to the one constituent of our precious marshmallows that we couldn't *participate* in. If two and two marshmallows came to four marshmallows, it came to that whether we toasted them or tossed them into the fire, diabolically—whether we relished them or underwent a diabetic episode at just smelling them. Two and two were four marshmallows was a mass of granite, contemptuous of our efforts to push, pull, or play with it or enter into a happy reciprocity with it. Sure, I've seen in Orwell,

Freedom is the freedom to say that two plus two make four. If that is granted, all else follows, but I deny it: if that's what freedom is, it belongs to a man who's scratching out his one, two, three, four days on his penitentiary's wall. And sure, I've seen how Gilbreth, of *Bricklaying System*, on being asked if his system wasn't slavery, answered, "Is it slavery to insist that a column always add up?" Well, dummy, of *course* it's slavery (a slave: a man who isn't free) and it's total slavery to bow to the four-marshmallow rule in all our earthly endeavors.

"But what if I *eat* them?" I asked my arithmetic teacher.

"If you eat two and another two—"

"Then there're none at all!" I said elatedly.

"No, then you've eaten four."

On hearing this, I felt crippled: I felt like a man in four hand and foot manacles and I don't think I'd overreacted, for Dostoevsky himself said,

Two and two are four is an intolerable thing. Two and two are four is a cocky young fellow who is standing across our path with arms akimbo. Two and two,

he went on, are four automatically without the accord of our own wills: immobile, immutable, and as immune as a pot of plastic ivy to our own idiosyncrasies.

Well, I must protest—I'd rather be a pagan to whom those marshmallows are God's holy ghosts and not an insensate sum. Now, I don't condemn my arithmetic teacher (and art and music maestros) for a dogged objectivity that, in fact, dated to the early seventeenth century and to Galileo, who ostracized out of Europe all that didn't, quote, unquote, exist. To *exist* meant to Galileo to be independent of eyes, ears, noses, to endure even if there are no men, women, children present to sense it. "A substance," he stated, "is great or small, is in this or that time, and is or isn't moving along but is not *necessarily* white or red, sonorous or silent, sweet-smelling or disagreeable. And therefore," continued the man who looked at the great caged chandelier at Pisa as $t = 2\pi \dfrac{l}{g}$, the pendulum formula, "the senses are names: nothing more, and if ears, noses, and tongues disappeared only the shapes would remain."

Only the solid geometry. "The world," he continued, "is written in mathematics: in geometric figures, and one cannot understand a word without them." In other words, the world is a silicon sphere of six sextillion tons and it goes counterclockwise in one year, five hours, forty-eight minutes, forty-five seconds: that's it, the ruddy world. As for me, I'd as soon inhabit a connex container, a wish anticipated in the mid-seventeenth century by Pascal, "Cast to the infinite immensities that I know not of, I am frightened!" He was happier in his old neighborhood, the biosphere, as there were no other benefits to the new philosophy (the words of Donne: *and new philosophy calls all in doubt*) than to have rolled away all the obstacles to efficiency there. If the odor of roses, color of crocuses, tone of the whippoorwills, if all our perceptions retire and the skeletons of the dead facts remain, the world will be one whose components no one can doubt—or can doubt the one best way to manipulate them. The world will be one that's accessible to computers, calculators, and our teacher's addition tables: to the criteria of what is and isn't efficient here. "For building walls," said Galileo, "the square is more perfect than the circle, and for wagon wheels the circle more than the triangle." Any arguments, anyone?

In the seventeenth century, the new philosophy made a tinker toy out of Europe. In politics, De Witt, in economics, Colbert, in oratory, De Fontenelle, in morals, Spinoza—I'll stop, but all sought the certitudes of solid geometry, even to writing in postulates, propositions, and QEDs. Each hedge at Versailles was planted like on a square-ruled pad, and the cities were in a square-shape at Freudenstadt, a star-shape at Karlsruhe, a nest of concentric nonagons in Palma Nuova, Italy. Concentric circles ran in Tintoretto's *Paradise* and Brueghel's *Tower of Babel*, I see. In the seventeenth century, a man carried compasses in his portrait, and Blake himself ("God forbid that the truth be confined to mathematical demonstrations") did one drawing of God with compasses too. The God of Milton

> *Took the golden compasses, prepared*
> *In God's eternal store, to circumscribe*
> *This universe,*

and God was the master mathematician to Galileo. "Why waste words? Geometry," said Kepler, "is God himself." Diderot, who didn't believe in God, was once cornered by Euler, the mathematician, who told him, "Sir, $\dfrac{(a+b)^n}{n} = x$, so God exists," and Diderot shambled away but I don't get it.

By my day, what wasn't geometry was "sickly sentiment" even to Marx. One Easter, I went upstate, and I was wide-eyed at the red, orange, and yellow-saturated mists (at the parrots in tropical storms) at Niagara Falls. "Mommy!" I shouted. "It doesn't stop!"

"It's like the sunshine," my mother said.

"The contour line," the tour leader interrupted, and his PA interrupted even the water's roar, "is 2,200 feet and the height is 176 feet. And ninety percent of—"

Jesus! The numbers came out of him like ticker tape! He seemed to see through a pair of lead-colored glasses—to see, according to Schrödinger, a very deficient picture of Niagara. "The scientific picture," said Schrödinger, "is ghastly silent about what is really near to us. It cannot tell us a thing about red and blue, bitter and sweet, physical pain and physical delight." It told us about the digits, nothing more.

At grammar school, I tried, I tried, to restore what the old philosophers called the first of the passions: wonder, and in wizard's robes (my father's graduation gown from Harvard) I got up in our vast auditorium to perform a Deft Demonstration of Deceptive Dexterity. A golf ball (got at a magic company, not at Davega's) was between my thumb and my index finger as I lied, "My father's a golfer and I'm his caddy sometimes. He hits the ball in the water sometimes, but I'll have another ball for him," and, abracadabra, there were now two in my quivering fingers. "And sometimes," I continued, "he hits the ball in the bushes but I'll have another ball for him, and you won't believe it: he hits the ball in an eagle's nest and I'll have *another* ball for him." By now, there were so many balls that my fingers looked like an egg-and-dart ornament until the balls disappeared up the sleeve of my father's graduation gown. "Abracadabra," I said.

"Thank you," the principal said, a Scot with a cairngorum on her shoulder and a haggis bag on her countenance. "*Up*," she now shouted, and we were marched to arithmetic class in spite of my deft demonstrations.

How dull! How drab! "I agree," Dostoevsky said, "that two and two are four is an excellent thing, but two and two are *five* is excellent too." At school, I was delighted to learn that a quarter moon is a half moon, a scissors is a pair of scissors, and a man who hasn't but two hands *has* but two hands too. I got some books, learning that two and two are four, *or more or less*, in noneuclidean arithmetic, that four and four are eight but eight and eight are four in modular arithmetic, like on a wristwatch dial, that aleph two and aleph two are aleph two in transfinite arithmetic, and that two and two are justice in Pythagoras. My older cousin, a mathematician, came up to Larchmont to sit by our flicking fluorescent lights to demonstrate that one was *already* two. If

$$a = b$$
$$ab = b^2$$
$$ab - a^2 = b^2 - a^2$$
$$a(b - a) = (b + a)(b - a)$$
$$a = b + a$$
$$a = a + a$$
$$a = 2a$$
$$1 = 2$$

and *quod erat*, everyone. No doubt there is a flaw there, but my cousin rose to manager of the GE computer division, where one and one are ten.

At school, I didn't contradict my candy-snatching teacher in her enumeration of marshmallows, fennelflowers, etcetera, but I did object to her cold-blooded count of snowballs once. It was a white-aired day in December: the air was having a pillow fight, and in the recess we had tossed snowballs, *whop*, but we might as well have tossed marshmallows as far as our teacher cared. "If," she said, showing us her empty hands, "there are two snowballs here and two snowballs *here*, there are how many snowballs, children?"

"None," I answered her.

"No, John. Not two minus two but two and two," our teacher said. "How many—"

"None! They melted, Miss Crockett!" I shouted.
"That isn't funny. How many snowballs, John?"
"Four," I said resignedly.
"How many sides does a snowflake have?"
"Six," I said resignedly.
"How many sides do two snowflakes have?"
"Twelve," I said resignedly—

OR one dozen, motherfucker, and I say, "So what?" No one cared that a snowflake was a six-pointed star (a bishop supposed it a crescent moon) up to the seventeenth century, except, of course, for the Chinese,

> The clouds float in the sky's four corners,
> And the snowflakes are six-petaled flowers,

a *shih* by a sixth-century prince. In the west, it was enough that the snowflake was one of one thousand water-items: so were the clouds, the constellations of the fish, the crab, and the scorpion, the summer showers, the dew on the daffodils, the Danube, and all but one third of ourselves: the world was water (and earth, fire, and air) and we were drenched in it. "A man," according to Barfield, "was rather less like an island, rather more like an embryo," and the earth wasn't just a carton of solid geometry.

All that began to change in the seventeenth century: in 1610 in Prague, Czechoslovakia. It had been snowing: the jolly people of Prague had been throwing snowballs, constructing snowmen, whatever, singing jingle bells, and Kepler, the astronomer, the one who announced that the planets go in ellipses (and I say again, "So what?")—Kepler was slogging over a stone-statued bridge to a new year's party when a *snih*-flake, a snowflake, fell on his overcoat. Now, Kepler hadn't had a good childhood. His father, I'm sorry, abandoned him and his mother was (or allegedly was) a card-carrying witch, the one who created pain in the butcher's hip and the teacher's leg, the one who once told the tailor's babies, "Oh little babies, bless you," the two little babies dying. By forty, Kepler had fevers, headaches, myopia, cholecystitis, dyspepsia, and in his words a mad dog's disposition: he gnawed bones and his motto was O *curas hominum,* "Oh, man's cares."

In short, he didn't consider himself an embryo, a part of the earth's ecology, but an observer with a pen, paper, protractor to try to fathom it. He didn't sing at the taverns,

Já piji a piji
Už jsem propil všechno,

a sort of *Roll Out the Barrel* in Czech, but sat and computed the barrel's capacity. He calculated the birthday of Christ as the year four before him, and he noted the music of the spheres as

 for the earth and

for Mars, I hope I've got that right. The orbit of Mars, he computed by adding, subtracting, etcetera, for one and one half thousand days (*ad insaniam,* he admitted) and he mailed his three hundred pages of computations and his one-sentence conclusion to Galileo, who never read it. Poor Kepler! He ought to have sent him a picture postcard, saying, "Dear Galileo, Mars moves in an ellipse, *arrivederci,*" and omitted the other geometry.

He once wrote, "The eye is for seeing, the ear is for hearing, the head is for understanding numbers," and, as that snowflake fell like a rare white midget moth, he observed (as no one in Europe had done before) that it had six little sides, thinking, "Why specifically six?" And flash, he forgot all his *curas hominum* (his kids were dying of smallpox and his wife of Hungarian fever, and Prague was being invaded, successfully) as his convolutions contorted in concentration but, not confining themselves to solid geometry, let the humanities in. He recalled how Olympias, the wife of Philip of Macedon, and Cornelia, a vestal virgin of Domitian's, the emperor of Rome, had both been assassinated: had clutched at their billowing togas so as to fall down decently. By analogy, Kepler asked, couldn't the snow compose itself in a hexagon so as to fall with decorum? Well, *couldn't* it? In his research report, he answered in Latin, "*Res mihi nondum comperta est*," "I don't know."

So much for Kepler and the six-sided thingamajiggers in Prague. A quarter century later, 1635, in Amsterdam, Descartes was in bed with the maid (whose name was Helen and who was four months pregnant, the philosopher's research for his *Formation of the Fetus*) as some more snowflakes fell. It was eight o'clock: sunrise, but Descartes (who generally slept until noon and, in fact, would die in his middle age on being awakened at four o'clock in the morning in Sweden) put his woollies on to go out and admire them. Now, there's lots to admire in God's jolly feather fights,

> *And then they grew so jolly,*
> *I did resign the prig,*
> *And ten of my once stately toes*
> *Are marshaled for a jig,*

Snowflakes, by Emily Dickinson, but Descartes was attracted just to their solid geometry. "The six sides were so straight and the six angles so equal that a man can't make anything so exact," he reported, for his toes weren't ready for a Dutch farmers-dance.

Not only that but he didn't *want* to admire them, for the total annihilation of admiration *(admiratio:* wonder) was the goal of Descartes's philosophy, "I hope we'll have no more occasion to admire anything." His fear of uncertainty owed to his mother's death when he was a *bébé* in Paris, the psychoanalysts say. In his early twenties, he hid himself in a hot room—a stove, he complained—until he had found a, quote, marvelous science,

> *The long chains of easy reasonings which the geometers use to*
> *arrive at the most difficult conclusions made me believe that all*
> *the objects of human knowledge are similarly interdependent,*

and that night he dreamt (among other things) of opening a poetry anthology to Ausonius's "What road shall I pursue?" His interpretation was, he must desiccate all of creation into the dry white bones of solid geometry, though a newer interpretation came at the Fifteenth International Psychoanalytical Congress, in Paris, as I was going to grammar school in Larchmont. A doctor said that Descartes was gay.

But like the true believers in *Tommy* in their earplugs and their eyeshades, he now stopped up his six senses to apprehend the earth, water, fire, and air as a pale calamine blueprint. He wasn't devout: he didn't like the Bible: it wasn't distinct, he said to a lady painter, sculptor, and tapester who was reading it in Hebrew and was also fluent in French, Dutch, Latin, Greek, Turkish, Arabic, and Aramaic. On seeing the six-sided *sneeuw*-flakes, he warded off an acute attack of admiration by attributing them to geometry: to the need of cents or florins, say, to assemble themselves in hexagons: incorrect, as was everything else in his text, a *beau roman* according to Huygens. A cloud, our philosopher said, is a bale of snow, it drops on another cloud and it sounds like an avalanche: thunder. Poor Descartes! He didn't know clouds at all, only their gassy geometry.

We proceed to the snowflake studies a quarter century later in London. In the 1660's, the secretary of the Royal Society, Hooke, who was looking at every little thing (at lice, mites, moths, spiders, flies, fleas, gnats, ants, and snake fangs and snail teeth) in his microscope, looked at a hundred snowflakes on his black velvet hat. "The branchings were six," he told the Society, "and were inclined to each other by sixty degrees. The lateral branches had collateral, subcollateral, and laterosubcollateral branches," enough that he too inclined to *insaniam* as he counted them. He went out to pee, froze it, inspected it in his microscope and ate it. "As insipid as water," he announced to the Royal Society.

He was hoping for Château Latour? I wouldn't know, but the man was mocked in the seventeenth century, too: a play was presented about him and Hooke himself saw it. In the second scene, two of the title character's nieces (a slander, for Hooke was sleeping with only one of his nieces) announced, "Were ever women so confined by a foolish uncle?"

"A sot," the other concurred, "that has spent two thousand pounds in microscopes to find out the nature of eels in vinegar, mites in cheese, and the blue of plums."

"One," the other continued, "who has broken his brains about the nature of maggots, who—"

Oh, Hooke was just writhing there at the Dorset Garden! The

other patrons pointed at him, tittering: at his crooked body, his face like the rake's descent, and his miserly, mistrustful, and melancholy disposition: he was despicable, said Waller. At the end, he didn't applaud but stamped away like Rumpelstiltskin to write in his diary in Latin, "Avenge me, God," though he still didn't write why a snowflake has six lateral branches.

In fact, all the Royal Society was the butt of *The Virtuoso*. Hooke had never weighed air but the title character did, "To what end do you weigh this air, sir?" "To know what it weighs!" To the seventeenth century, a scientist was an Ariel who just flitted about,

> *These were their learned speculations*
> *And all their constant occupations:*
> *To measure wind and weigh the air*
> *And turn a circle to a square,*

On the Royal Society, Butler, and the king himself laughed at his own society for weighing ayre, said Pepys. No matter: it was still weighing wind and was counting up snowflake sides as I entered kindergarten and, *at last*, announced that the six-sided symmetry owes to solid geometry, indeed: to the molecule, a hexagon of oxygen atoms at 2.76 angstroms apart and of hydrogen atoms at 1.01 angstroms and 1.75 angstroms from the oxygen atoms.

And that ended that, or so it seemed to the Royal Society.

> *Or so it seems. Yet who would dare*
> *Deny that nature planned it other,*
> *When every freckled thrush can wear*
> *A dapple various from his brother,*
> *When each pale snowflake in the storm*
> *Is false to some imagined norm,*

Phyllis McGinley. The wild west wind: it says hurrah for humanity with a shower of white confetti, each as diverse as our pinkie prints, though (as mathematicians admit) there were a hundred decillion in this earth's history. In spite of Galileo, the language of solid geometry is not enough for the snowflakes, even less for the whole blessed world. It's not only written in its predictable angles but in the curves of the wind-driven wheat and the swallow's swoops, or as Goethe insisted, "What is exact in mathe-

matics except for its own exactitude?" Have another marshmallow
now, Miss Crockett.

Aʟᴀꜱ, I can count on a snow-
flake's sides the Americans who will think of themselves (or two
thirds of themselves) as the same matter as snowstorms: as em-
bryos in their amniotic fluid. Our environment is the hard-edged
thing of Galileo, a construct of sines, cosines, etcetera, a concatenation of catwalks, an atlas of area codes and zip codes, a
machine for living inside: though as someone said of the Bauhaus,
"Who wants to live inside a machine?" A world with no perch for
the human heart, a world with the weltanschauung of one old
twentieth-century chairman of the German General Staff. On ma-
neuvers in Prussia, his aide admired the red-rippled sunrise on the
Pregel River, "Ah, look at that river there!" The general looked
through his iron-rimmed monocle, answering, "An unimportant
obstacle."

It was just fifty meters wide, as our arithmetic teacher might
say. At one-thirty, anyhow, the buzzer would buzz, we angle irons
would be uprights and we would troop like an army platoon
through the right-angled halls. We were being brought up like
soldiers: like the German general or our own defense secretary in
the Vietnam War, "I want percentages, I don't want poetry!" To
my soul's salvation, though, my last class of the afternoon was in
poetry and I thank you, Miss Hulda Hegge! If it weren't for you,
I'd have gone from grammar school with the head of an iron
computer but the heart of the Tin Woodman. Once, we were
listening as you were reading from Wordsworth's *Daffodils*, and I
asked you, "Miss Hegge? What are the daffodils, anyhow?"

"Oh," you told us, "they're lovely flowers!" You didn't tell us,
"They're bulbous herbs of the species *narcissus pseudo-narcissus*,"
and you didn't do what teachers did to Stephen Spender, in
England, who hoped to become a botanist until he enrolled in a
botany class at Oxford. You didn't test us, "How many daffodils

did Wordsworth see? One hundred? One thousand? Ten thousand?" No, you didn't give a fig for our written responses to number-numeral relationships on the abstract level, one of five hundred categories, so help me God, on the report cards in Dallas. You simply said, "I was once in England and I was where the daffodils were. I saw very far, and as far as I saw was this golden sea: the daffodils, and they were nodding as if they were talking to me. They were nodding this way and the other way," and you nodded too, Miss Hegge, as though in a gentle trance, telling us, "and I had Wordsworth's emotions too." And then you concluded from *Daffodils,*

> *And then my heart with pleasure fills*
> *And dances with the daffodils,*

and you asked us, "Who else wants to dance with the daffodils?"

"I do, Miss Hegge!" I cried.

God bless her, I say. In poetry class, my one reservation wasn't the small, sweet, round-faced teacher but the poetry itself, most of it. Wordsworth had stayed a feeling human being (as had blacks and women, involuntarily) by absenting himself from the world of relentless efficiency: by fleeing to a $30-monthly cottage in a perfect republic of shepherds, unquote, of men who promised, "We're verra nee oot o' t' warld, ye'll see." But mostly, the poets were as loath as the mathematicians to contaminate creation with an infusion of personal sentiment. In the early seventeenth century, Shakespeare had written,

> *Where the bee sucks, there suck I,*
> *In a cowslip's bell I lie,*

in *The Tempest*, in the same year as Kepler's snowflake. But after that, the poets contracted a bifurcation of intellect, said Nicolson, or dissociation of sensibility, said Eliot: "The language became refined, the feeling became crude." By the end of the seventeenth century, if I'm not too *too* pedantic, the poets were people like Dryden, who (abetted, perhaps, by the recent downers: by coffee, chocolate, tobacco) wrote with a dazzling disregard of the soul, again according to Eliot. Dryden, I'm told, composed a second edition of *The Tempest* by scribbling in such codicils as a trio of singing imps,

> *In hell, in hell, with flames shall they reign,*
> *And forever, forever, shall suffer the pain,*

and then confessed in his epilogue that it was, quote, rotten poetry, and Pepys concurred with him, "No great wit."

Descartes killed poetry, people said. In the seventeenth century, few of our poets detected a sand grain's infinities as they adjusted to the new euclidean world,

> *As lines, so loves oblique may well*
> *Themselves in every angle greet,*
> *But ours so truly parallel*
> *Though infinite can never meet,*

Marvell, and Cleveland even parodied the "eyes like astronomy" and the "straight-limbed geometry" of the then heroines. By the twentieth century, the most famous poem at my grammar school was in the sine lined cadences of Kilmer, "I think," said Miss Hegge,

> *I think that I shall never see*
> *A poem lovely as a tree,*
> *A tree—*

"Miss Hegge?" I interrupted her. "If the poem's right, we should study the *tree*, shouldn't we?"

"Well, John, I do like some other poems better," our teacher sighed.

My heart didn't leap at that tree that looked at God. I couldn't even see the blasted thing—an apple tree? a maple tree? a shoe tree, perhaps—though it no doubt bloomed at the poet's former home in Larchmont. Our poets (according to Hazlitt) had had their wings clipped by our scientists, who, in fact, often monitored them to try to imprison them in a rock-solid reality: to restrict them to what would precipitate in a test tube.

All right, I won't protest that Gauss had corrected the compass point in his own copy of Sir Walter Scott, "The moon rises broad in the northwest." But what of the man who corrected the undocumented nomenclature in Whitman? Who read,

I hear you whispering there O stars,

and then wrote, "He was interested in the stars though he produced no adequate catalog," and who read,

Solitary the thrush,
The hermit withdrawn,
Sings by himself a song,

and then wrote, "I strongly suspect that the hermit thrush is the wood thrush." And what of Babbage, who objected to Tennyson's

Every moment dies a man,
Every moment one is born,

writing him, "Sir: It must be manifest that if this were true the population would be at a standstill," and who recommended instead,

Every moment dies a man,
Every moment one and one-sixteenth is born,

and what of Buckminster Fuller, who objects to *most glorious sunset* in Wordsworth, writing, "The sun doesn't set: the earth revolves. How about sunclipse?" It is a beauteous evening, calm and free, the sun is clipsed in its tranquillity.

Of such people, I say tar and feather them. Well after grammar school, I read in *Geomorphology*, by Oscar von Engeln, "A case is the lake district made famous by Wordsworth. Its features are the product of pleistocene glacierization, of which the poet shows little comprehension," and I was inspired to blue-pencil one of the man's inadequate odes and to interpolate an emotion recollected in late-cenozoic tranquillity. As follows,

She dwelt among the untrodden ways,
* Beside the springs of Dove,*
And let me stop right now to praise
* Them as a product of*

The pleistocene glacierization.
* This is proven through*
(1) the parallel striation
* On the pebbles, (2)*

Erratics out of Ennerdale's
* Granophyric sill*
At Ullock, (3) the hanging vales,
* (4) morainal till,*

And (5) the roches moutonées.
* The maid above*
Was one whom there were none to praise
* And very few to love:*

A violet by a mossy stone
* Of autobrecciated*
Andesite inside a zone
* Of rock incorporated*

Early in the Borrowdale
* Series and supine*
Conformably upon the shale
* Of Skiddaw's anticline*

And issued in the Ordovician
* Period. On these hills*
Of andesite are, in addition,
* Golden daffodils.*

She lived alone, and few could know
* When Lucy ceased to be,*
But she is in her grave and geo-
* Morphologically*

In early paleozoic strata.
* All the very aptest*
Fossilized invertebrata
* Like the dichograptus*

Octobrachiatus (Hall)
* Keep her company.*
It makes a mountain, after all,
* Of difference to me,*

or anyhow to the Brotherhood of Efficiency, a character calls it in Wells's *Things to Come*.

Well, I suppose what's to come is objective poetry (just as there's minimal art and aleatoric music) such as appears in *We*, by Zamiatin,

> *Two times two, eternal lovers,*
> *Inseparable in passion four,*
> *The hottest lovers—*

blah blah blah, which the protagonist calls, "A work of rare beauty. There is one truth and one path to it, and that truth is: four, and that path is: two times two," but I say no. The dew-diamonds on the daffodils, the ruby-throats on the goldenrods, the cirrus clouds: the world is a rock-candy mountain, there's more than the cold coordinates of two and two rock candies come to four rock candies, and to hold to that ascetic diet: to mere efficiency, is to wizen into the white-skinned, white-shirted, alienated men. To know what we're told, not a morsel more, and to never hear the question of Eliot, "Where is the wisdom we have lost in knowledge? Where is the knowledge we have lost in information?"

N̲o̲t long ago, I looked in on my hard-headed grammar school in Larchmont. It was spring again: the dogwoods bloomed like an orchard of marshmallow trees, and in the old brick building the ferns, philodendrons, and pothoses (and the paper maple trees on the windows) made a hothouse of my old schoolrooms. On the walls were drawings of one man, two cars, three ducks, four squirrels, instead of such mud-colored reproductions as Meissonier's *Campaign in France, 1814*, and the children sat in such wonderful which ways as the *vajra asana* of hatha yoga. To my disappointment, though, a teacher (in denim, same as the children) held up some elbow macaroni, uncooked, to demonstrate that two and two elbow macaronis come to four elbow macaronis, and her large-lettered books said,

Sue had a butterfly collection. In one box she had nine and in another she had twelve. How many butterflies did she have?

I told myself, Ah, *plus ça change* . . .

My old teachers weren't at their raucous blackboards. My history teacher was dead and my geography teacher (her voice like a marathon runner's in the twenty-fifth mile) was just marginally alive with Parkinson's disease. My arithmetic teacher lived in a mobile home in Sarasota, Florida, and my health teacher in an insane asylum in Valhalla, New York. My one beloved, my poetry teacher, was a vitamin saleswoman, and my gym teacher was a gold prospector in California. A heart attack had my art teacher at the hospital and a stroke had my music teacher in the old folks home in New Milford, Connecticut: and I drove up one afternoon to say hello and, in my forties, to try to discover which of her licorice lollipops was *do*. One's never too old.

But alas. The home seemed and it even sounded like the mental institution in *One Flew Over the Cuckoo's Nest*. On the women's floor (with the odor of old linoleum like a sinus spray) one of the old folks rendered a tuneless tune as though accompanied by a tongue depressor, all of her upper lip as lined as the Palisades and her lower lip going, "Ahhh! Ahhh! Ahhh!" Another woman with the somatotype of a laboratory skeleton called to me, "You! Can you wheel me to my own room right now?"

"I don't know if I'm allowed to," I apologized.

"Oh, go to Hades," the woman said. A third woman sat in a corner crying, and I went there compassionately. "Arthur," she cried, clutching my hand almost hopelessly. "They took my Arthur away!"

"Your husband?" I said understandingly.

"No," she sobbed. "Oh, how come you don't understand?"

On the surface, it wasn't the same environment as my old music class, but my teacher was in fine fettle, comparatively. Her sentences parsed, even if they were delivered like an old shortwave radio, so ragged it couldn't curdle a boy's own blood anymore, and her cold talons (as boneless now as a fillet of frog's legs) lay on my own accommodating arm in a rather romantic manner. In her chrome wheelchair, she had her turkey à *la mode de Gerber's*, her mashed potatoes, and her applesauce (with a dash of grated aspirin inside) by being fork-fed, and, as the food dribbled out of her brown-toothed mouth, my retired teacher told me, "I think I'll bug another cigarette."

"I'm sorry?" I said.

"I said I'll bum another cigarette. But," she sighed, "the nurses tell me I can't accept it."

"What will they do if you do?"

"I don't know. Scold me."

"So tell them shove off."

"That's easy enough for you."

I gave her a pot of white gardenias from an outdoor stand in Connecticut. "Miss Rofinot," I began uneasily. "I went to school forty years ago, and I still don't know where the *do* is."

"Where what is?"

"*Do.* You remember? As in *do*, a deer, a female deer?"

"Oh, there's a scale they've called the chromatic scale," my teacher explained. "And that means every note like C, C sharp, D, D flat—"

"D flat, Miss Rofinot?"

"Yes, E flat."

"Yes, Miss Rofinot."

"E, F and F sharp is a half step up, G and G sharp is a half step up. Every sharp is a half step up."

"Yes, Mrs. Rofinot."

"And every flat is a half step down. And then the naturals take the sharps and the flats away. It is so complicated, heh."

I frowned. In the sinus-sprayed dayroom, one of the old women slept, one of the old women wept, and one without teeth in her oval mouth started to shout in One! Word! Sentences! "Miss Rofinot? I still don't know where the *do* is," I confessed.

"It changes. If there's a flat in the signature then the key is F."

"Then—then—" I stuttered. "What happens then?"

"I think I should show you." She sighed at the old piano there, for her arm was paralyzed and she couldn't play (or even tap out the *one* and *two*) and her leg was unusable too. Instead, I put the five lines of the staff on her paper napkin, and she put the letters there in her tremorous hand. "E," she narrated, "and G and B is the third one up. Is that this one?"

"Yes, Miss Rofinot. Every good boy," I recalled.

"My glasses aren't good. All right, the B is flatted in F, and," she continued as she kept lettering, "and D and F."

"*Nurse*," the one-word woman shouted. "*I! Cannot! See! The! Clouds!*" The nurse turned her a little counterclockwise to the now orange clouds.

"And the spaces are F and A and C—"

"Miss Rofinot," I said softly, for she wasn't lettering them as at grammar school: from the bottom up, she was lettering them from the top down, so that incorrectly the top line and the top space were F's. "Miss Rofinot," I whispered. "You're going down, not up."

"*I! Can! See! The! Clouds!*"

"And finally E," my teacher said. So now there were E's on the bottom line and the bottom space.

"*But*," the woman continued. "*I! Cannot! See! The! Clock!*" The nurse turned her a little clockwise.

"Miss Rofinot? I still don't know where the *do* is," I pleaded.

"*I! Am! Bored!*"

"Oh, shut up," another woman shouted.

"The *do* is F in the key of F."

"The *do* is F?"

"In the key of F. Of course, there are two F's and—"

"*Bored! Bored! Bored!*"

"Yes, you're bored," the nurse repeated. "Aren't you?"

"So there are two *do*'s," my teacher said. And pointing them out, she was aghast to discover them on the top line and the top space of her musical staff. "Heh," she gasped.

"*I! Cannot! Stand! It!*"

"It's gotten so I've forgotten it," my teacher lamented.

"No," I said. "I think I'm just very stupid."

"No, I'm the stupid one," she moaned.

"*I! Want! Some! More! Ice cream!*"

"I'm not very good anymore."

The nurse went to get some vanilla, and I said farewell to my two-wheeler teacher in Connecticut. Outside, the maple trees were paper trees in the starlight: the stars seemed a stone's throw away, and the night was a cool face-cloth at a Japanese restaurant. On the lawn, I looked up at the south-headed swan: the northern cross, and at that brightest, bluest star in the summer sky, at Vega,

Thou brilliant lustrous one,
More shining than the Cross,

said Whitman. The poet, I recollected, went to astronomy classes on Broadway and was taught that the star number sixty-one in the northern cross was, in fact, sixty trillion miles away, as calculated by a Prussian astronomer. "He commenced measures," the teacher said as Whitman listened. "He referred the central point to the intersection of another perpendicular. He had to fix a point to which to refer that point—" anyhow, it worked out to sixty trillion miles, *clap*, and the class applauded but not Walt Whitman. He was just tired, he wrote in *When I Heard the Learned Astronomer*, and standing up and slipping out of the classroom,

I wandered off by myself,
In the mystical moist night air, and from time to time
Looked up in perfect silence at the stars.

And I—I was now looking at Vega, a refugee from the five-lined diagrams and the ABCs of Miss Rofinot. A pox on Galileo, I thought, a finger for my old grammar school in Larchmont. The world is solid geometry: agreed, and it's the orderless glory of the stars, snows, and the golden daffodils too. Our eyes, ears, nose are its only portals, and to stopper them in efficiency's service is to divorce ourselves from all but our God-forsaken thoughts. I didn't want to: I'd rather participate in the planet, thanks, and I walked away from the old folks home and its new white cemetery, crooning (in the wrong key of B, undoubtedly) the first familiar bars of Mozart's Variations in C. Twinkle, twinkle, little star, how I wonder what you are!

4 / Do A Good Turn Daily

Or, Is Intellect Idiotic?

In the summers, I went to a boy scout camp in the hills behind the New York State Hospital for the Agrarian Insane. At the foot of our precarious camp was a mist-hidden lake, the den of one-legged herons as still and as silent as patinated statues. To clap one's hands at this mystical lake was to produce a fop-topped bird, a crested kingfisher: it crossed like a powerboat until it called *kkkkkk*, as if it were stopped by an iron ratchet. On the shore, the black-masked yellowthroats went to a mardi gras, and the barn swallows barnstormed up on the hill, thrilling the black-eyed susans by the American flagpole. In the sky were sharp-shinned hawks and, on one unforgotten morning, eagles, a pair that balanced on two-yard wings as stiff as two tightrope poles. The sun was white on their crowns, and I shouted up to the nearest tents, those of the Seminoles, "*Eagles.*" The boys there shouted up to the Delawares, "*Eagles,*" and the shout swept up the hillside like a forest fire, "*Eagles! Eagles! Eagles!*"

At the last light, the nighthawks came out in the steel colored sky. By then, we weren't working on merit badges: on bird badges, on basket badges, and we wended up to the star-shadowed top: to the old oak grove, its mistletoe moss, its abundant acorns: to the site of our council fire. To light it with paper matches (or as we were taught to: with flint) would be too profane, and a boy camouflaged in an oak created one of Jove's fireballs instead. A roll of wet-with-kerosene toilet tissue, it fell like lightning (on a guy wire, confidentially) into the crisscrossed logs of our council fire. "*Ohhh,*" we gasped as it flashed aflame to silhouette one of the older scouts in a deerskin shirt, a deerskin clout, and two red-beaded deerskin moccasins and to redden his eagle-feather head-dress. "Imagine," the man began solemnly, "that we are all Pawnees in South Dakota. From one of the teepees there comes the medicine man, he walks to the fire with dignity, and he lifts up his arms to Manito for his assistance with a story of our remote past. He begins—"

No one spoke. The crickets themselves were quiet. In the fire, a log collapsed and a column of red-hot sparks ascended to Manito.

"Many moons ago," the man in the deerskin continued, "a couple of brothers went to sleep in some unexplored woods. A few hours later, the older brother awoke to the sound of a rattlesnake's rattle. It came from close to his feet, which seemed to be stuck together and, in fact, couldn't be pulled apart. He flipped off his robe to discover there were no feet there: in their stead was the tail of a very large rattlesnake, and his own toes were the rattle!"

No one didn't believe it. We wiggled our Keds to assure ourselves that they were separable.

"The older brother thought," the man continued, "Oh, something terrible's happening to me! What should I do? He woke up his younger brother, saying, 'I'm changing into a rattlesnake. So listen, as I have a lot to tell you. First off—' " At the end of his spooky story, a tom-tom sounded in the darkness and the old scout lifted his arms to Manito, singing in his ram's-horn voice,

> Hail to Mighty Gitchi Manito,
>   Manito!
> Hail to Mother Earth and Things That Grow,
>   Things That Grow!
> We are gathered in the glow—

"In the glow," we whispered reverently.

The whole world breathed. The forest floor, the blueberry bushes, the dome of the oak boughs themselves—in the orange glow, all of them swelled with a thing transcendent of their formal dimensions. A poet would call it God, discerning him in all living things just as we boy scouts did: as Dickinson,

> Some keep the sabbath going to church,
> I keep it staying at home,
> With a bobolink for a chorister
> And an orchard for a dome,

or as Millay,

> *God, I can push the grass apart*
> *And lay my finger on thy heart.*

After all, as scouts we had hiked in these brilliant hills with the wide-open eyes of Hopkins, who had explored (in the words of his red-edged diary) a painted-napkin valley in Wales and had scribbled one day,

> *The world is charged with the grandeur of God.*
> *It will flame out,*

our very sentiments under the orange-scorched oaks.

Now, Hopkins had been called pagan and I'll admit it: we were pagans at boy scout camp. In spite of perfunctory prayers to the great scoutmaster, unquote, we had that oldest religion: the worship of mother nature, of orbiting eagles and of all creatures under them. Our grove of glow-dappled oaks was the age-oldest temple: as many as five thousand years ago, the stone-agers of Russia (the ancestors of the Goths, Greeks, Romans, and now the Gipsies, Germans, Irish, Italians, Slavs, Scandinavians, Iranians, Indians of India, and the English) had worshiped the oak gods too, and their word for the oak, *perkwu*, became the name of the storm god in Russia, Prussia, and India: Perunu, Perkunas, and Parjanyah, and even today a Finn who hits himself with a hammer says, "*Perkele!*" In Greece, Odysseus consulted an oracle oak, in Rome the vestal virgins watched over an oak-wood fire, in Britain the druids (from the stone-aged word for a tree: *doru*) adored the you-know-whats, eating the acorns, too. As for our council fire, it was a god to the same stone-agers of Russia, whose word for a fire, *egnis*, still is the name of the red-faced fire god of India: Agni.

In those 1940's, we still believed with the Roman, Seneca, "There is nothing void of God." Even among the Jews, Moses had worshiped a blackberry bush, but, in his later years, he had done the most unprecedented act (the most *unlikely* act, says Barfield) in all human history: he had announced that God didn't inhabit the earth but the far-off clouds, out of our reach. To revere any real entity, even the two companions of God: the sun, the moon, would be to be stoned, according to Moses, and three thousand people who did it were massacred one day. But there's more in the golden sun, the silver moon, and the pulse of all living things than in the dead letters of Exodus, and the heirs of Moses couldn't look on their world without wonder. In spite of his ten commandments, even the high priest worshiped the sun, moon, and the planets in the reign of Josiah, and David listened to God in the rustling of the mulberry trees. In Jerusalem, the Jews even worshiped snakes, until a thousand years of stonings converted them to teletheism: the doctrine of a god who was somewhere else. By the birth of Christ, the Jews didn't dare to *draw* a terrestrial creature: an adder, crocodile, dragon, though the rabbis had no unanimity on dragons without fins. To the Jews, there was no God in the here and now.

Now, Christ, to his disciples, was a god who practiced in our own community but who departed, on Easter, and denuded it of its divinity. To detect any now was abhorrent to the church's fathers, such as Eusebius,

> The gospel teaches us not to be awed by the visible parts of the cosmos, as they must be of perishable nature,

and Lactantius,

> Why do some men of dull heart adore the elements as though they're gods? It's because as they gaze at God's works, namely: the sky, the mountains, the rivers, the sea, in their admiration they do forget the Maker and worship his works, instead. The men who prefer these to God are ungrateful to God.

It was sinful to Augustine to appreciate even the music of biblical chants, "I confess I have sinned," Augustine said. Nor were the herons, etcetera, sacred to Francis, who saw himself as a missionary to the lower chordata and as their private preacher,

> O creatures! Praise the Lord! And grateful be
> And serve him in a deep humility.

"What presumption," a character says in Huxley, as we would have said in our bird-loud camp. "Why couldn't he let the *birds* preach?" At times, Francis had told his feathered friends to just shut up ("My sister swallows! It is now time for me!") and, even deafer, the Metropolitan of Dol once ordered them to cease and desist eternally, as they interrupted his Pater Nosters.

But like the Jews, the Catholics weren't content with a world disowned of its inner light. So they knelt down to worship stone— if it had been sculpted into the Virgin—or to worship wood if it had been chipped from the Holy Cross. At our boy scout camp, it baffled me that they worshiped a cracker: on Sunday, the priest (a man in sad black apparel) displayed it and chanted in Latin, "*Hoc est corpus meum,*" "This is my body, which—" His church was an open grove, its walls perpendicular pines, its floor swamp-soft in the needles, subsiding like an old trampoline under a boy scout's foot. In between the resin-sided pines, one of the sun-shafts lit on a wooden cross: there, to the ovenbird's song, the priest proclaimed that the flat little cracker, *and nothing else,* was God. He was blind, apparently.

To the Protestants, if God weren't in the steepled trees he certainly wasn't in a cracker box. To discern him in any pied-à-terre was a madness, a monstrous dogma, a disgrace, an impious lie in the language of Calvin: a fiction of the corporeal presence of Christ. Why, didn't he ascend to heaven? And didn't he depart from the earth, therefore? To return him to terra firma was to *drag* him out of his uncorrupt element into the rot, the rust, the mortality of our biosphere, according to Calvin,

> So let there be nothing derogatory to the glory of Christ, as happens if he is coupled to any earthly creature.

By the seventeenth century, there was no *glow* to our god-forlorn world, just as there were no white lights in Rembrandt. We worshiped in nice neat churches not in cathedrals (the "piles" of Smollett) and our clothes were the color of death: the hangman's black. Our land submitted to miners, drillers, developers as our flora and fauna succumbed to the DDTs. Where there was no God was nothing but solid geometry, just as Galileo demanded.

No wonder our children converted to the pagan religions of

Asia! Its gods were imperfect, impermanent: its gods were *perishable* but at least were in the vicinity. The roshis say in Japan, "Where's Buddha? In three pounds of rice." In China, Chuang Tsu was asked where the Tao is,

> *It is in the ant,*
> *It is in the weeds,*
> *It is in the manure,*

and the lamas say in Tibet, "All sounds are mantras, all sights are yantras, all the world is Nirvana." In India in the *Upanishads,*

> *Thou art the fire,*
> *Thou art the sun,*
> *Thou art the air,*
> *Thou art the moon,*
> *Thou art the red-eyed parrot,*

and one conscientious swami sat in manure because the manure was God. Ramakrishna, the priest of a nineteenth-century temple to Kali, in Calcutta, was offered food for Kali and fed the cat instead. "The idol, the altar, the temple floor—even the cat is Kali," Ramakrishna explained.

The indians in America believed that the flora and fauna were the stopping places of God: and we their disciples believed it at boy scout camp. In the glow of our council fire, the skin-colored circle of oaks nodded to one another like a council of tribal elders, an owl called from one of their redskinned shoulders, and, as the embers dimmed, we interlocked arms for the creed of our old-time religion: the whispered words of *Taps.* Day was done, gone the sun, and God wasn't up on high, somewhere, but God was nigh.

I₋N the night, we went to our lantern-lighted tents to sleep on a horse's mouthful of hay and, at sunup, to wake up to bugle sounds from a creosote-colored tower:

it wobbled like a couple of two-story stilts to the throbs of "You gotta get up." We washed in cold water before running down to the morning mess and its intense smell of Bond Bread, to pray perfunctorily to our absent host: the gracious giver of all good, and to start shouting, "The bug juice, please!" "The moo juice, please!" The bug juice being the apple juice, the cherry juice, or the grape juice the color of spiders and the moo juice coming from cows, and our uproar lasted until, say, the nature director rose to announce the annual animal hunt: for an eft, one point, for a toad, two, for a frog, three, and for a skunk a well-deserved one hundred points. The nature director started, "I want to announce that—"

He said it! He said announce! As though he had dropped a conductor's baton, we started to sing simultaneously,

> Announcements! Announcements! Announcements!
> A terrible death to die,
> A terrible death to die,
> A terrible death to be talked to death,
> A terrible death to die,
>
> Now when you're up you're up,

we sang, standing up like soldiers,

> And when you're down you're down,

sitting down on the wooden benches: wham,

> And when you're only halfway up,
> You're neither up nor down!
> Announcements,

etcetera, the corn flakes decomposing, the cartons of moo juice toppling, the nature director sitting as impotently as Job to such second verses as Row, Row, Row Your Boat. And life was but a dream at our boy scout camp.

Do not ask me, ask doctors how the bread went down and the words went up simultaneously, but the breakfasts had to have been more serene at the Hospital for the Agrarian Insane. The only lull in our pandemonium came on each second weekend, when we sat clam-mouthed as a half-dozen scouts came to breakfast with a hand on each other's shoulder and a foot in some unseen ball and chain, proceeding like the personnel of a Georgia chain gang. The previous night, we had watched as the six were tapped for the boy scout secret society: the WWW, at its special fire at Three-Finger Rock. On that occasion, no meteor lit the council fire but a boy in white feathers trotted out of the night and lit it with torch fire. It flamed up like dynamite and it disclosed a second feather-dressed boy on one of the lichen-crusted ridges (the lichens the colors of white peeled paint, of burnt brown toast, of gold in a panner's pan) on Three-Finger Rock. "Hail," he chanted, "to Mighty Gitchi Manito! Hail," as still other indians ran to our wide-eyed circle to tap, rather, to wallop the shoulders of the six chosen ones. And whisked in back of the living-lichen rock, the six simply disappeared for the coal-black night, to reappear as they limped into the stone-silent hall for an ascetic's breakfast of water and one white slice of Bond Bread.

What happened in back of Three-Finger Rock? I never knew till I was fifteen and I, too, was tapped for the WWW. Away from the fire's light, we heard the boy in the eagle feathers finish his Gitchi Manito,

> Hail the North Wind and its Winter Breeze,
> Winter Breeze!
> South Wind,

so forth, then we were guided down to the lake, a big black pan of stars, and to a pair of silver-sided canoes. As we paddled off, the sounds were as crisp as the white light of Venus: the cricket's chirp, the wood frog's croak like a duck's quack-quack, the whippoorwill's call, the ripples of the ink-black water as we did J-strokes into it. Gone, gone beyond, gone beyond the beyond: correct, the world was a mantra, a whisper of God that soothed us as the cool water would. And sssss, we slipped into the cattails on the far shore, there to encounter a tribe of the eagle-feathered indians in the flare of their orange torches. One little indian said, "Brothers—"

Ah, but this was a secret society and I must be silent, except that a part of our ritual was so close to *Hiawatha* it surely falls in the public domain. Its narrator was a boy in a leather clout and a white-beaded leather vest, in epaulettes of ermine tails and a brooch of eagle bones, in buffalo horns on a rabbit cap: the indian medicine man. He was earnest (if rather eager to get to each verse before he forgot it) while telling us with crossed arms,

> *You who love the haunts of nature,*
> *Love the moonlight on the water,*
> *Love the sunshine on the meadow,*
> *Love the shadow of the forest,*
> *Love the wind among the branches,*
> *Ever murmuring, ever sighing,*
> *Love the rushing of great rivers,*
> *In their palisades of pine trees,*

in fact he said *pasilades*, though we didn't mind it,

> *Listen to—*

but there the secrets start, such as the very meaning of WWW. My lips are locked, for I in time would become the medicine man and I, too, would stand on the torch-shadowed shore to scour out of my own cerebrum the words of "You who love."

But with the exception of one benighted boy (to be met here imminently) we really loved the haunts of moonlight, sunlight, shadow, of spittlebugs in their bubble baths and of wasps in Japanese lanterns. At our far remove from the A&P, we boiled, boiled, and boiled the skunk-cabbage salads and we cleaned our teeth with the horsetail stems. We knew what the temperature was by the rate of a cricket's chirps. In the mole holes, we lowered a cattail to catch a tenacious mole, and we *reeked* of the wide outdoors when we scooped up a tall-tailed skunk for one hundred points in the annual animal hunt, to lose to a boy who scooped up two hundred efts. We conversed with the chipmunks, too, "Do you want a Ju Jube?"

"*Chip!*"

"What sort of? A lemon one?"

"Chip!"

We lay like cadavers to lure in the turkey vultures and we walked on the nature trail, too, so called from the sheet-metal signs that an oak was *quercus lobata,* etcetera. If the signs (the pride of the nature director) were to be credited, we weren't in any arcadia but in some frightful jungle, the lair of a red-toothed nature. Our holy oaks were the hostages of the die-all viruses in their trunks and the gall-wasp eggs in their twigs: in their monstrous growths. The bark beetles ate the xylem, inscribing it with cuneiform, and the woodpeckers took off the bark to get to the glutted beetles. The little infant acorns, the filbert weevils ate, the white-tailed deer ate the acorns and the filbert weevils, too, and each wretched oak had a cloak of murderous mistletoe like Medea's poisonous robe. To read the sheet-metal signs was to see these trees as Hardy had, combatants all,

> *Sycamore shoulders oak,*
> *Bines the slim sapling yoke,*
> *Ivy-spun halters choke*
> *Elms stout and tall.*

Why, even the chickadees there were as sociopathic as any gang on the West Side of Manhattan. The birds didn't sing a madrigal, as we had been promised by Marlowe—no, the meaning of their unpremeditated art was "Stay off my turf, motherfucker!" The signs said the long-eared owls ate the cute chipmunks, too.

We didn't detect this. We were at peace on that trail, though the interrelations were ones that we wouldn't tolerate from our own neighbors in Larchmont. In that village of six-sided bricks, we living things were as isolated as illegal aliens: though not on that twisting trail. Up, around, down were nothing but other living things: the leaves as silver-lined silhouettes in the eye-searing sky, the white-breasted nuthatches on the upper trunks, upside down, the boat-bottom-colored moss on the lower trunks, the nut-colored fans of fungus on the old toppled trees, the white termites there, and the leaves on the forest floor: the mulch for the solomon's seal. At one point, a hemlock rose out of solid rock: out of a crack that it elbowed open, an affidavit that we living things were as potent as Samson. We were more at home on that palpitant trail than in our homes in Larchmont: our life delighted in life, in the language of Blake.

But even the stones seemed as alive to us as to Christ, "The very stones would cry out." Once, I was going on the nature trail with a boy whose name was Klots and his famous father, the author of *The Field Guide to the Butterflies*. We had passed— well, a thousand stones of every lichen-crusted color when one of them must have cried out to Klots's father. "Hmm, there ought to be mice under that one," the man said casually, he tilted up the flat gray stone and lo: a couple of mice were peering up as though telling us, "My God! How did you *find* us?" But more than we stared at those white footed mice, we stared at the reticent top of Klots's father's Rosetta Stone. We were in our childhoods, when, says Spender, the pebbles amaze, but I'm fifty now and I'm still overwhelmed by that silent granite. "I don't know, I just listened to it," Klots's father explained.

A minute later, he pulled a small pebble out of a *creek* to show us a caddis worm in its mobile home. In time, Klots, Klots's prestidigitatorial father and I had completed the nature trail and had arrived at the nature director's office, a cabin on whose masonite walls were the ragged integuments of old dead opossums and a sign saying do not touch. An open bottle, its contents the color of muddy water, released the corrosive odor of formaldehyde. for the nature director (a boy of about eighteen with a pocked and purpled complexion) was at a table counting the scales of an old dead ribbon snake to ascertain that it wasn't really an infant garter snake. It was scandalous, but the nature director would go to his sunless recess (as Goethe had said of Newton) to contemplate what was the glory of all the hills and dales around him. As we entered, he didn't glance up but greeted us, "Hullo."

"Guess what?" I shouted. "We went to the nature trail and Mr. Klots—"

"Good God!" Klots's father said. I turned to him apprehensively as he bent to the wooden floor and, in the dust, inspected a dead white moth as small as an arbutus petal. "But this is an African moth!" Klots's father gasped.

"Mm," muttered the nature director, preoccupied by the wet-with-formaldehyde scales of the old rigor-mortised ribbon snake.

"Mr. Klots? It may have fallen out of the moth collection," I volunteered, conducting him to the forty small boxes of old dead *phorma pepons* and *macroplecta meriodonalises*.

"God, they *all* are African moths!" Klots's astonished father said.

I tapped the purple nature director on his round shoulders. "How come they're all African?" I asked.

"One, two, three, *four*," the nature director said. "All right, it's a ribbon snake."

You're right: the one boy who wasn't in love with nature was the intent nature director. A zoology major, his tragedy was to accept that the *animalia* constitute sort of a solid geometry that we cannot understand if we don't reduce them to Arabic numerals. A little snake: was it a northern brown snake or a red-bellied snake with an off-color belly? The nature director counted, for the former had seventeen scale-rows and the latter had only fifteen. A pretty bird: was it a white-eyed vireo or a red-eyed vireo? The nature director counted, for the former had two white wing-bars and the latter hadn't any. And what was the big, black, feather-legged, finger-length, pincer-faced, and really detestable insect, the monster out of some steaming meteorite that a boy once brought to the nature director's den? "*It bit me,*" the boy scout stammered, and the nature director used a magnifier to ascertain that the hideous thing had six thoracic legs on its three thoracic segments, prolegs on none of its eight abdominal segments, a cephalad-directed not a ventrad-directed head, a pair of claws on its six thoracic legs, and a pair of mandibulo-suctorial mandibles as he consulted his *Key to the North American Insects*. "A hellgramite, *corydalus cornutus*," he announced, and he smothered the foul fiend in his sodium cyanide prior to pinning it in his insect collection like a note on a bulletin board.

Now, I don't fault the nature director for his onomatomania:

that is, his total obsession with the *names* of all living things. After all, God authorized man to declare that a rose is a rose, whatever, the stone-agers did it and indians do it as consummately as any taxonomist: the Seminoles coining names for two hundred plants, the Hopis three hundred plants, the Navahos five hundred plants, so I'm informed. In the Philippines, the Haununóos, who file their betel-black teeth to repugnant stumps, refer to the *líyamlíyam* and another 1,800 plants, more than the botanists do at the University of the Philippines, in Manila, as well as to one dozen snakes, spiders, crustaceans, as *well* as to sixty fishes, seventy birds, eighty molluscs, and one hundred insects. To walk on a nature trail with a Haununóo is like batting about with the ghost of Linnaeus. No, where these indians and the nature director differed wasn't in christening all living things but in considering them as spatial relationships, as dead as the dodecahedrons. In the Philippines, the pigmies distinguish the bats by their natural habitats: in the bamboo, the *litlit*, in the banana trees, the *dikidik*, in the palm trees, the *tididin*, and in their haunts a dozen more. To tell them apart, the pigmies do not violate the chiropterous right to life, liberty, and the pursuit of fruit flies by grasping the aghast animals and by pulling their furry ears in front of their noses, as the nature director did in America. The director would tell us, "See? If the ear is one millimeter longer it's a *little brown bat*, but if it's four millimeters longer it's an *Acadian bat*."

And saying so, he would relocate them in a more efficient habitat: a bottle of fresh formaldehyde, where the relative length of a bat ear and a bat nose would be obvious to the most nearsighted boy. The contrast between a bat that's alive and one that isn't wasn't as clear to the nature director as to us (or the little critter itself), for the two modes had the same measurements, and the nature director became the collector of nature's debt by his continually killing them. In his course for the insect merit badge, he "destridulated" a male little cricket: he cut off its wings, to demonstrate that the females weren't turned on if a male couldn't crick. On netting a tiger swallowtail, he dropped the sun-colored specimen into a jar of sodium cyanide, amputated its abdomen, dropped it into another jar of hot caustic potash, pushed out its sexual organs, and grinned like a peeping tom to show us the swallowtail's penis with a 400-power microscope. It was blasphemous, but I had to gas fifty insects for the merit badge, whose name was Insect Life but ought to be Insect Death.

One afternoon, I was gassing a dreamy dusky-wing at the nature director's office when the sound of Mexican maracas commenced, and I noticed a four-foot rattlesnake, a very alive rattlesnake, on the nature director's desk, the span of my hand away from the butterfly and me. Its eyes were vertical slits in its arrow's head and its black-banded neck was in S-shapes, and as I edged away I said, "Gee, there's a timber rattlesnake there."

"I got it from someone at Schaghticoke," the nature director said.

"Gee," I repeated.

"It was three dollars—watch, I'm going to milk it."

"But that's just a superstition, isn't it?" I asked.

"It's not going to milk a cow, dope! I'm going to milk the rattler!" So saying, the nature director put a small microscope slide in my fingers and he himself pinched the serpent's neck in his own enterprising fingers. And *rrrrrr*, it rattled again like a new year's razzle-dazzle, and I swear I saw steam come out of its nostrils as I waited impatiently to see that rattlesnake's tits. "The slide, hold it in front of its rostral plate," the nature director said. "In front of its nose."

"Is this close enough?" I asked.

"No, closer, closer—*there*," the nature director said as the openmouthed animal bit at my microscope slide with its two scimitar-shaped fangs. The venom crept to my fingertips but I tilted the wet little slide to repel it.

"Oh, that's what the *milk* is," I said.

"That's right." And putting the viper into a padlocked box, the nature director injected the venom into a three-point frog from the annual animal hunt. It croaked, and one month later the culpable rattler got *his:* the nature director dropped a rag sogged in chloroform into its padlocked box and it thrashed about like a bullwhip, biting itself on its writhing sides with its dripping fangs. It breathed for one more minute, its belly plates like a deck of cards, spread, unspread, until it was motionless as a length of waterlogged rope. Its agonies over, the nature director coiled the openmouthed corpse into a bottle with the label *crotalus horridus horridus*, where for one hundred years the boy scouts could see it strike at the brown formaldehyde. "On second thought, it might be a *crotalus horridus atricaudatus*," the nature director said.

He didn't think of that reptile as one incarnation of God. A tube: that's what it was to the nature director and the other servants of science (of science with a capital scythe, says Jarry) as long ago as the seventeenth century, such as the Royal Society. Three years old, the Society had reported how to kill timber rattlesnakes, which was to press a wild pennyroyal plant to their rostral plates for a half hour's time, a way of such feeble efficiency that it was soon mocked in Hill's *Review of the Works of the Royal Society,*

If the world should wish to see this discovery paralleled, we have the ever-remembered powder for killing fleas. The flea was to be held between the thumb and finger while the powder was to be applied to its trunk.

Nor did the Society confine itself to the study of man's worst enemies, for it used goose quills to inoculate opium into a dog, tobacco into a dog, and spaniel blood into a mongrel, an act that was caricatured in *The Virtuoso,* "So gentlemen, the spaniel became a bulldog and the bulldog a spaniel." In my own boy scout days, a doctor put two dozen dogs on a table in Manhattan and, after petting them, after comforting them, beat them a thousand times with a half-pound mallet to study shock, successfully. "We were able to produce fatal shock in a high percentage," he reported in the *American Journal of Physiology.*

No aberration, the nature director saw God's creations as saltpeter, pasteboard, and catgut (three words of Carlyle's) and his heart didn't leap up at the red, orange, yellow locus of Airy's Rainbow Integral. He understood that the poison ivy wasn't ivy, the red cedars weren't cedars, the ladybugs weren't bugs, the house sparrows weren't sparrows, the jack rabbits weren't rabbits, and the flying squirrels didn't fly, but he didn't delight that the flora, fauna, and boy scouts were one and the same miracle: were *life*. The flower in its crannied wall, the hemlock in its clefted rock, the swift in its sooty chimney didn't remind him how all living things—among them, him—will flourish in the most inhospitable circumstances if no one interferes with them.

> Sweet is the lore which nature brings,
> Our meddling intellect
> Misshapes the beauteous forms of things,
> We murder to dissect,

but the nature director saw as a dissector would: with the *meddling intellect* of Wordsworth.

The intellect: our most tragic illusion, said Jung. It pretends to know everything when it knows nothing except what is scornful of our own sentiments, like the two ten-millimeter mandibles of the hellgramite: everything else, it repudiates as irremediably immeasurable. To be like our nature director, to cling to the intellect not to the passionate intuition, is to condemn ourselves to irrelevance and to waste away like the seventeenth-century president of the Royal Society: Newton, a mental incompetent at all that didn't reduce to the one-two-threes. He once proposed to a woman but, her hand in his hand, started to contemplate the binomial theorem, too. So $(a+b)^n = a^n + na^{n-1}b + \frac{1}{2!}n(n-1)a^{n-2}b^2$, he thought, tamping his hot tobacco with a pipe-tobacco tamp—*no*, it wasn't a tamp but the lady's dainty finger, the seventeenth century story went, and the lady screamed and Newton said, "My dear, I beg your pardon!" He died of chronic virginity, the doctors reported.

As someone said, a man doesn't get as stinking drinking as he does thinking, but the nature director swilled at his own 200-proof intellect all of July and August. *Il penseroso*, he hid in his odorous office and—the next summer—at one in the reptile department of the Museum of Natural History in Manhattan. There where the birds didn't sing, I visited him and he said proudly, "I discovered a new semi-poisonous snake in Brazil."

"Gee, you've been to Brazil?" I said, surprised. It was unlike the nature director to paddle down the Amazon or to use his arms, legs, or pale gray eyes to participate in the outdoors: only to ponder it.

"No, I discovered it at the museum here," the nature director said, and he showed me a black-banded snake in a bottle of muddy formaldehyde. "The black bands aren't as long as on other *erythrolampruses*, so I've called it a new subspecies, *erythrolamprus aesculapii bogerti.*"

"Who's *bogerti?*" I said.

"Dr. Bogert. The curator here. It won't be a new subspecies if he doesn't endorse it."

"Gee, good luck," I said.

The intellect: a fatal disease, said Wagner. In his twenties, sent to Korea, the nature director caught a two-foot copperhead on the central front, and, in his crusade for the international recognition of his *erythrolamprus aesculapii bogerti*, he donated it in formaldehyde to Dr. Bogert. In his thirties, sent to a mental hospital in Pennsylvania, he wrote in his autobiography that he had discovered a new semi-poisonous snake, the *erythrolamprus aesculapii bogerti*, and in his forties down to a $100-monthly flophouse in Baltimore he wrote to Dr. Zweifel, the new curator at the Museum of Natural History, to tout his *erythrolamprus aesculapii bogerti*. "The bands shorter than in *erythrolamprus aesculapii monozona*," the nature director insisted, and I must report with a heavy heart that at fifty years old he killed himself, his ultimate act of irrelevance in his cut-and-dried world.

His name was Stewart. As nature director, his retirement from the boy scout camp was no red-letter day for the animals there, for his successor was an insect exterminator in his civilian life. To donate a common amber-wing, a silver-spotted skipper, or even a ruby-throated hummingbird to his office was as unintentionally sinister as to donate cats to the ASPCA. The next summer's nature director was a premedic, a boy whose monomania was the dissection of fat green frogs. A frog's little wiggling legs in his fist, he would tell us, "Now, what's the first thing to do to dissect a *rana clamitans?*"

"Give it some laughing gas?"

"No, *kill* it," the nature director cried as he slammed its pop-eyed head on his desk-edge like a judge's gavel, to sentence it to terminal hematoma. A pin in its brains was his coup de grace.

Now, I don't think that our boy scout camp was a haven for all the psychopathic personalities in Larchmont. After all, our right to use and abuse the fish, fowl, and all living things had been established in Genesis, and our saints practically had a *zoo* of subservient species: the lion of St. Mark, the bear of St. Euphemia, the wolf of St. Sequanus. "It was wonderful," says a thirteenth-century report, "to watch as this wolf pulled the plow and did everything like a domestic animal." To the seventeenth century, *nature* was the one obstacle to efficiency, or, in the words of one founder of the Royal Society, "The veneration [of] nature has been a discouraging impediment to the empire of man over the inferior creatures." We have to master it: Descartes, to establish an empire over it: Bacon, to administer it as the Japanese do with their *bonsai* trees. Soon nature, according to Dewey, was something not to enjoy or endure but to control like a tiger tamer's herd, and the nature directors directed it into formaldehyde, where it wouldn't bite. The nature directors weren't nuts.

But they seemed so. By August, Stewart was known to us lesser intellects as the Mad Doctor. Another nature director put a live little brown bat on the line of his fishing pole to eat up the cursed mosquitoes. Another put one hundred frogs from the annual animal hunt into a burlap bag and *hip, hip,* emptied them on the desk of a man who bothered him. As they hopped on the paperwork like a horde of wet rubber stamps, the nature director shouted like Moses, "Behold, I've delivered a plague of wet-footed frogs unto the hard-hearted man!" Another director belted himself to his lintel: there to flap his arms massively like a ring-necked pheasant, saying, "Squawk!" He did this, he told us, to celebrate the great sighting of one of these *rarae aves* in his class for the bird merit badge.

One nature director took to drink: domestic port, a violation of our boy scout oath. The worse for a bottle of Gallo, he rose at a council fire to officiate at a vesper service for (he professed) a Siamese fire god. "Howa Taho! That's the fire nod's game," the nature director roared to two hundred wide-eyed boys. "The fire god's name, repeat it!"

"Howa Taho!"

"Sesa Siam! That's the sand of Liam!"

"Sesa Siam!"

"Now louder," the nature director roared as the fire reddened his blood-reddened eyes.

"Howa Taho! Sesa Siam!"

"Now louder," the nature director roared, and he stumbled off to the cookie jars at Sakajawea, the girl scout camp, as we sat and chanted that we were horses' asses—*oh, what a horse's ass I am!*

The next day, I was called down to the camp director's office off the ping-pong room. "I've had to let the nature director go, John," the camp director, an ex-state trooper, said, as he watched me with his straight-shooter eyes.

"Gee, Morty," I said, surprised.

"I think you can hack it, John."

"Morty?"

"I can pay twenty dollars per week," the camp director said, and I wasn't out of high school when, for my sins, he installed me as the new lunatic there.

But let that pass. A summer ago, I stopped in at my boy scout camp and saw the same swallows (no: their great-great-*thirty*-grandchildren) do the same swoops on the black-eyed susans by the American flag. The oaks stood as changelessly as God, but the pines on the parade grounds that, in my childhood, rose to the tip of my neckerchief, reached to the chimney swifts today: to thirty feet, a reproof to my own comparative inertia. The new camp director was a mere sperm when I was an eagle scout, and the Catholic priest was an African, in whose home of Ngwo, Nigeria, an ancient ebony tree is God and the populace dances around it. Not emulating them, the priest believed in the wafers which came by parcel post from the Congregation of the Holy Ghost, in Pittsburgh, saying on Sunday, "Diss iss my body, which—" At the insistence of Christian ministers, the two-horned medicine man for the WWW had purged the pagan things from the poems in the cricket-chirping night.

At the nature director's office were a coral snake in formaldehyde and an albino frog in Clorox, the result of a recent experiment in what would befall a common frog in Clorox. The nature director himself was an odd-eyed individual (on his desk was a packet of Zig-Zags, I saw) who was conducting a class in the tree merit badge, telling the twelve-year-olds, "Another method of mensuration is occulation, correct?" A moment later, he was summoned down to the camp director's office, and I was over-whelmed by my déjà vu to discover that he had been fired for smoking cannabis in violation of the *Boy Scout Handbook* ("A serious problem today") and for telling the boy scout commis-sioner, "So you don't like it, faggot?" On hearing this, I did my day's good deed by pinch-hitting for the depraved director in his afternoon class in the reptile merit badge.

My luck was to have a real live reptile as an audio-visual aid. A ribbon snake, a shoelace long, a catch in the annual animal hunt, it slid in and among my gentle fingers as I said hello to a dozen boys on the former nature director's porch. But unlike a cat that scratches its back against me, the ribbon snake was at *home* in my fingers, evidently, as if they were cattails or some other natural habitat. It licked at my little finger to test if this weren't really a tender salamander, and I was, well, *flattered* that the intuitive creature thought of me as part of its real world. Then carefully, I passed it to one boy scout, doing my duty as pro-tem nature director by asking him, "Do you know the name of this snake?"

"Yes sir: Herman," the boy scout said.

"No, I mean—" I began.

"Hello, Herman," the boy scout said, his nose stroking the snake's smooth nose.

"I mean what species is it?"

"Oh Herman! You're licking me! A garden snake," the boy scout answered.

"No, not garden," I said. "The word is garter: *garter*, like the red little things that the camp director wears, but I don't think this is a garter snake. A garter is bigger—"

The boy scout interrupted me. "How much bigger's the biggest snake?"

"In the world? Well, there's a python that's twenty-two feet at the Bronx Zoo—"

"How did they catch it?"

"How did they *catch* it? Uh—"

"How long is twenty-two feet?"

"Twenty-two feet?" I said, grateful for a more soluble problem. "As long as this porch is."

"I caught a milk snake once," the boy scout said. "I saw him and I had this rope, and I roped him and I put him into a burlap bag. He was big!"

"Mm," I said. "But this I don't think is a garter snake. I think—"

"Oh Herman! Oh, what big eyes you've got!" The two were still eyeball to eyeball, the boy and beast on that creosote porch.

"I think this is—"

"You don't have any eyebrows!"

"A ribbon—"

"You don't have any eyelashes, either!"

"Snake," I said.

"You don't have any eyelids!"

"No," I agreed. "A lizard does, but a snake doesn't have any eyelids."

"So how does he keep things out?"

"Huh?"

"So how does he keep the gravel out?"

"Gee, I don't know," I said.

"He doesn't have any ears, either."

"No," I agreed. "His eyes are his only holes."

"His nose!"

"I forgot," I confessed. "But how can I tell it's a ribbon snake, not a baby garter snake?"

"Hey Herman! You're crawling up my shirt sleeve!"

"I'll tell you: I'll have to count up the snake-scales. One, two, three," I began as Herman emerged at the boy scout's collar in search of some toads there. "Gee, this isn't easy."

"Hey Herman! You're tickling me!"

"One, two, three, four, I'm getting lost," I confessed. "One, two, three, four—"

"Is it safe if I tie him into an overhand knot?"

"It's safe," I said. "I don't think I remember this. Uh, there's something about the fourth scale but I don't remember what it is. So—"

"Herman untied it! Herman untied it!"

"It should be a ribbon snake but—"
"I'll tie him into a figure eight!"
"It might be a baby garter snake."

And come and get your beans, boys, come! As the bugle blew on a Panasonic, the boy scouts sprinted to dinner and I put the species *sauritus sauritus* or the species *sirtalis sirtalis* into its concrete pit. I promise you, I felt like a real horse's ass. The boy who was nose to nose with that trustful creature of God knew much more than I did, his nature director emeritus. As his wide eyes met Herman's, as his life met life, he participated in this planet like an Ojibwa indian,

We know who the animals are: the bear, the beaver, the rest, because we married them long ago and learned from our animal wives.

To this honorable estate, I had come like an old pornographer with my pointing finger, my wagging tongue, my intrusive intellect, to expound the barren facts of the reptile merit badge. To earn it, the boy's perceptions had to limit themselves to that small fraction —according to Dostoevsky, a twentieth—that all his four billion contemporaries shared. So *what* if the whole world called it a ribbon snake, a garter snake, a gutter snake, a garden snake or a Gorgon? The snake itself didn't know it!

Our intellect! It's impotent even in its own domain: it can't locate an electron, said Heisenberg, it can't do a QED on some simple things in *arithmetic*, said Gödel, it still hasn't demonstrated that an even number must be the sum of two prime numbers, though no one doubts it. Nor was intellect part of our constitutions for 99.9 percent of our history, says Jaynes. We hunted, we planted, we built the damn pyramids and the Sphinx, we *spoke* to each other without any cogitation about it, Jaynes maintains. In the *Iliad*, Agamemnon commands a hundred thousand men to sharpen their spears, to wield their shields, to hop on their fleet-footed steeds, and at their defeat he flares up, "Fie upon you, Argives!" But never do his commands come out of his intellect: he doesn't think in the *Iliad*, he simply listens to Zeus. In the oldest book of the Bible, Amos serves as a spokesman for God, the Almighty Arsonist, "Thus saith the Lord! I will send a fire on Moab!" "Thus saith the Lord! I will send a fire on Gaza!" "Thus saith the Lord! I will send a fire on Judah!" But never is Amos the conduit for his own thoughts.

No one was intellectual (for chrissake: no one was even *conscious*) for the first three million years of human history, says Jaynes. And then something occurred: the eruption, perhaps, of the only volcano in Greece, in 1470 B.C. on Thera. "In one day and night of misfortune, the island vanished into the sea," said Plato. The shock of three hundred hydrogen bombs and a tidal wave as high as the Empire State hit the old civilization on Crete: recent computations, and at the hill city of Gournia the carpenters left all the hammers, nails, on the floor as they fled, unsuccessfully: the wood burned to charcoal, the trim melted down to chaotic gobs, the bricks baked to vermillion in the fire that followed (or perhaps, preceded) the horrible sky-high wave. And four hours later, it *still* was higher than a two-floor house as it smashed into the Holy Land. Civilizations collapsed and men, women, and children—among them the Jews of the exodus— became a mob of displaced persons, the instructions of Zeus were no longer reliable, and we began to use intellect, instead, just three thousand years ago: says Julian Jaynes.

By three hundred years ago, Descartes could say, "I knew that I was an entity whose entire essence consists in intellect." The next century was the one of Reason,

> *Two principles in human nature reign:*
> *Self-love to urge and Reason to restrain,*

said Pope, and Robespierre's only god was Reason. In the *next* century, all that wasn't intellect was "the beast within us," and currently we are the monocerebral men, says Fromm: the men whose bones are the buttresses of two-eyed, two-eared computer chips. On television at seven every night is a wax museum of these creatures: the chess champion, the astronaut, the president's assistant with a zombie's one-note voice, the president's assistant with the hair that's not cut but calibrated, the secretary of our defense,

The real threat is to let some force other than reason shape reality. That force may be greed, aggressiveness, hatred, inertia,

or *love*, the man didn't remember, and, too often, the correspondents themselves, telling of one hundred deaths as though they're reciting the *Statistical Abstract of the United States*. "Good evening! One hundred persons died on a DC-10—"

Our intuition capitulates to our totalitarian intellect, though, as Bergson said, "Intuition goes in the very direction of life, intellect in the inverse direction." The next century will be no more footloose or fancy-free, if I must judge from the eggheads of *2001*, *THX1138*, *Futureworld*, and the Futuramas at the 1940 and 1965 world's fairs in New York City. In my second childhood, I'd gone through the tunnel of love once more: the Futurama, 1965, and I'd listened to muzak-music (the sound of some orchestra in a fathom of olive oil) as my armchair approached a lemon-yellow glow: the City of Tomorrow. It lay underneath cement like an automobile lot, and the trees (which were few and far between) were in more cement, recalling the dismal prediction of Joni Mitchell's: They put all the trees in a tree museum. And seeing them, I felt that if *I* lived there I'd scratch out a human heart on those potted trees or I'd scribble *hello* on those concrete walls— on those monuments that in the summer sun, oh, God, would be hot, white, and hostile to all human aspirations, would be the same solid geometry as in Brasilia, Islamabad, and Century City in California. After all, on the marble walls of Pompeii it was written that *Paris Was Here*, so why were there no graffiti in the concrete city of Tomorrow?

Were there really people there? If there were, it was obvious none of them smoked, chewed gum, chewed candy, chewed cookies, or blew their noses in Kleenex, as there were no paper wrappers— well, so there weren't litterbugs in Tomorrow but there were no wastepaper baskets, either. "Do you think there's anyone there?" I asked one of the other armchair travelers.

"Anyone where?"

"Anyone *there*," I said. "Do you think there're people there?"

"People there?" The man was disoriented, as though the presence of real flesh was a concept that he hadn't entertained. "Of *course* there're people there, aren't there?"

"Where?"

"Well, I say they're watching television. And going bowling on Friday."

He didn't believe it, I don't believe. In the sixteenth century in Utopia, we were quick, witty, merry, and partial to Plato, in this twentieth-century utopia we had evolved, evidently, to an ectoplasm of invisible intellect: to machines, says Clarke, to patterns of little electrons, says Watts, to vortices of pure thought, says Shaw. Nor did this inability to sing, to shout, or to see swallows at all dispirit the three intellectuals. "If this happens—and I think that it must—we have nothing to regret," says Clarke. "If all this ends," says Watts, "why should that trouble us?" "The day will come," says an old woman in Shaw, "when there will be only thought." "And that will be life eternal," an old man elaborates.

At the Futurama, we seemed to have reached the omega point of Father Teilhard de Chardin, the French philosopher. By his definition, our intellect had at last freed itself from its material matrix: an ecstasy, he predicted. As one who says thank you, God, for my own material matrix, I've wondered how a utopia so hollow, so heartless, and so *impious* could owe to someone who was an avowed agent of God. Father Teilhard de Chardin, I've learned, was a man haunted by the one ultimate inefficiency: death. At five years old, he had a traumatic episode as his hair (a snippet, since he was having a haircut) curled like a fallen leaf in his fireplace, disappearing, and, as he said much later, "I knew then that I was perishable." He started to sob and, after that, was as leery of real flesh as Plotinus, a third-century philosopher who was never sketched, since (he insisted) it would perpetuate his existential degradation.

Teilhard de Chardin didn't care for the "delicate" and "destructible" butterflies. He preferred beetles, the harder the better, and he collected stones: the indestructible ones of France's volcano country. He collected, too, an iron newel, an iron plow pin, and a six-sided iron nut and worshiped them as his immortal god of iron until they rusted: then, at ten years old, he collapsed at his chateau, sobbing again. At forty years old, he was transfixed as a dog-tooth tuna ate a flying fish and a gull nibbled up the last little morsels in the Red Sea. "Who will deliver us from death?" Teilhard de Chardin wailed.

Alas, death is one of two certain things: the mayflies live a few hours, cecropia moths a few days, and half of our universe decays to pions and positrons in one one-hundredth of one decillion years. In time, everything dies but death itself, and Teilhard de Chardin couldn't abolish it without at first abolishing life. In his utopia, he killed all our inefficient viscera to sublimate us to the one immortal element: the intellect, the loveless and lifeless intellect, says Mumford, the mud-colored computer tape, the roll that encodes all the facts, facts, facts, but the ones secreted in our own hearts. The good father called it superlife, but I beg your indulgence if I simply call it death: if my eyes, ears, phallus are to be amputated, thank you, no, I'd rather be a little brown bat in the nature director's formaldehyde.

And that reminds me: a summer ago, I put the congenial snake in its concrete crib and I ran downhill to our evening mess. In the tumultuous room, I was introduced to the two hundred boys and I said diabolically, "I have a short announcement." And instantly, the baked potatoes decomposed as two hundred unintellectuals sang, "Announcements! Announcements! Announcements! Mary had a little lamb, little lamb, little lamb—" An hour later, in the glow of our council fire the mouths of these babes demolished the whole philosophy of Father Teilhard de Chardin,

> Every time you're near a rose,
> Aren't you glad you've got a nose?

The following morning, a heron balanced close to the mist-ridden lake and a yellowthroat bounced in a dew-dappled bush. In the rafters of the nature director's porch was a brood of new little swallows, open-mouthed as though caroling the Hallelujah Chorus. As their acting director, I was careful as any mother hen as I set a mirror over them to awe everyone at my boy scout camp with a living vision of God.

5 / See Here, Private Sack

Or, The Inefficient Element

Call me Sad Sack. I was out of the boy scouts into the army three short days of the red-menaced 1950's and I was already screwing up. But honest, it hadn't been my intent to comport myself other than in accordance with the almost talmudic rules of *The Soldier's Handbook*. To begin with, I had placed my polyethylene soap dish at the front of my foot-locker tray. One inch behind it (*one inch behind it:* by order of the army's adjutant general) was my polypropylene comb, and in their appointed order were my polystyrene toothbrush (its stiff bristles to the left: *left*) and my razor blade and my razor—oh, my locker looked like the Union's order of battle at Gettysburg in the early morning of July 1, 1863. In one corner was a red-hatted sentinel: a tube of my shaving cream, in one other corner was—

"Sad Sack! And what," the sergeant shouted, "in da holy hell is dat ding dere?"

"Sergeant sir? It's my toothpaste," I replied. It was seven o'clock or just after reveille on a snowy day, and I was standing at iron attention at this very important locker at Fort Dix, New Jersey.

"I ain't sergeant sir! I'm good as anyone here and I'm sergeant, sergeant, got it? And dere ain't anywhere dat it says toot paste in *Da Soja's Handbook!*"

"Sergeant sir? I mean sergeant—sir, it says on page sixty-some-thing that in the far upper left of the footlocker is—"

"Powder! Powder!"

"Is tooth powder, sir? Oh," I explained. "I use toothpaste myself."

"Not any more," the sergeant shouted. "Ya uses powder! Ya uses powder like it directs in *Da Soja's Handbook!*" I was appalled. Of course, I was aware of how such matériel as pink-tinted toothpaste can be the undoing of the most resolute armies. In grammar school, I had heard of the infamous horseshoe nail,

> *For want of a nail, the shoe was lost,*
> *For want of a shoe, the horse was lost,*
> *For want of a horse, the rider—*

etcetera, until the whole kingdom fell to the Huns—to *someone*, we weren't told at my grammar school. Nor did this seem paranoia—no, in 1812 someone forgot to put calkers (or one-centimeter cleats) on the eight hundred thousand horseshoes of France's *Grande Armée*. On the ice-ridden road to Moscow, the slip-shod horses fell on their *derrières*, the poor horses couldn't get up (and were eaten by the famished enlisted men) and it was *finis* for Napoleon. In 1588, there were no well-seasoned staves in Spain, and the tide of battle turned when the water ran out of the water barrels (at their bottoms: a few uninviting inches of sea-green slime) in the Spanish Armada. And great ghost of Caesar— I was aware that the very decline and fall of Rome is attributable to the lead plumbing pipes in the better homes, for Rome's better people (the ones, according to Juvenal, who dined, alone, on seven-course dinners) died of lead poisoning, inadvertently. In 1942—to illustrate that my own army wasn't secure from the treachery of the trivial—we put ten thousand men on Papua who weren't equipped with the usual ditty bags. In the mud, the quinine pills in their pockets became a lint-like thing, the soldiers had no more quinine pills and a third of them caught malaria: it took them another half a year to throw out the Japs on Papua.

No sirree. On my third day at Fort Dix, New Jersey, I was content that the war effort in Korea (we were at war in Korea) had been compromised to a greater or lesser degree by my thoughtless use of Pepsodent in its gummose form in direct disobedience of *The Soldier's Handbook*. I mean it—suppose that my toothpaste and I went "over there" and the former froze over in the mountains of Frozen Chosen. A cold cement, it wouldn't come out of its toothpaste tube, and I, its dirty-toothed owner, would be evacuated to some rear-area "mash" with a case of gross carious lesions. My squad would be one man short, and as our slit-eyed enemies came up the mountain we— Listen! It wasn't impossible! It wasn't the "mickey mouse" in our orders—the razor here, the razor blade there (and the razor's head to the *left*, trainee)—that so upset me at my big boy scout camp, it was rather the utter impossibility of carrying all of those orders out. For Almighty God! I was only human! I had two hands, that's all! I had two feet that marched to the two-four time of *over hill, over dale, and* to the different drums of the drives within me. I wasn't just a machine, set to squat when it said ready, squat, in *The Soldier's Handbook.* Certainly not, and if any exercise of my self-determination—if any unscheduled use of my toothpaste, shower soap, or horseshoe nails was a threat to our war effort in Korea, we were better off if I slashed myself with my well-placed razor blade and, at reveille, bled to an early death in my sergeant's arms as I murmured, "My only regret—"

"And Sad Sack! *And,*" the real sergeant said (it was still seven o'clock at my egregious locker at Dix)—"and where in da holy hell are ya cigarettes?"

"Sergeant, I don't smoke cigarettes," I said.

"Well, lamebrain! It don't say to smoke cigarettes in Du Soju's *Handbook!* It only says to dispose dem in da lower left of da locker!"

"But sergeant, I think—" I began.

"Ya what? Ya what? If da army wants ya ta think, nincompoop, it will issue a goddam box of brains!"

Oh Sergeant McHugh! I do not dislike you, sir! The man, reader, wasn't a big gorilla but a few inches shorter than me—a man who chewed tutti-frutti as he indulged in his fad, furor, madness to end inefficiency: to stop us from tossing wooden shoes in the machine to Win the War. In this crusade, he was more often than not as benign as St. Francis. "We are now gonna count off," he had said as the buses brought us to our dorm in the Garden State. "We are gonna count off by calling out, One, Two, One, Two, One, Two, One, Two. Is dere anyone here—" and the man stared at each acne-dappled one of us—"who doesn't know how ta count ta Two?" Our sergeant was no less considerate when he saw at this seven o'clock that we (no, it wasn't just me) weren't just the toy soldiers with the Winchesters on their right shoulders and the Chesterfields in their lockers that he knew were needed by Uncle Sam. He presented a saintly patience, instead, and far from having us ready, aim—far from having us shot at the sunrise, he just directed us ("Ta ya left! Ta ya left! Ta—Gallagher! Ya still outa step") to march to a dim auditorium and to a one-hour movie on what might betide us if we wouldn't bow to the One Best Way, as specified in *The Soldier's Handbook.*

The movie's name was *The Late Company B.* The lights going out, we saw the late company as two hundred crosses (and two stars of David) in a white cemetery and in the flawless formation that the sergeant tried to impose upon *us,*

> *Dress it up and cover down,*
> *Forty inches all aroun',*

the sergeant would say. As the mist slipped by (and the cellos played on the soundtrack) the unit started to reincarnate itself like the see-through characters in the movie of *Our Town.* It stood at its wooden crosses and in its hollow tones said, "Boggs? Boggs?"

"Here! Where's Moon?"

"Moon? Moon?"

"Duffy? Duffy?"

"Sack? Sack?" No part of the soundtrack, the words were those of a boy in our dim auditorium.

"Who said dat? Quattrocchi? Den gimme ten," our sergeant shouted, and Quattrocchi did his ten pushups on the auditorium's concrete floor as the ghosts in the movie muttered on.

"Hanks? Hanks?"

"How did it happen to us, Duffy? I can't figure it," another mass of ectoplasm said. "I can't figure it!"

And those cellos, crescendo. As the late company resolved itself into a dew again, an announcer called for a sort of coroner's inquest into the cause of its total catastrophe. And flashing back to its infantry camp in Louisiana, he announced that the fatal flaws were a number of boys whose philosophies were "The little things don't matter." One such defect was Boggs—he had lost his canteen ("I'm sorry, sarge") and another was Moon, who wouldn't eat the mess sergeant's meatloaf ("Aw, this meatloaf stinks") and who pushed the six-sided solid aside as we all applauded and as our sergeant shouted, "*Stop it!*" The hero, though, or the villain of this verisimilar movie was a soldier whose name was Brown. Brown, who was white, incidentally, as was everyone (no doubt even the boogie-woogie bugle boy) of *The Late Company B*, had two pairs of combat boots but he only used one. "He saved the other pair for inspections," the tittle-tattle announcer announced, and I thought, So, who doesn't?

To the music of tubas, trumpets, and big brass drums, the company got on its gray-sided ship, and, *cut*, it was slogging over a hot little island in the Pacific. "*Awk. Awk,*" the parrots called as Brown sat down underneath a mahogany tree and, in pulling off one of his boots, discovered a hole in its well-worn sole of silver-dollar dimensions. He was rubbing his metatarsals as the captain came by.

"Hey Brown! Why don't you use the other pair?"

"They're with the supply column, sir."

"Well, they don't do very much good there!"

"*Awk,*" a parrot cried.

A bird of ill omen, obviously, but Brown just stuffed an old handkerchief into the troublesome hole (a *little* thing, the announcer repeated) and he stood up to— Tatatata! Tatatata! It was the Japs!

"*Banzai,*" the yellow devils cried.

"*Sir,*" the old sergeant cried. "We can't hold them!"

"*Fire whatever you got,*" the captain cried.

"*Ohhhh!*" A moan arose in the dim auditorium as the combatants began to go brown on the hitherto silver screen. The film was on fire, unfortunately, and our own sergeant took us outdoors for an hour of deep knee bends. And although we never ascertained how the two hundred soldiers died for the want of one soldier's shoe, we did devote lots of our time-until-taps (as our bottles came out of our not-wholly-official lockers) to the joys of conjecture over it. We thought up infinite possibilities. For instance, what if the captain wrote, *We need reinforcements,* on some scrap of paper that—to get to his higher headquarters—he entrusted to Brown, who misused it to reinforce the hole in his well-loved boot. It wasn't impossible—on September 9, 1862, an order to the Confederate army came from General Lee,

> *The army will march tomorrow, taking the Hagerstown Road. Jackson will take the route to Sharpsburg, cross the Potomac, and intercept such as may escape from Harper's Ferry. Long-street will—*

and there were paragraphs for General Walker, General Anderson, General McLaws, General Stuart, and General Hill. General Lee, who had issued it, entrusted a copy of the top-secret order to a man who apparently had no cigars (we know nothing of his tooth powder, sorry) in the lower left of his locker—no, his three cigars were on his person, he wrapped the order around them and, not caring for the aroma, apparently, he set them aside at his campfire, where, the next day, the weeds and the top-secret wrapper fell in the possession of Private Mitchell of the Twenty-Seventh Indiana Volunteers. "Lee has made a mistake, and he will be punished for it," the army wired to President Abraham Lincoln. It then intercepted him at Antietam ("The longest day," a Confederate captain said) and Lee retreated into the South and eventually lost the war. It really happened. It really did.

THE thought that one of his men might singlehandedly lose the war in Korea was one long nightmare for our Sergeant McHugh. For everyone else, it wasn't beyond belief but, Jesus, we were just human and we couldn't chasten ourselves (we couldn't reduce all our wills unto one, in the seventeenth-century phrase of Hobbes) to insure that we wouldn't be the monkey wrenches in the big green machine—well, it was then olive drab. We saw, among other things, that the tooth-powder cans (or in some recalcitrant cases, the toothpaste tubes)

in our footlockers came in such clown-clothes colors as red for the
Pepsodent and green for the Chlorodent and that their dissimili-
tude was a blot on our company's colors—we saw that but we
weren't pleased with the sergeant's solution of one tooth powder
for all and all for one. For starters, he strolled into the barracks
one day (the beds parallel as sarcophaguses, the bed rails meeting
at infinity, the blankets brown as our mother earth) to call for a
democratic vote on whether we ought to adopt a red, orange,
yellow, green, blue, or indigo toothbrush handle, and we were
speechless at this invasion of our own discretion until a so-called
colored soldier spoke up. "Sergeant, I vote for red."

"Ya vote for red?"

"Cause sergeant, we gonna put the mothers right up your rosy
rectum."

"Now dat's insubordinate," the sergeant began, but he was
shouted down.

"Red! Red! We vote for red!"

"No, de're gonna be *green*," the undemocratic sergeant said.
"And dose cigarettes gonna be Kools, and—"

"No they won't," a man shouted. "I don't smoke mentholated
cigarettes!"

"Now dammit! No one says smoke da Kools," the sergeant
retorted. "I just say *get* da Kools!"

"Sergeant? Get them from where?"

"Da damn cigarette machine!"

"On whose money, sergeant?"

"On *your* money, meatball!"

"Never happen! I'm not using no twenty cents for no fucking
faggot cigarette!"

"Me neither," we shouted. "No!"

It was mutiny! It was the Second American Revolution! In the
course of human events, we just walked away from the man whose
authority over the tint of our toilet articles came from the very
president of the United States. Oh, we were no dumb driven cattle
at Fox Company! We weren't the one-dollar cartons of chemical
elements (of ten gallons of water and of enough iron for a nail,
enough phosphorus for two thousand matches, enough carbon for
ten thousand pencils, enough gold for the Nazis, and enough cal-

cium to whitewash a chicken coop) that—in theory, anyway—all the king's horses and men could create a man of. No, we weren't the living machines of Reich, the big and the little wheels with the size, shape, and the right set of teeth to transmit the torque from the input end to the output end. We had free wills, and we were more evolved than the gears in a jeep transmission.

I mean, Jesus Christ! It was taught since the seventeenth century that a man, woman, or what-have-you is a mere machine. Our heart was a mere machine according to Harvey, our body (though not our sovereign soul) was a mere machine and was nothing but a machine to Descartes, and our whole frolicsome self was a mere machine to Hobbes. "For what is the heart but a spring," the philosopher wrote in *Leviathan*, "and the nerves but so many strings, and the joints but so many wheels?" And what, I reply, is this philosophy but so much engine exhaust? We vomit if we eat rotten food, said the doctor-philosopher de La Mettrie. Our pupils close in the daylight, our pores close in December, and our bodies recoil if we're approaching the parapets of Notre Dame. To quote de La Mettrie, "Is more needed (for why lose myself in the passions) to prove that a man is nothing but a collection of springs?" Well, doctor—we weren't springs in that infantry camp and we didn't go like jack-in-the-boxes as soon as an index finger hit us. In spite of our sergeant's efforts, we weren't just the self-balancing twenty-eight-jointed adapter-base bipeds that we are called by that prodigal son of the seventeenth century, by Buckminster Fuller. I ask you, Professor Fuller! On their wedding day, did your father look at your mother as a twenty-eight-jointed biped? If he did, today there would be no Professor Fuller!

Oh, we were incorrigible at Fort Dix! We had bourbon bottles (the dull-looking lumps in our laundry bags) but we hadn't half of our red-capped quota of Brasso cans. But don't call us unpatriotic, please: it didn't delight us to aid and abet the red menaces in Korea by not hanging ourselves from the barracks beams like so many marionettes. An army of traitors we hadn't wanted to be— no, I must disagree there with Dostoevsky. He wrote that out of *perversity* we people do dirty tricks to demonstrate that we aren't piano keys. If, he continued, it were proved that we are piano keys, we would go and cause chaos to prove that we aren't piano keys, and if this were predicted to prove, again, that we are piano keys we would go mad deliberately to shout to the gods above that we aren't: aren't: *aren't* piano keys! By this assessment, we GIs were the same willful rebels as the heroes of *Player Piano, The Invisible Man, The Magic Christian,* and *One Flew Over the Cuckoo's Nest,* but I contend we were *patriotic* and it wasn't on communist orders that we were loose screws in the war machine. No, we couldn't help it!

Because! We were alive! We weren't dead, and our apathies, antipathies, and our passions were a bar between an officer's order and its instant implementation. Oh, we would do column right like a parade of the wooden soldiers if our sergeant said to. We had been taught to ("Sad Sack! Ya know which hand is ya right one?" "This one, sergeant, sir." "Ya know why?" "Uh—" "Well, knucklehead, on account of da regulations say so")—we had been told to and, hell, there was no added advantage to straggling off to the left in the eastless and westless wastes of Fort Diddle Doo. As our two hundred boots hit the dirt simultaneously, we may have seemed (to look at and listen to, two, three, four) to be nothing more than the con rods of some olive-colored machine, but we were as liable as you yourself to trip, fall, faint, forget that we hadn't closed our fly, or go AWOL instead of column right, for as living things (as hemlocks in their clefted rocks) we were more obedient to our own imperatives than to the rules of Simon or Sergeant Says. Oh, listen to us as we're marching by! Do you suppose that the cadence call was one in *The Soldier's Handbook?*

> *I knew a gal and she was willin',*
> *Now I'm takin' penicillin—*

oh, we had wills of our own, everyone!

At the end of this semi-successful indoctrination, we were awarded the rifle merit badge and we were marched to the local airport in Newark. I wore a suntan uniform and (in place of a neckerchief) a scarf of infantry blue as I and the other doodle-dandies got on a passenger plane for the first thousand miles to Korea. On my shoulder straps there were no bars, tree leaves, or eagles—no, but there was a sun-shined set of white heraldic devices, the regiment's insignia, and oh! they were fine fine fine! Or would have been if they weren't upside down.

"As usual," I muttered.

"Oh," my girlfriend said at the airplane ramp. "You look like General MacArthur!"

"I shall return," I said as I kissed her. "So long, Sally."

She staggered as my fine visor hit her between her beautiful brown eyes. "*Ow ow ow*," she screamed.

"I'm sorry, Sally. So long," I said, climbing up, stumbling in (I had my combat boots on) and sitting down at a window seat on the 100-passenger plane.

The four propellers started. "Ladies and gentlemen, welcome aboard," the stewardess said—the stewardess stood like a wac company commander in her three-button suit (and three-button sleeves) and her own gold insignia: wings, and she spoke as intellectually as the super computer (or, for that matter, the stewardess) in *2001*. To listen to her could convince someone that a man-machine (or the end result of equality: a woman-machine) is, in fact, possible, even if there wasn't one on our company roster. In fact, there was at Bell a new machine—a *vocoder*, so they called it—to put ten telephone calls on one thin telephone line by strangling all of the joy, sorrow, zest, lethargy, love and loathing out of the ten conversations and by just transmitting the facts, ma'am, and the stewardess spoke like one of those damn contraptions. Nor was her grammar that of a living being—no, her throat was a pipe organ's pipe without any note that wasn't in black and white in the *In-Flight Manual*. "In the seat pocket," the stewardess said in her *which*-ridden sentences, "is a card which illustrates the safety features of our aircraft. It points out the location of, *giggle*, of your nearest exit and—"

Huh? Did the girl giggle? Yes, the girl giggled, and I sat and wondered why. Had she had any alcohol in the past twelve hours in defiance of section five of the *Manual?* Had she done scuba dives, and had one little bubble of nitrogen risen to her sweet medulla oblongata? I didn't know, but her one moment of mirth betrayed that the stewardess in her ten-inch-below-the-knee uniform was as human as any GI Joe. And the pilot too?

And *arrrr!* We rolled down the runway and we ascended out of that haunted airport in Newark. Haunted, as it had had three crashes in the three winter months— the planes crashed into a waterworks ("The roof fell on me," the watchman said) and an orphanage of sixty sound-asleep orphans ("Oh God! Not another one," a neighbor said) and, as strange as it seems, practically into the pilot's own dining room and a birthday party for his mother-in-law, and in these monthly crashes a total of fifty, thirty, and thirty people died. Nor could any authorities account for it—a gremlin, perhaps, had gotten into a governor solenoid valve of a near right propeller, and (and I'm quoting) the propeller had inadvertently reversed at fifteen hundred feet and

the violent maneuver created an emergency of such attendant urgency that the crew didn't make a correct analysis of the difficulty

and crashed on the two-story houses on Salem Avenue. God, it seemed to us lap-strap wearers that the soldiers were safer in the Second World War in *The Late Company B.* On the sea-level ship, at least they got to Guadalcanal! Or wherever!

Now, I didn't die on my three-mile-high trip to Chicago, Oakland, Tokyo, and Seoul, Korea, but thirty thousand people have died in their foam-rubber seats since then, and—as our unit is winging west to its destiny in the inscrutable east—let us allot twenty minutes to the causes of those catastrophic crashes. If you didn't know it, propellers do not conduct themselves like in Dostoevsky and reverse themselves out of sheer perversity at fifteen hundred feet. Oh, agreed, a near right propeller came off a passenger plane in the 1960's in spite of the laws of centripetal force —the plane, which it then harpooned like a big gray whale, crashed in the wheat fields of Marseilles, Ohio, and thirty people died in its crushed aluminum. Do not berate the poor little propeller, though, for the real culprit was a man—a *man*, a fatal insertion of human uncertainty into the chemical elements—at the propeller plant in Indianapolis, who had forgotten to "nitride" the helical splines of the torque piston of the pitch change unit of the helpless propeller. In spite of his best intentions, he could reproach himself in the too-true words of George Gordon Liddy, "I goofed."

Now, I've done some research here. In the sixties, a man at the rudder plant in Teterboro had gone against regulations when, to put eight wires into a servo unit, he had used tweezers and not his softer fingers. A few months later, the wires parted, the rudder went left, so did the plane and it crashed in the choppy waters of Pumpkin Patch Channel, in Queens, and ninety people died in their sudden submarine. A man at the hangar in Tulsa forgot the two-inch aluminum tag for cylinder number twelve of engine number two—it cracked, it caught fire, the plane crashed on Fort Leonard Wood, Missouri, and thirty people died in its soot-colored debris, and a man at the hangar in Kansas City, Missouri, forgot the one-inch cotter pin (a *little* thing: a one-inch cotter pin) in a one-quarter-inch bolt in part number 290790 of the linkage to the elevator boost—the nut fell off, the bolt fell out, and the elevator began to wallow like a child's kite at the wheat-stacker city of Chicago. As the song went in the sixties,

> *It was just a little tiny teeny,*
> *Just an eeny meeny weeny,*
> *Just an honest mistake,*

but for want of a one-inch cotter pin, the plane crashed and the seventy people died in their crumpled seats. And turned into news, says the Brazilian poet Carlos Drummond de Andrade.

They were telling the truth, apparently, in *The Late Company B*. If the intent is efficiency, the nemesis is the average man, the one who isn't above forgetting one of the one million little things —like the teeny weeny screw in Cheltenham, England. It was eeny meeny enough to have fitted into a Timex but went instead in the upper left of the pitch indicator on the pilot's instrument panel— well, a man in Cheltenham, England, had screwed in this microscopic screw but (to use a word in *The Wealth of Nations*, by Adam Smith) he had "sauntered" and hadn't screwed it the last half turn. In one half year, it wiggled out and it caught the pitch pointer at seven and a half degrees. So the pilot thought he was taking off at seven and a half degrees when he was taking off at forty-five degrees—he stalled over the dome-topped mosques of Ankara, Turkey, he crashed and his twenty passengers died. Are you ready for the $100 one? A man at the hangar in Minneapolis had not read paragraph (1)(a)(1)(e) of the aileron cable pages of the *Electra Maintenance Manual*,

> *Using turnbuckles, adjust cables as necessary to align rigpin hole in booster input and—*

but the man himself hadn't read it. So the turnbuckles weren't turned—the right aileron went up, the left aileron went down, the pilot shouted, "No control," he crashed in the big-shouldered city of Chicago and thirty more people died. The responsible party's name was Mr. Brehmer. He was fined $100.

In my research, I've learned that the pilots themselves (at up to $100,000 annually) are no less susceptible to dumb blunders. In the 1970's, a pilot came in so spiritedly that his 100-passenger plane fell in two on the sand-sided runway at Fort Lauderdale, Florida, but glory to God! No one died! A pilot came in to Cincinnati at six hundred feet, but Cincinnati is eight hundred feet and his fifty people died. At sixty feet, a pilot deployed the spoilers and at once apologized to the other pilot, "Sorry! Oh sorry, Pete," but the plane didn't forgive him, it crashed in Toronto and his one hundred people died. Oh Christ! It's insane that the inorganic ingredients of these machines: the aluminum, titanium, and stainless steel are efficient enough to do Immelmans, literally, while at the very steering wheel is the one inefficient element, the one unpredictable part, the one-headed body of Captain Capriccio. Man, as Eliot wrote, betrayed in the maze of his own ingenuities, condemned by the irrepressible presence of life, is the one incompatible component of his own apparatus, and its motors roar at this flesh-filled flaw in the words of Kipling,

> *We are not built to comprehend a lie,*
> *If you slip in handling us, you die,*

and one hundred others with you.

I've already said, I didn't die in my ten thousand miles to the tinkly temple bells—is it not obvious? but twenty-two years later the longer end of the odds overtook a friend whose name is John

Merriman. A tall thin man (in spite of his fondness for hot dogs—he had ten before lunch, sometimes), he had stepped onto a passenger plane to Chicago at Charleston, South Carolina. He had been south to see his old mother and he was going north to get married—anyhow, he sat down in economy class, and a stewardess in a red vest and six gold buttons said, "Ladies and gentlemen, welcome aboard." As she rattled on, a curious case of aphasia seemed to have seized her and to have deprived her of the definite article *the*. To operate the safety belt, the stewardess didn't say to insert the metal end in the metal buckle—no, she was more concise as she told everyone to insert metal end in metal buckle, period. The stewardess spoke to John and the other passengers like a lady dictating an international cable.

Oh reader! I'm off again on a digression in a digression in a twenty-minute digression! My apologies, but the grammar of red-vested stewardesses would be of concern to John Merriman. As editor of the *CBS Evening News With Walter Cronkite* in Manhattan (I was associate producer, and we worked in the same well-lighted room) he was dizzy enough from the sentences of his own swift writers. If one of them wrote of a pall that descended, my friend used to ask for some color film of that troublesome pall, or if one wrote of a country in dire straits he would want a map of the world with the dire straits identified by a maltese cross. "The dire straits used to be in South Africa. And now they're in South America," John would complain. "Are they drifting?" Now, time was money at CBS—one half second was $500, but no one had ever saved it by omitting the *the* and writing for Walter Cronkite, "And that's way it is." As he listened that day, the stewardess seemed like no earthling but an extra-terrestrial entity to the ears of John Merriman.

But buckling belt, he did what stewardess said—he relaxed in his foam-rubber aisle seat. And *arrrrr*, the two jets roared and the plane took off at seven o'clock in the morning (by his 25-year-employee's watch) on September 11, 1974. And now let's look in the cockpit, devoted reader.

"Gear up, please," the co-pilot, who, in fact, was doing the flying, said. The co-pilot was a close-cropped man in his middle thirties.

The pilot, a mustached man of fifty, perhaps, pushed up a wheel-shaped lever on his instrument panel. "Up," the pilot said.

"Flaps up, please," the co-pilot said.

The pilot pushed up a flap-shaped lever. "Up."

"Slats up, please," the co-pilot said.

The pilot pushed up a slat-shaped lever. "Up. You know, there was this colored gal," the pilot said as he watched the altimeter pointer rise. "She got on this bus, you know? She sees this ole gal almost as dark as she was, but her hair was as straight as a string! So she walks over and she says, Who is you? The ole gal says, Well, I'm a Navaho. Oh, she says, you is? How's business, I's a Nigaho!"

The co-pilot laughed as he looked at his engine pressure ratios —at his *eepers*, so called—and as his left hand adjusted the throttle levers. "Got one boy in the schedule," the co-pilot said. "Is sayin' about his wife, says, Well, she's dirty, you know? She never cleans anything up? Says every time he wants to piss, the sink is full of dishes!"

And thank you, Mr. Gallagher, and don't mention it, Mr. Shean. We shouldn't be surprised that the fun-loving boys in the cockpit weren't the close mouthed ones of *Airport, Airport 1975, Airport 1977,* or *Airport 1979.* On the official log, the two together had ten thousand hours of flying time—yes, and 750,000 hours of living time, and had other compulsions than the sub-sub-paragraphs of the *Flight Operations Manual.* The two were alive, like a couple of horses with an inclination to slip their reins: to upset absolutes and to overload equations with x's. It wasn't remediable, but the two were the only spontaneous parts of the big silver-sided bird—a bird, incidentally, that was by now at eight thousand feet.

"I can't tell a story," the co-pilot laughed as he looked at his gyrocompass and (his right hand on the omega shape of the wheel) turned northwest to Chicago.

The pilot looked out his left window. A mile and a half below him, the sun was slanting into the tulip trees, the tupelos, the moss-covered cypresses, and the cottonwoods of Four Hole Swamp in South Carolina. In that morass there were black bears, the pilot knew—he had shot, skinned, and stuffed one ten years earlier, and he had consigned the huggable thing (his grandchildren called it Mike) to the floor of his television room till the dogs began on its big black ears. At which time he removed it—but still there were so many papier-mâché-mounted animals on the room's knotty pine (an elk, coyote, antelope, bighorn, squirrel, mink, sika, two boars, two goats, ten mule deer, and two moose) that a man almost needed a system of mirrors to look at *Little House on the Prairie*. As if this weren't enough, enough, he was about to overdevelop by mounting another boar, and, in fact, on the day before (and in his oldest clothes) he had worked on this pigskin till six: he had used epoxy to fasten the two-inch tusks to a fiberboard frame from a mail-order house in South Dakota. His wife (who had helped with the two evil-looking eyes) had served him dinner at six o'clock, and at seven o'clock he had watched the *CBS News With Walter Cronkite,*

Good evening. A public opinion poll indicates a two-to-one disapproval of the pardoning of Richard Nixon. The survey—

and the tired headhunter went to bed at eight o'clock: dusk.

He had got up at half past three like a matin-saying monk, and (his wife having fed him cold cereal) had driven to the jet-black airport in his boar-hunting car, a Bronco. "I'm dog tired," he had confessed to the co-pilot, who had got up at three himself and, not eating anything, had driven in in a Toyota. At seven, as they roared down the runway he had been saying, "Okay! Let's go to Chicago! And *rest*—that's what I need! I don't need this damn flying!"

"Damn right," the co-pilot answered him. "All this damn noise!"

"Well, this is a decent trip," the pilot was saying now as they reached a final altitude of sixteen thousand feet. "Except for that getting up early!"

At three miles high, the sky everywhere was as clear as a flute's music. By the flick of his left thumb, the co-pilot turned on the automatic pilot, and the pilot reached up and turned off the seat-belt sign. In economy class, the stewardesses stood up and served coffee, cola, and Fresca to my word-aware friend and to the other passengers at their xerox documents or the *Charleston News and Courier (Watergate Pardons Under Study)*. All was well—the swamp seemed a golf course's green now, and the two pilots relaxed (the pilot was even whistling) as they explored for the suitable stuff for small talk. As who wouldn't?

"Well, whattya think," the pilot said, "of Ford givin' a pardon to Nixon?"

"I was surprised," the co-pilot said.

"I'll tell you, if he gives *amnesty*," the pilot said, meaning amnesty to the draft dodgers, "he gonna hear from me."

"Yep," the co-pilot said. "I'd say this, that if they come to the country and take their lumps—"

"Yeah, I'll go along with that," the pilot said.

"But to come back and say, Ha ha ha," the co-pilot said. "See what I did!"

"No sir, boy," the pilot said. "He gonna hear from me."

"He's committed suicide," the co-pilot said.

"Yeah," the pilot said, and he turned to another item he had watched on the *News With Walter Cronkite*. "And you notice? Ole Kennedy got booed at? Splattered with eggs, that sonofabitch? Boy, they don't like busin' there."

"And that tickles the shit out of me," the co-pilot said.

"I don't know anybody likes it," the pilot said. "Why the hell do we have to do it? Eleven for ten," the pilot said—he meant that the airplane was at eleven thousand feet on its descent to ten thousand feet, for the co-pilot, who had flicked his left thumb to turn off the automatic pilot, was now coming down for a scheduled stop at the old gold-mine city of Charlotte, North Carolina. Two miles below, the two could see the ground fog on the oaks, beeches, maples, and pines by the trout-filled water (the co-pilot didn't fish, but the pilot had a porpoise, snapper, bass, trigger fish, and two northern pikes on his living-room wall)—the water of Fishing Creek in South Carolina. As the co-pilot pulled the throttles back, the pilot reached up and turned on the seat-belt sign and, his microphone in his right hand, said, "Ladies and gentlemen, would you please recheck your seat belt? Well," he said after putting the microphone down. "What they're doing is, they're forcing the whites to go to private schools."

"They really are," the co-pilot said.

"Then they'll say, Okay, we're going to integrate the *private* schools. You whites gonna pay for all those blacks. Seven for six," the pilot said—the plane was at seven thousand feet on its descent to six thousand feet in a cloudless sky.

"One thing that kills me," the co-pilot said as he kept pulling the throttles towards him, "is Arabs are takin' every damn thing. Shit, they bought an island for $17,000,000 off of Carolina."

"Yes sir, boy," the pilot said. "They got the money, don't they?"

"It's coming in at such a fantastic rate—"

"Yeah."

"—if we don't do something by 1980, hell, they'll own the world."

"They owned it *all* at one time."

"That's right. I'd be willing to go to one car and get—"

"Four for three," the pilot said.

"—rid of my little ole money. I think I'll keep that Toyota of mine—it's a piece of shit," the co-pilot said as he turned to align himself with the north-south runway in Charlotte. "But it's cheap to operate."

A half mile below (looming up in the ground fog like a couple of Loch Ness Monsters) the co-pilot saw the humps of the Scooby Doo and the Goldrusher, the up-and-down and the spiral roller coasters at the amusement park of Carowinds. His twin daughters had a thing about roller coasters—a trip to the wild blue yonder was no longer scary enough (he had flown them to their grandma at two weeks old) and now their hair wouldn't curl if they weren't on the wet roller coaster in the waterfall at Disney World, in Florida, the spiral roller coaster in the oak-tree tops at Opryland, in Tennessee, or the ("Ooooooo") the ten-floor drop on the world's worst roller coaster, the Great American Scream Machine at Six Flags Over Georgia ("Daddy, let's do it again!" "No!"). At this hour, there were no shrieking boys and girls on the two roller

coasters at Carowinds, but the co-pilot hoped to do them some-
time with the sandy-haired twins.

"By God," the pilot looked out the left window and said. "That
looks like Carowinds!"

"Carowinds is supposed to be real nice," the co-pilot said.

"Yeah, that's—" the pilot said.

"Gear down, please," the co-pilot said.

"—what that is," the pilot said as he pulled the wheel-shaped
lever down. "That's Carowinds."

"Carowinds," the co-pilot said.

A trio of red lights went on. The three gears deployed—the
lights went off and three green lights went on. At one thousand
feet, a yellow light and a beeper went on, and tapping them the
pilot turned them off in accordance with the *Flight Operations
Manual*. He turned on the no-smoking sign—a chime went on. He
turned off the radar in the black-colored nose so as to not sterilize
the airport personnel at Charlotte. He pulled up a stick-shaped
lever to set the automatic spoilers. "No smoke," he reported to the
co-pilot now. "Radar up. Gear down. And spoilers armed." Alas
—although he had gone through the SOP ten thousand times (and
two dozen times in that week alone), he wasn't a tape cassette and
he hadn't complied with the second part of the twelfth paragraph
of the flight operation policy part of the first volume of the *Flight
Operations Manual*. In his only infraction of that four-pound
book, he had tapped out the yellow light and the beeper without
announcing, "A thousand above."

"Okay," the co-pilot said. His eye on his eepers, he didn't know
he was now eight hundred feet from the pine-tree tops. "How
about fifty degrees?" As the flaps deployed, the wind became
louder and he sensed he was dropping faster now.

"We're ready," the pilot said, and he peered down into the
ground fog. "All we've got to do is find the airport."

"*Oh damn*," the co-pilot shouted. As soon as he saw the trees
underneath him, his right hand pulled on the wheel and his left
hand pushed on the throttles—it didn't avail, the right wing hit on
the two-story trees, a hurricane of pine needles went by the windows of the tossing and turning plane, and the tree trunks tore at
its gay-painted walls. In economy class, the belt broke and John,

my friend from the well-lighted room at CBS, hit his chest on the seat ahead of him at 140 miles an hour. He continued through the great scream machine until, as it shuddered and stopped, he himself stopped by a little ravine. His chest was a rotten watermelon—he and seventy others were dead on their early arrival in Charlotte, North Carolina.

JOHN, I had cared for you. And five hundred miles away at the sound of the bulletin bell and the tat-tat-tat of the teletype, a pall descended upon the studios of the *CBS News With Walter Cronkite*. The art department got an old photograph of John, and that evening it was projected onto the studio's wall and, by the grace of one hundred thousand watts, into the pilot's home and his small museum of natural history. His widow sat by a sad-eyed moose as a man on her color television said of the late editor,

He loved simple sentences. He insisted on clarity. He revered words. And—

My friend John Merriman. A victim of that unpredictable entity, the one hundred pounds of clay that (according to Aldrin, a pilot who flew to the moon) never, never will be a machine.

Well, I'm sorry if I've cast doubt ("So what am I doing?" John would ask as he flipped an invisible frisbee into the studios of the *CBS News With Cronkite*. "I'm casting doubt!")—I'm sorry if I've thrown doubt on my own viability over the Pacific Ocean. In our fine visors (and ultimately in our fur-lined hats) we got without harm to Chicago, Oakland, Tokyo, and the ice-cold airport of Seoul, Korea, but aboard the olive-drab airplane to the western front a PFC in the air force committed an error of no little importance. In one more proof that the plumeless genus is the one crimp in our ever-efficient society, he committed a real gaffe—he gave me my parachute telling me, "Oh, this is a new-release parachute."

"A new-release parachute," I repeated.

"To release it, what you've gotta do is hit this thingamajig."

"Is hit this thingamajig," I repeated.

"Correct. Is do it and you'll release it."

Alas, the airman was no devotee of crystal clarity. He hadn't meant (as I had supposed) that a man would release the *parachute* by hitting the little circular thing—he had meant that a man would release the *parachute pack*. By that action, he would unstrap it, and that thirty-pound parachute pack—and its cloud-colored parachute—would simply fall off his aching back. In principle, the thingamajig would be hit right after, *and only after*, the soldier was on the old terra firma again, but I had understood incorrectly that it should be hit after leaping out of the airplane at fifteen hundred feet. "Well, happy landing," the airman said.

"Happy landing yourself," I laughed.

And *arrrr*, the airplane started, started rolling, and rose to those fifteen hundred feet. In my innocence, I sat placidly in a bucket seat and, by twisting myself, looked at the snow-covered hills. At acres of snow-white powder,

It floats like the butterflies,
It croaks like the frogs,

say the Koreans, in reference to the driven snow and (as they stomp across it) the fallen snow, and the snow on the thatch-topped houses below me may have creaked like the crickets, too. It practically camouflaged them, but I could discern that the houses there were in L shapes, and the L angle faced to the south-east and the L-back faced to the northwest: to the skin-chilling winds from Siberia. The houses seemed of ocher-colored adobe, and a wall of adobe surrounded them, and—

"Get ready to jump, gentlemen," the sergeant said.

"In the name of the father," a soldier began.

I was the third one out. At once, a 100-mile-an-hour hurricane assailed me, and I didn't even say "Geronimo" as I hit my fist against the thingamajig in panic, actually. It was scarcely a split second later that my parachute pack was a little tarantula in the air ten, twenty, forty meters above me, and I was alone in my green fatigues and my red-and-white shoulder patch. My flesh froze, and I myself was a man who seemed, to my own disoriented eyes, to be ten feet away from me. "Oh God! John is falling down," I thought in my unutterable horror. "He is rolling and he is shouting something, is shouting something, is—"

Oh, I'm exaggerating. I'm shoveling it, in the army jargon. We really flew to the western front in a mud-colored plane, but, as God would have it, we didn't jump out—we landed on landing gears on a snow-swept runway, where, on my left shoulder, my wide eyes discovered a D-ring ("What does this do?" "It opens the parachute, son." "No, this little circular thing—" "No, that releases the whole damn parachute pack." "Oh no!"). As the truth of the word *release* appeared, an ice-cold wind from the northwest—no, it was from somewhere between my shoulders— seemed to sweep over me. I thought, Oh no! Is this the last legacy of Orville and Wilbur Wright? A world where a PFC who isn't efficient at oral communication is God himself? And can cast a mother's beloved son out of the heavens like an insurgent angel? The parachute passer-outers, the pin putter-inners, the pilots themselves—until we have hanged them all on the tallest apple tree, we must accept that to try for total efficiency is to fly after wild geese and to fly in, quote, the friendly skies is to open ourselves to the tragedy of *The Late Company B*. For these are the days when anyone's inefficiency (as we were warned by Huxley) is nothing short of a sin against the holy ghost, and, to err being human, sooner or later there will be one who commits it.

Listen, I'm not against airplanes. I've sat for one, two, three hundred hours in those luminous tubes, and I say verily, verily, when my encyclopedia calls them one of the world's seven wonders. A while ago (be patient, we'll be in the trenches presently) —a while ago, I even inspected the airplane assembly line in Long Beach, California, and I was agog as a wide-eyed owl. In one enormous room (so help me, there could be a cloud inside) a number of men were making a wide-body airplane, a DC-10, for the McDonnell Douglas Corporation and, ultimately, for Malaysian Airlines. It was just awesome, for I was there at that indispensable operation when the two wings are put on: or rather, the wings themselves (a set of samurai swords of 7075 aluminum alloy) were on the football-field floor, and I was there in my wide-eyed wonder as the fuselage was put on. "Okay, Henry. We need to come down twenty thousandths," said a pink-shirted man at a surveyor's instrument.

"On the aft?" Henry asked. He was operating a monumental hydraulic jack.

"On the aft," the man in the pink shirt confirmed. "A little more. A little more. A little more. And hold it, Henry!"

"Is it good?" Henry asked.

"It isn't good," the man in the pink shirt answered. "We got to go up again."

Oh *wow*, to move a whole fuselage (or actually, an eight-ton element) a fiftieth of an inch, everyone, which is what happened as I and three little brown-skinned men in black mustaches stood on a scaffold, looking on. No secret agents, the three were inspectors for the Malaysian Airlines. One wore a red plaid tie, the second a gold paisley tie, and the third a sapphire pin on a white-on-white tie, and, coincidentally, all of them thought that the fuselage (made in San Diego, California) and the wing agglomerate (made in another country: in Toronto, Ontario)—the two components were like the jigsaw puzzles at Selangor's in Kuala Lumpur. As they interconnected (so accurately that the pinholes lined up, and rigpins could be put through them), the Malay in the red plaid remembered the local proverb about the *ikan* and the *sayor*, saying, "Ah, the fish and the vegetable! A thousand miles apart, at last they meet in the frying pan." And congratulating the pink-shirted man, he went home for his rice and his cuttlefish (the other two had hot *sayor sawi* and *kuay teow*) as the workers used a double-margin thirty-gauge bit, burrer, and counter reamer to put in three thousand holes to attach the sine qua non—the wings, ignoramus—with the Hi Loks and the Huck Bolts. As the work went on, the room reverberated to the huck gun's sound. Shboom! Shboom!

I ask you! Is that efficient or is that efficient, please? And yet (and there's the rub) how ominous that the three hundred thousand parts (and the three million fasteners) would be in the two-thumbed hands of the same imperfect species as in *The Late Company B*. For almost anyone, *anyone*, like the baggage man in Paris, Mohammed Mahmoudi, who didn't close the rear baggage door, is able to disannul all the three million fasteners and to chop three hundred passengers to eighteen thousand pieces—one of them being a doll in a little girl's wristless fist. As long as real people are in the concatenation of circumstances, there can be no earthly empire of Efficiency, I'm afraid. In fact, I was still at the airplane assembly line as a gray-haired inspector came on one of those teeny-weeny errors that can be the one rotten one. The inspector, whose name was Dolly and who had other things to think of (she was doing afghans for Christmas), had been pushing and pulling the left outboard aileron to ensure it went twenty degrees up and down in accordance with the *Test Procedures Manual*. And tinkle, there was a sound like a screw loose.

"Oh, there's a foreign object in it," Dolly said.

"A foreign object? What would it be?" I asked.

"A nut, a bolt, a washer," Dolly said. "A man once left a flashlight in it."

"Do you just leave it in?" I asked.

"*No*," Dolly almost shouted. Or the nut (or whatever) would rattle until it had chafed the epoxy primer paint. The metal would rust, a hole would form, the aileron wouldn't work, a roll would initiate itself, the plane would crash in Malaysia and—

"Holy smoke," I said. "Thank you for finding it, Dolly!"

"Someone would find it if I didn't, I'm sure," Dolly said.

"I'm sure," I said. And saying goodbye, I left the assembly line to go tootling off in a green-colored automobile at altitude naught. *O tempora*, I thought. A nut forgets about a nut in Long Beach, California, and three hundred passengers turn to *lembu satay* in Kuala Lumpur. Of course, there were forgetful men in centuries past, and I didn't think that the ascent of our species retrogressed to where we are empty-headed apes—no. In the words of Plautus, to fly without feathers isn't easy, and we can stand tall at accomplishing it and, 999,999 times in a million, statistically, living to pop our ears while telling about it. But this efficient century is the first, surely, and the last, perhaps, when a nut-forgetter is not just liable to kill himself but to kill—well, what about a hundred million incredulous casualties? The trouble is, our "system" is nothing but the old martingale system of Vegas: to double your bet if you lose your money to be almost,

almost, sure of winning a silver dollar but (if the other color comes up ten times consecutively) to lose $1,000 instead. To buy an airplane ticket is to buy a high chance of no one's dying and a low, though ultimately inevitable, chance of a real bloodbath. If you wonder how, a scenario for the inadvertent death of one hundred million people is to be goggled at in *The Coming Dark Age*, by Vacca.

Suppose, according to this alarmist author, that a passenger plane with a nutty aileron crashes into an electric line in Chicago (the real plane with the turnbuckles in its aileron did, in fact, crash into one in Chicago) and then suppose that the power goes out in Chicago. And suddenly, the trains aren't running and—as the gas pumps aren't running either—the cars aren't running either, and it's one big parking lot on the Eisenhower Expressway. The office workers have to camp out in their offices and (I didn't say, but it's January) to light their fires in their baskets and—*fire, fire*, but the streets are a parking lot and the fire engines are out of gas, re-member? Oh Mother Leary, it's the Second Chicago Fire! And there's a hot time in town tonight as people die in the fire, the smoke, the panic, the snow, and (the trucks aren't running either) in the riots at Dominick's and the A&P. Not only that, but the entire east has a run in its stocking and the power's out in Indi-anapolis, Cincinnati, Pittsburgh—

> *Some millions of people will die. As survivors attempt the timely removal of corpses, an epidemic will be the new phenomenon. The decisive fact: half of the population will die of bubonic plague,*

and *quod erat demonstrandum*, the imminent death of one hundred million people due to one nut-forgetful man. In *my* opinion, it won't happen tomorrow but it will eventually, sure as God made little pink-colored people. Or *something* will—for the trouble in three hundred thousand perfect parts is, the more perfect they are, the more imperiled they are by the one imperfect one. In the words of Roderick Seidenberg, "As science advanced, man alone appeared a wayward and unpredictable entity in an otherwise tractable universe. Such a situation becomes in time intolerable and—" *Ecrasons l'infâme*, there will be those who say.

6/All Quiet on the Western Front

Or, The Anarchist Manifesto

And *meanwhile* in Korea, a few other privates and I were camping out in a sand castle made of sandbags, a so-called hooch (from *uchi*, the Japanese for *maison*) on the mountaintop south of Old Baldy. In our man-made cave, the only light was a pale gray shaft of sunlight from the one embrasure (or, after dark, from a candle in a C-ration can) and the dim furniture was of early ammunition crate—it said *explosive* on every splinter-ridden table and chair. But here beneath the almond eyes (and the 82-millimeter mortars) of our enemies, we *still* were human beings and not the copper-coated robots that the army's tables of organization called for. Our thoughts weren't of dame duty—no, we sat around (in the words of Cummings)

> *in the deep mud et*
> *cetera*
> *(dreaming*
> *et*
>   *cetera, of*
> *Your smile*
> *eyes knees and of your Etcetera)*

and listening to *Dear John (Oh, How I Hate to Write)* on radios rigidly tuned to Radio Station Nomad, the GI's own sympathetic station—for Sally, my girlfriend, was already married to someone else. On our *explosive*-stenciled shelves was a commissary of tamales, pumpernickel, anchovies, sardines, shrimps—caught, the label said, in the pure waters of the fjords—kippered herrings, and two cans of after-dinner mints from the Gourmet's Club of Goshen, Indiana, for we relished the mess sergeant's meatloaf as little as did those soldiers of *The Late Company B*. And (most infamous of all) our topless tubes of toothpaste, of *toothpaste*, weren't in any well-kept lockers but to the left of the Karvi Cheese! Have mercy on us, Sergeant McHugh!

The world outside (as seen through the six-inch slit) was practically all Old Baldy: a sand dune owned by the sand fleas, ostensibly: the distant army of China. To dispossess it, we had some orders which were, if anything, categorical, stating that the first battalion, thirty-second regiment, would—no, will, will—attack the enemy's trenches on hill number 266 or, as we called it, on Baldy, and will capture *(will*: the orders weren't to try to, do your damnedest to, or even pretty please, everyone)—it will certainly capture the treeless, shrubless, flowerless, and, in words of one syllable, the dirt-dump hill. But though the tense of those confident orders was the same one as *the sun will rise tomorrow*, today it just seemed to make realism out of idealism and God's will out of wishful thinking. It now was noon (on my birthday, thank you), and Baldy looked like the mise-en-scène of some fast-paced farce—in scene one, the GIs ran into the trenches there, in scene two the GIs ran out and the Chinese ran in, in scene three the Chinese ran out and *and* and *and*. And really (as viewed from a few hundred meters away) the battle on Baldy did seem something out of the *Comédie Française*. To look at, the GIs weren't the flawless men (the ultimate weapons, the army called them) who had been drawn as rampant lions on every objet d'art—on the insides of our teacups, even—at our infantry camp in America. "Now, they ain't osservin' *orders*," a boy in our fortress said.

"They usin' their orders for bum wad," for toilet paper, another said.

"Well, I'd have the GIs myself," another said: the GI's disease, diarrhea.

We were at ease in our home sweet home—until, at noon, the idyl was interrupted by the surprise visit of three great generals. Now, I'd been to grammar school and I was aware that a general is no less susceptible (is more susceptible, historically) to a man's weaknesses than a private is. Alexander had had the opinion that a one-yard snake was his father, and he had killed thirteen men for not saying yes, you are accurate, sir, and Caesar (the same as those people in Kepler) had tightened his own *toga laticlavia* (he used his left hand, we're informed) so his ding-dong wouldn't show when he told everyone in Greek, "Then fall, Caesar." Napoleon had eaten in fifteen minutes (his preference was the *poulet à la marengo*) and, in the forty-five minutes saved, he had collapsed on the floor complaining of gas, groaning, and vomiting until the empress came with a cup of her camomile. He tried to kill himself once ("Goodbye, Louise. Kiss my little son for me," he wrote to Marie Louise. "Goodbye, Louise") but he just vomited up the opium, hellebore, and belladonna.

Nor are the flaws of our star-shouldered men so far from momentous ones. I'm thinking now of the four great generals on the losing side of the Battle of Balaclava, on the Black Sea. On the hilltop there, the first general saw the Russians (but the old general, who had fought at Waterloo, was still calling them the French)—the enemy ripping off his cast-iron cannons. At his orders, a second general scribbled, on tissue paper, that the cavalry was to try (to try: at least he appreciated that the men weren't machines)—to *try* to rescue the guns, gurus, finns, or *finis*, it wasn't especially legible. As soon as he scribbled this, a man galloped down to the valley like an avalanche to carry the tissue paper to general number three—a general who was up at four every day to issue orders on belt buckles, bootstraps, boots (and yes, and tooth powder too) and yes, and horseshoe nails too.

Well! On seeing the tissue paper, the finical general number three (who had not, remember, the same panorama as one and two) said, "What guns, sir?" But saluting, he galloped to general number four to order him to those invisible guns. "Certainly, sir," the general said, and he galloped off in the wrong direction with his six hundred men, who, incidentally, were in their cherry-colored pants (like the red pants of the French, in the First World War, who marched at the German machine guns at a French general's orders, *"Les pantalons rouges, c'est la France"*)—in cherry-colored pants in spite of the *Times*'s editorial that they were as malapropos as the cavalry women's costumes in Auber's opera *Gustavus III*. In their lollipop-colored clothes, the six hundred men and their general rode at the whole delighted army of Russia. Oh, the wild charge they made!

"Forward the Light Brigade!
Charge for the guns," he said,

but five hundred soldiers died. For someone, in the considered opinion of Tennyson, had blundered, and it wasn't a private like you and me.

And Jesus! How had I ever forgotten about the generals there in Korea? The one who had thrown the typewriters out the window, saying, "They're dusty!" The one who had toilet seats in the shapes of thunderbirds, saying, "Well, this is the thunderbird division, isn't it?" The one who had run around and around his $30,000 hooch in hot pursuit of Marilyn Monroe. Our absolute rulers in Korea had their heads screwed no more securely than the men in the trenches, rumors were. So why, *why*, were the other soldiers and I so wide-eyed at twelve o'clock noon to see our division commander, our corps commander, and our army commander come up the one hundred sandbag stairs to our unimportant hooch? A two-star general, a three-star general, and a four-star general—what was it that made soccer balls of our eyeballs as they approached us? Was it the sun, perhaps, on their forty-five stars—on their right shoulders, left shoulders, right collars, left collars, and fur-lined caps?

"Jumping Jesus! Look outside," a boy hollered at us. "Look outside!"

WE weren't (thank you, God and the little fishes) eating the kippered herrings. We weren't putting the Brasso on our belt buckles, either—we were watching the comic opera on Baldy and singing along to *Grandma's Lye-Soap* on Radio Station Nomad. For months, we (and everyone else in Korea) had requested it one, two, three times every hour, and the announcer at Nomad—on the edge of a lye-soap-occasioned insanity—had been broadcasting it nonstop, confident that we would eventually die of OD,

Mrs. O'Malley! Out in the valley!
She suffered from ulcers, I understand!
She swallowed a cake of grandma's lye-soap
And had the cleanest ulcers in the land!
So let's—

And snap! I turned the radio off as the four-star general (a man who played tennis in Seoul and was steps ahead of the two other generals) presented himself in our dim potato bin in his starch-saturated fatigues. Now remember: I was just twenty-two (by eastern standard time) and as tongue-tied as if I had won some contest in *Stars and Stripes* for tea for two at the White House. My only thought was, Oh, there's mud on my boots, although there was mud (and a number of pine needles) on the general's pair of clodhoppers too. By the grace of God, a boy with presence of mind in our circle cried out, "Attention!"

"At ease, gentlemen," the four-star general ordered us. "Can you see Old Baldy?"

"Yes sir, out the window, sir," a boy replied.

"Appreciate it." And striding there, the general began to look single-mindedly out of it, indicating to our indescribable relief that he wasn't here to inspect the anchovy cans but to *observe* as the first general did at Balaclava. "Uh, where do you think the front line to be? The most advanced troops," the four-star general said.

"I think, sir," a boy replied, "I *think* they're at that bunker with the large aperture with—oh God!" As he talked, an artillery shell fell on that very bunker.

"Uh, that round is pretty short there," the four-star general said.

"That's incoming, sir," the boy replied.

"Oh," the four-star general said. He went athletically to the two other generals (the two other tottering generals were at our eagle's nest now) and he declared, "We should go down to stimulate those boys. Now shouldn't we?"

The two-star general grinned as if he were saying, "Oh, how jolly, general." But the three-star general, a man whose face was a bag of butter beans, sat on an ammunition crate as though the bell had rung, panted for air, and spat, sometimes, into the cartridge case of a 175-millimeter artillery shell—a knickknack like an umbrella stand on our muddy floor. He was silent, otherwise—he was clearly *hors de combat* at this moment in army-navy time. And that meant a question of etiquette that no one could answer short of transmitting an international cable to Dear Abby. To appreciate this, do you remember when the artillery shell fell out of the ten-meter cannon, *plop*, in the first reel of *The Great Dictator?* The colonel, remember, told the lieutenant colonel to please pick it up. The lieutenant colonel told the major, who told the captain, who told the lieutenant, who, to relieve everyone of the hot potato, told it to Charlie Chaplin. See, the army's etiquette is that every order is issued by a four-star general to a three-star general to—but whoops, the three-star general was a missing link in this daisy chain today. "Uh," the four-star general said to the two-star general, unable to order him to do this, that, or the two together at the winter's biggest battle in Korea—"Uh, I'm not here to announce how to run this operation," the four-star general said. "It's your show here, but if I were you—"

"Yes sir?"

"—I suppose I'd pull everyone off of Baldy," the four-star general hinted. "I'd send in some smoke today," send in some artillery today, "and I'd work it, uh, *really work it*, over tonight. And then attack tomorrow."

"Yes sir," the two-star general answered.

In our dim-lighted room, a bear rose slowly from its winter sleep. The three-star general, a man who would rather die of cardiac arrest than of the fade-away disease, stood up and hobbled (he used a cane, honestly) to the two-star general to reinstate himself in the Great Chain of Being. "*Now, general,*" the three-star general said so threateningly that the two-star general came to army-academy attention—"the attack has failed, general! All you're doing is fooling around on Baldy! Is fooling around and is fooling around! Is," spitting into the un-umbrella stand, "is fooling around on Baldy!"

"Yes sir," the two-star general said. He stood as stiff as an old cigar-store indian.

"Do you follow me? Is fooling around, general," the three-star general shouted, the spit dripping out and the beans in his face becoming as red as kidney beans. "So call your people off Baldy!

And pound it with your artillery! And when you're ready, call me and we'll attack it!"

"Yes sir," the two-star cast-iron general said.

"But stop the fucking fooling around!"

The two-star looked unhappy. The three-star looked as though he wanted to hammer his knot-covered cane on the two-star, shouting, *"Du dummkopf! Das ist nur spielerei,"* and the four-star, forced, by his officer's code of conduct, to dissociate himself from the three-star's delirium, looked out the six-inch slit as preoccupiedly as one who had spotted a rare olive warbler on Baldy. We peons—we privates stood in the shadows of our little citadel like the hoi polloi that the noblemen seem so oblivious of in Shakespeare.

> *Why, look you, I am whipped and scourged with rods,*
> *Nettled,*

Hotspur is screaming to the turrets themselves with no never-mind to the pages, heralds, beadles, and other sundry attendants whose ears (we must assume) must be as big as wassail bowls. In our more modest hooch, the sound of our loud-mouthed leaders did the same metamorphosis, converting our eyes, ears, noses, and open mouths into ears—we were entirely ears. To us, the cane-carrying general was no less immune to the lower passions of man, apparently, than a man with three yellow stripes instead of three silver stars, and his hysteria reconfirmed that the rank is but the guinea's stamp, as we were told by Burns: a man's a man, unquote.

Our sympathies were with the little fellow, the two-star general. Our own closest commander (as of the day before: he had just arrived in Korea), he now looked as if he wanted to cry—yes, really. His eyes were wet, as my own eyes were a year earlier when an old master sergeant shouted at *me* ("Now sound off!" "Sack!" "Louder!" "Sack!" "Do you unnerstand me, Sad Sack? I said louder!" "Sack!" "Louder! Louder! Louder!" "Sack!" "You little fruit! You have a cunt where a cock oughta be") or really, as anyone's are if someone with no more cerebrum is not only ordering him—in itself, an invasion of his most private property:

himself—but is *screaming* it. I don't doubt that a decade ago in Athens, the eyes of the orchestra conductor were, at the very least, wet, as an army officer (the officers were the absolute rulers then) —as a colonel tried to arrest inefficiency in the orchestra, shouting, "*Kirie!* You have one hundred men! And only seventy-eight of them signed in! Why?"

"We are doing a comic opera, colonel. The men aren't in—"

"So write them in!"

"But colonel—"

"Or cancel the comic opera!"

"But colonel! What happens when we do Bach? There are no trumpets, trombones, tubas—"

"Cancel Bach! Cancel Bach!"

Oh, I am sure there were tears in that music-maker's eyes. As there were in the two-star general's, and I can conceive of our clamorous hooch if he weren't taught at his military academy that a big boy doesn't cry. In my imagination, I can see the tears rolling down his fatherly face, and I can hear him say, "Oh sir, don't shout at me. It hurts to be shouted at."

"*Crybaby,*" the three-star general shouts. "I wouldn't shout if you weren't fooling around on Baldy! If you pounded it with your artillery, instead!"

"But sir," the two-star general says. "*Sniffle,* I've already pounded it with twenty thousand artillery shells."

"So dummy! So pound it with twenty thousand more!"

"I can't, general, sir," the two-star general cries. "I can't because—"

"I say you can! I've half again as many stars and I say you can! You little fruit!"

"I can't, I can't," the two-star general cries. "Oh, *sob,* you aren't smarter than me just because you're bigger than me. I can't because—"

"You *can* because—"

"I can't because there *aren't* any, sir," the two-star general (the tears rolling down and the salt streaks scarring his soft-skinned face) —the general cries. "The army is almost out of artillery shells!"

"*What?*" At the six-inch slit, the four-star general turns as athletically as a man hitting a backhand overhead, saying, "Are you alluding to *my* army, general?"

"Yes sir, general, sir," the two-star general says, and he blows his red-rimmed nose in a Kleenex. "It's almost out of shells, general, sir."

The four-star general glowers. "Now, general, there are hoi polloi in our presence here, and you are not stimulating them by suggesting that."

"*Sob*," and the two-star general starts to cry once more. "Oh, general, I've tried to behave like a model major general—"

Enough. For the record, the men in our echo chamber were General Taylor, General Kendall, and General Trudeau. And furthermore, let the record show (as it will in, oh, ten minutes) that the whole army was, in fact, practically out of artillery shells, and the more chrome-covered stars that a general had, the more wrongheaded the general was. Oh, those crew-cutted clowns in Korea! We stood up (our heels together and our pigeon toes at forty five degrees) in their awesome presence. We sirred them, we saluted them, and we didn't use a bore-patch on our ear wax in the presence of one, two, three, and four-star generals. But honestly, can it be argued that we were such utter incompetents that we really *needed* them?

It can be argued, friends. And was in the mid-seventeenth century by Thomas Hobbes.

Now, Hobbes (I have looked this up)—Hobbes was just twelve years old at the start of the seventeenth century, and, as a gentleman's secretary, he did nothing to boast about (oh, he did learn the cello pretty well) for the next thirty years. In 1630, though, while a guest at a minister's home in Geneva, he experienced what was a bolt-from-the-blue-above in his uneventful life. In the minister's library, the finger of fate directed him to an open book and a sentence in Greek, Ἐν τοῖς ὀρθογωνίοις τριγώνοις τὸ ἀπὸ τῆς τὴν ὀρθὴν γωνίαν ὑποτεινούσης πλευρᾶς τετράγωνον ἴσον ἐστὶ τοῖς ἀπὸ τῶν τὴν ὀρθὴν γωνίαν περιεχουσῶν πλευρῶν τετραγώνοις, and he read it and suddenly gasped. "By God," Hobbes is recorded as having said. "It's impossible!" The book was by Euclid, and the sentence alleged that in any right-angled triangle the square of the hypotenuse equaled the sum of the squares of the two other sides.

Now, this wasn't bulletin news to the western world. It had occurred to Pythagoras, who had sacrificed an ox (or according to Galileo, a hundred oxen) in honor of that quadratic equation, but it was like lightning from Mount Olympus to Hobbes, who hadn't majored in mathematics at Oxford. And poring over the proposition, he was referred to the forty-sixth, the forty-first, the fourteenth, and the fourth propositions and—as he went backwards, backwards, and the sun started to set on Burgundy—to the first indisputable postulate that a line could be drawn from A to B. All right, agreed—and Hobbes, his red goatee trembling, his finger a fat brown bookworm, started to go ahead to the many cheerful facts about the hypotenuse, and God! It was accurate what was in Euclid! Life, for Hobbes, had begun at forty and at the perception that, ahhh, that squared and squared equaled squared! His face, which so far had been yellow, became (and for fifty years, remained) a ruddy red, for he had been born again as a convert to plane and solid geometry.

At dinner that day, he didn't cut his *petit pain* into a cone, cylinder, or parallelogram as everyone on the flying island did in *Gulliver's Travels*. He didn't use a transit to measure himself for a doublet as in *Gulliver's* or in Woody Allen's *Sleeper* ("Okay," the tailor says of a suit that's ten or twenty sizes too big, "Okay, I'll take it in"). But that night, he did indeed sit in bed drawing a little pinkprint of triangles on his thighs, just as Archimedes had drawn them (in the olive oil on his thighs) at the baths at Syracuse, Sicily. He did this night after night, and Hobbes—in many months—came to look at our good green earth as a concatenation of lines, triangles, rectangles, of rigid geometry as reliable as any watchmaker's watch in Geneva. It was *efficient*—or rather, it would be efficient but for the endemic incalculability of one little element. And this little element was so addicted to spilling out of its proper sphere that no rulers or compasses knew how to circumscribe it. A living thing, it went about on our planet on four legs in the morning and two legs at midday and—you have guessed it!

People! The people (our man would write in *Leviathan*)—the men, women, and children of our silicon sphere are, in the last analysis, madmen, for like actual madmen (or drunks, he would write) we are often possessed by our passions, and our passions unguided are, for the most part, madness, unquote. As closet lunatics, we become pale if we love someone or black if we hate someone—we laugh and cry in any six-hour afternoon to a degree that no right-angled triangle would, and to laugh and cry in our clockwork world is just double trouble to Hobbes:

> *The passion which maketh laughter is incident most to them that are conscious of the fewest abilities in themselves. On the contrary [there] is the passion that causeth weeping, and they are most subject to it that rely principally on helps external, such as are women and children.*

To love, to hate, to laugh, to cry—to *feel* is to let ourselves overflow the mathematical measures of the six-foot fathom and the sixty-minute hour. It is generative of everything evil, like

> *war, which is necessarily consequent to the natural passions,*

and is corrosive of the golden goal of society: efficiency, in the considered opinion of Mr. Hobbes.

Well, what can I say? All people do have passions—there's no prescribing them not to, and there seems to be no solution to the people problem but the final one of the Queen of Hearts, "Off with their heads," or of Lieutenant Calley, "Waste them." But our man, Hobbes, was more tenderhearted (he also learned the six-stringed lute) and he wanted to institute efficiency by some other means than one of benevolent genocide. Accordingly, he moved to Paris, he woke up at seven every day and (after his breakfast of buttered bread) he went walking in the *jardin*, thinking, thinking, dipping the tip of his quill into an inkwell in his walking cane, and, in spite of his palsy, writing, until by the mid-seventeenth century he had concluded and, in *Leviathan*, had announced that to have farms, factories, and the other desiderata—to have efficiency, we must subordinate ourselves and our mad, mad, mad, mad passions to some absolute authority,

*as if every man should say, I give up my right of governing
myself,*

and I am yours, sahib. All right: I do agree. No one can harbor
doubts that the one thing wrong in the world (as the seventeenth,
eighteenth, nineteenth, and twentieth centuries see it) is that
there're people in it, or that something, *anything*, has to smother
them if they're ever to be as efficient as an Accutron. Nor can
anyone fault the philosopher's verdict until, in his seventeenth
chapter, he swallows a so-called camel in his announcement that
the absolute authorities will be people too.

What? What? The blind will be leading the blind, sirrah? No, I
can accept that I must accept a vegetable—a calm coconut on the
mantel, say—as my absolute authority, or even some species of
dull, listless, and passionless animal like the hippopotamus who,
a few years ago, was elected to the city council of São Paolo,
Brazil. But people? Is it not circular that if I'm human and if I'm
mad, accordingly, it behooves me to surrender myself to a creature of the same human condition? Of the same species as the two,
three, and four-star neurotics in my once-halcyon home in Korea,
the men who were standing at catatonic attention, shouting at mad-
hatter-party pitch, and staring out of the six-inch window at the
spring migrants on Baldy? I who don't drink (and Hobbes, who
was drunk a total of once every year) am to sir-and-salute a
creature that he himself likens to a drunken bum? Oh, you're
putting me on, Mr. Philosopher!

Of course, I say this with twenty-twenty hindsight. For unlike
me, Hobbes did not sit—correction, stand—in the mad generals'
presence, although, having done a satisfactory translation of
Homer,

*Tell me, oh muse, the adventures of the man
That, having sacked the sacred town of Troy,
Wandered—*

he ought to have known from the poor sportsmanship of Ajax, the
peevishness of Achilles, and the prattle of Nestor—to have known
what a lot of fools those officers could be. And doubtless, if
Hobbes (or the cavalier-collared ghost of Hobbes) had floated up

to our wobbling hooch in Korea, he'd have resolved his cognitive dissonance by calling the generals irredeemable madmen that a really, *really*, absolute authority has to enforce efficiency on. Alas —the president of the U.S.A. and the commander over the two, three, and four-star keystone cops was, in that month, a five-star person himself. The next president (the big-toothed president) was one who once called the Pentagon to complain that a sailor didn't stand at attention for him, the next president (the big-eared president) put his feet in his administrative assistant's lap, and the next president (the big-nosed president) sat in his oval office worrying, worrying: should the secret service sing the *Star-Spangled Banner?* And thumbing his autobiography, saying, "It makes fascinating reading."

"Yeah," his administrative assistant said.

"I want you to reread it," the president said.

"Okay," his administrative assistant said.

"And everybody else," the president said. "I want them to reread it."

"Sure," his administrative assistant said.

"The book reads awfully well," the president said.

Oh, God's wounds, did Hobbes ever actually *see* any absolute authority? We are informed that he did indeed in the very year, 1651, as *Leviathan.* One day in Paris, the sun was shining outside of his oriel window when the most absolute authority in one thousand years went by on a yellow horse—an Isabella, so called from the yellow color of the archduchess's sheets. The trumpeters in his train were in black or blue velvet doublets—the tune itself wasn't reported, but the march from the second act of *Aïda's* appropriate, isn't it? And there were the queen mother's horsemen (one hundred horsemen) and the king's personal horsemen (two hundred horsemen) and the King of Siam's elephant men (two hundred elephant men, but I've made those up) and, well, enough's enough, a character with a heron feather in his scarlet satin hat. The king himself, the most absolute authority, wore so much golden embroidery that no one knew what, if anything, he wore underneath it, though later he wore a $30,000,000 robe for the real ambassador of Siam. Magnanimously, he kept tipping his indescribable hat to the *petit monde* on the rooftops, at the windows (and at the new windows cut for the great parade), and in the stone-cobbled streets of Paris. Oh, I can almost see Hobbes in his linen-and-laces, shouting, with all of Paris, "*Vive Louis Quatorze! Vive Louis Quatorze! Vive—*"

The king was thirteen years old. His mother was (or was until recently) spanking him, and for saying *merde* she was shutting him in his room forty-eight hours. At the *école*, he had written,

> A *king can do as he pleases*
> A *king can do as he pleases*
> A *king*—

in his schoolbook, but he was still called dull on his royal report card. A few years earlier, he had absentmindedly spat on his younger brother's bed, and—oh, his brozzer he spitted on Louis's bed, and Louis spitted on his brozzer's bed, and his brozzer he did his oui-oui (*et pissa dessus,* my sources say) on Louis, and Louis did his oui-oui on his brozzer, and Louis hitted him in the *bouche,* and Louis—

And this was the man without whom (to listen to Hobbes) our whole lives will be nasty, brutish, and short. And yeah, and there will be bats in the Eiffel Tower!

Wᴇʟʟ, I say claptrap. For even a one-eyed look at human history (a hand clapped on the other eye in horror, like the man's hand in the Sistine Chapel, in Rome) is quite enough to suggest that the kings, queens, and the big cheeses were, *at the very least,* as nasty as anyone else ("A great inconvenience," Hobbes confesses). Nor were the rulers themselves in all ages ignorant of their existential incompetence. As many as five thousand years ago, Gilgamesh, in what today are the Arab lands, wanted to go to war against the King of Kish, I'm serious. "*Gaammasigendeen,*" "Let's smite him," he cried in his mud-walled chambers, but he didn't smite till all of his men unanimously voted, "*Gaammasigendeen.*" Gideon, on being urged to be ruler of Israel ("Rule thou over us, thou, and thy son, and thy son's son")—Gideon said in one-syllable words, "I will not," the Bible tells us. Alas, there isn't anyone now as modest as Cincinnatus, who was once dictator of Rome but, after saying do this, everyone, do that, everyone, for the better part of a day, said just forget it and abdicated. No, the only known parallel in this century (and one that would hardly qualify for Plutarch's *Parallel Lives*) is Mr. Gumbert of Omaha, Nebraska. A nominee for state senator, he withdrew since it was impossible to (*quote*) to represent the men, women, white, black, rich, poor—the twenty thousand individuals of the Ninth Legislative District. "I recommend," he announced to the openmouthed reporters, "the voters refrain from voting in the hope that no one will hold this office."

Amen. And with those trumpet-tongued words, let us bid adieu to Mr. Hobbes. In his last thirty years, he kept trying to shore up the universe by squaring the circle, unsuccessfully—so unsuccessfully that the result of his ruler, compass, and pen ("If we consider the benefit, which is the scope at which speculation should aim—") was not even printed by the Royal Society. Instead, let us now return to our storm cellar on the western front in Korea. Our own loud absolute authorities—the two, the three, and the four-star window-rattling generals—departed by the sandbag stairs, and a day later (the generals, remember, had to tell their colonels to tell their lieutenant colonels to tell their captains to tell their lieutenants to tell us)—a day later and a few dead soldiers more, the GIs were finally told to stop fooling around and to get themselves off of Old Baldy. To no one's astonishment, they did and (*one two three*) as fast as cottontail rabbits too. In utter refutation of Hobbes, the men didn't go on making war and go mad, potted, and passionately to the crest of the hill, yelling, "*E pluribus unum!* And death to the yellow belly!" As we are reminded by Koestler, a man who thinks war is consequent to our natural passions is one who was never a private himself—a private like us, who killed or were killed on Baldy because the authorities told us to. Abolish authorities and

> *We will live,*
> *And the war will end,*

promised a prior philosopher to Hobbes: Chuang Tsu of China. And silence. For ten minutes, there were no sudden sounds on Old Mount Acomia. A balloon—red, round, model fifty-one (aren't the other models round, a man must wonder)—a round balloon rose to the god of Korea, Hananim. No doubt, it went there to ascertain where the wind was (it was still northwest) and to report this to the artillery. For suddenly there was the big brass drum and the tin whistle of a 155-millimeter shell (a shell a half-foot wide) on its way overhead to Old Baldy. It was followed, like a snow goose, by another thousand, till it sounded as if the whole primum mobile was in fragments, falling like the 1908 meteorite on the poor communists—*boom*. In the valley, the 90-millimeter shells were put in the mud-colored tanks, and, as the motors roared like at demolition derbies, the tank drivers started to no-man's-land to put the contents of these umbrella stands on Baldy. Myself, I had volunteered (ah youth, as someone says in Conrad, my deepest secret was to have volunteered for the army, the Far East Command, and Korea)—had now volunteered as assistant driver on tank number twenty-four, the real assistant driver being sick on a fifth of Jim Beam Bourbon. Ah youth.

I had never driven (or ever driven in) a tank until now, but I had been issued a 700-page manual,

When crossing a ditch, shellhole, or trench, release the accelerator momentarily, then—

and I had wiggled into the assistant driver's seat. And closing a manhole cover over me, I found myself in the black hole of Korea—oh, there was a "window" as wide as a post-office slot to look at creation through. And through it, I saw our mud-colored tank go through the western front (no more than a roll of concertina wire) to the spear-shaped grass at the base of Old Baldy. On top, I saw people—communists, who were shooting an 82-millimeter mortar at us. "And they're hitting the road right behind my ass," our assistant gunner declared.

"Man, I'm just going to fire too," our gunner said. "On the way!"

He pushed a black button, and a 90-millimeter shell went out of the cannon's end—a dragon's tongue of fire accompanied it, the whole world (as seen in my special-delivery slot) was, for one second, yellow, as though it were drenched in yellow lemonade. The tank rocked from the recoil, and the red-hot shell (as against the new improved shells of the 1980's, which, to the army's consternation, do a loop-the-loop as they bound from the cannon's mouth) hit the very crest of Old Baldy. It kicked up a dry dust storm and one less transparent item.

"It looks like a body going up," our gunner said.

"No," our assistant gunner said. "It's bigger than a body, isn't it?"

"No, not with a hundred pounds of lead up its ass," our gunner said.

He was laughing and I laughed too. On reconsideration, it seems schizophrenic to go into stitches at the dismemberment of someone of my age, sex, and species (though of another political party), but the smell of his viscera and the sound of his scream didn't penetrate to my compartment, and the sight of him was filtered by my two periscope mirrors and was framed (in yellow-lemonade color) in a tight little rectangle there, like a Terry Toon. No doubt, if I had beheld that boy as intimately as the one observed by Wilfred Owen,

> *If you too could pace*
> *Behind the wagon that we flung him in,*
> *And watch the white eyes writhing in his face,*
> *His hanging face—*

if I had studied him, I don't think I'd have laughed aloud. But one thousand meters away, I was aware of him *intellectually* like the nature director's insects, and he was just the Objective. The Object. They.

"On the way," the gunner reported, and his second shell hit the same place on Baldy. "Boy, that's a pretty round, isn't it?"

"What do I do as assistant driver?" I asked.

"Nothing," the driver told me. "Me, I just wrote a letter home."

"Where did you mail it?" I laughed.

Ah youth. It is so transitory, though. My day as the happy assistant driver of a 50-ton medium tank was, as it happened, my last adventure in the army's armor branch. As soon as our forty shells were on Baldy, we pushed on the wobble stick and we returned to the western front: to the old ammunition dump to get forty more. But when we got there, the cupboard was bare—it was no figment of my imagination that the army was out of 90-millimeter shells and its generals were a collection of blithering idiots. So we parked in our parking lot—a mud-crusted quarter acre— the gunner and the assistant gunner got up a pinochle game, the driver did the inevitable by turning on Radio Station Nomad,

> Mrs. O'Malley! Out in the valley!
> She suffered from ulcers, I understand!
> She swallowed a cake of grandma's lye-soap,
> And had—

and the intrepid assistant driver went to his immobile home in the infantry corps. To my righteous indignation, I now looked out of the six-inch window to see those godless communists in the fresh shellholes of Baldy. And digging in, but our orders were to ignore it if we saw one, two, three, or any but fifteen communists together—to not call artillery, for the army was almost out of 105, 155, and 175-millimeter shells. On the brighter side, it still wasn't out of red balloons, and at sundown one of those floated like at a birthday party over the enemy trenches on Mr. Clean Mountain. Hail to thee, blithe spirit.

Of course, the order that we shouldn't shoot if we didn't see the whites of their thirty eyes was a secret one. I myself didn't tell (I am no tattletale, to quote the immortal words of a five-star general: of General MacArthur)—I didn't snitch but I'm sure someone did, as it soon appeared at the top of *The New York Times*. The secret was out, and, reading it, the secretary of the army himself flew to Korea to see if there was no ammunition in our only ongoing war. An ex-textile executive, the man was chewing on chewing gum as his chopper dropped on the 630th ammunition company. And popping out, he said to a soldier name of Dabravalskas, "Do you have plenty here?"

"Yes sir," the soldier said.

Well Jesus! What is he *supposed* to say to the secretary and all the four-star generals in the Far East Command? No sirree, sir, the situation is all fucked up? One morning, a mere lieutenant colonel came to us Willies saying, "Is the food satisfactory, men?" "Oh, yes sir," we chortled, though it was noon and we had had nothing but a hard-edged quadrilateral of toast apiece, black as a brick in a chimney—there was a food shortage too. I mean really! A man is mad who exposes himself to forty lashes by telling the truth to his massa, and it was in self-defense that the soldier said, "Yes sir. We have the normal number of artillery rounds."

"Thank you, sir," the secretary said, and he departed at twelve o'clock noon—or two hours before the deadline for *The New York Times.*

The reporters asked, "Did you see any shortages there?"

"One," the secretary answered. "An enlisted man told me he'd had trouble getting color film. And that was the only shortage—"

Oн, fuck you, Mr. Secretary! On that whole western front, there wasn't a PFC (a chicken on his knee, a can of kippered herring on his crates, whatever) who wasn't a better authority on the non-being of 105, 155, and 175-millimeter shells than you. But thank you too (and thank you, two, three, four-star, fourflusher generals) for the timely reminder that an expert is, to quote from *The People, Yes,* by Sandburg, a damned fool a long ways from home, and an authority is not our rock and our redeemer, necessarily. He doesn't descend on two white wings but a chopper, just as we—he has two eyes, two ears, and teeth for his tutti-frutti just as we. For men are men: I'll say that again, says Brecht, and their genius is just enough, sometimes, to regulate themselves but is never enough for one, two, three, or two hundred million more.

I'm older now, and I'm writing this in a two-room hooch in the Rockies: in Ketchum, Idaho, but I'm still virtually a stump (a stupid troop under military protection) in Korea. It's eight o'clock —I've had eight hours sleep but I still can't sleep in the outhouse (by order of more damn authorities: *stamp*) in San José, Cali-

fornia, I can't sleep in my trash can in Lubbock, Texas, my dog
kennel in Wallace, Idaho, my bathtub in Detroit, Michigan, my
refrigerator in Pittsburgh, Pennsylvania, or in the Kentucky State
House. A bed isn't dangerous, though, said a judge in St. Louis,
Missouri, and I've slept in a bed, providentially, but I can't snore
(according to more authorities: *blop*) in Dunn, North Carolina.
At eight o'clock, I rise, shine, and go to the tile-walled bathroom
to brush myself with Crest and wash myself with Zest.

The top of my toothpaste tube: of my Crest, is approved by the
food and drug commissioner if it doesn't melt at 320 degrees or
dissolve in antioxidated xylene, and the aquamarine of my Zest
was approved after being fed, *fed*, to three thousand rats, to eight
hundred mice, to one hundred rabbits, and to four dozen om-
nivorous dogs. Well, thank you, Mr. Commissioner! Now, I can
eat my Zest without cancer but I just wash with it this morning,
singing, *Oh, What a Beautiful Morning!* I can't sing in the shower
in Philadelphia, Pennsylvania, I can't sing off key (the revenge of
Miss Rofinot, I suppose) in Charlotte, North Carolina, and I can't
sing,

> It ain't gonna rain no mo', no mo',
> It ain't gonna rain no mo',

in Oneida, Tennessee. Jesus, do they *enforce* it?

Drying myself, I put on my pants of American upland cotton as
it's defined by one more authority, the secretary of agriculture, in
his section twenty-eight. To keep them up, I can't wear suspenders
in Nogales, Arizona, and I can't tuck them into my cowboy boots
in Madisonville, Texas, if I do not own cows. I mean it, I ought to
go to bed again but I can't in Minot, North Dakota, if I'm in my
cowboy boots. In the seventeenth century in Paris, France, I
couldn't wear pants if there weren't forty threads (or forty-four, or
forty-eight: it fluctuated) in each square *pouce*: by order of Louis,
and that same century in Boston, Massachusetts, I couldn't wear
pants with lace: by order of the General Court, "Under penalty of
the forfeiture of such clothes." In China, I couldn't wear pants if
they weren't white or black in the Sung Dynasty or white or yellow
in the T'ang Dynasty or blue or green in the Han Dynasty on

penalty of ten, twenty, thirty, forty, or fifty lashes on my bare bottom, though

> *Sound old rulers, it is said,*
> *Left people to themselves, instead,*

according to Lao Tse. At half past eight, I do some omelets for me and my girlfriend here in the Rockies.

It takes me—oh, ten minutes. It *ought* to have taken me 4.932 seconds to put in the eggs, 2.340 seconds to pour in the milk, 6.480 seconds to beat them, and 24.336 seconds to cook them or 76.176 seconds for our two omelets, according to the secretary of agriculture in a $40,000 report—$40,000 of your money, *amigo*, though he spent $300,000 more to caution you to "Avoid cholesterol." I can't have a rotten egg in Indianola, Iowa, and my chicken can't lay an egg before eight o'clock in Norfolk, Virginia. Why won't a chicken cross a road in Quitman, Georgia? Because, "It shall be unlawful to allow chickens to run on the streets," and I can't eat a sausage along with my omelet in Bnai Brak, Israel, or in Helena, Arkansas, in June, July, and August, "It shall not be lawful to sell in the city, sausage," but the law was called unconstitutional by the supreme court of Arkansas. Our breakfast over, my girlfriend must do the dirty dishes: that, or be drowned in the twentieth century B.C. in Babylon.

We water the pothos: we can't have a marijuana plant but we can have henbane, hellebore, and poison hemlock, and we can't have a dandelion in Pueblo, Colorado. We feed the parakeets: we can't have a parakeet in Atlanta, Georgia, if we haven't a parakeet permit from the Poultry Association. We can't have a hippopotamus in Los Angeles, California, a wild lion in Alderson, West Virginia, a little brown bat in Stillwater, Missouri, a wild camel in Galveston, Texas, and we can't hitch a crocodile to a fire hydrant in Ann Arbor, Michigan. At nine o'clock, my girlfriend sits at her loom and I write on my yellow pad, "I write on my yellow pad," all permissible: though there was an absolute authority in *Phaedrus*, by Plato, who was opposed to the *abc*'s, "It will produce forgetfulness." The man's name, I'll politely omit.

My friend's name is Maria. She can't sit on my lap (without a pillow on it) in Norman, Oklahoma, I can't tickle her in Norton, Virginia, or use a feather duster to tickle her in Portland, Maine. We can't do the turkey trot in Iowa City, Iowa, or the angleworm wiggle in Belt, Montana, or go and play shuffleboard in the seventeenth century in Hartford, Connecticut, "Much precious time is spent unfruitfully," said the General Court. We can't play poker, hokey-pokey, or rouge et noir but we can play stocks-and-bonds in San Francisco, California. We can't put a penny in our pretty ears in Honolulu, Hawaii—Christ, do they obey that in Honolulu or do they worry as in *The People, Yes,*

> *Why did the children*
> *Put beans in their ears*
> *When the one thing we told the children*
> *They must not do*
> *Was put beans in their ears?*

I can't call Maria a bitch in Torrington, Wyoming, and she can't call me a sonofabitch in Paducah, Kentucky, "Such words excite violent resentment," said the chief justice of Kentucky. And meanwhile in Washington, the Senate has voted on a motion to table a motion to reconsider a vote to table a reconsideration of a ruling that a point of order wasn't in order against a motion to vote on a motion to vote on—I'm not inventing this! It happened!

Maria again: I can kiss her for one second only in Halethorpe, Maryland, for five seconds only in Holstein, Iowa, but I can't even hug her in Macon, Georgia. Here in Ketchum, Idaho, I can't put my ding in her dong without a $10 license from the county clerk: if I do, I'm liable for $300, and three thousand men are convicted each year in America. Even licensed, I can't put it in her mouth— to our north, a man who did it in Wallace, Idaho, got five years minimum for his most heinous crime, unquote, and it's also heinous in South Dakota. It's bestial in Alabama, morbid in Kansas, depraved in North Carolina, degenerate in Indiana, detestable in Mississippi, loathsome in Missouri, loathsome in Florida ("The punishment was death, sometimes burning alive," said the supreme court of Florida, "but such punishment has been modified") and it's filthy in Oregon, filthy in Delaware, filthy in Maine, but all right in Pennsylvania if I've been licensed by the county clerk. I don't know why the county clerk cares, and I can't even have my *wife* in Florence, Oregon, "No person shall while in or in view of a public or private place perform an act of sexual intercourse," or do they mean in a private place in view of a public place? I can't do my oui-oui on Maria in Salem, Oregon, and someone who did it in Salem got fifteen years in the state penitentiary. I can masturbate in Reno, Nevada, but Maria can't.

Sonofabitch! Excuse me, Paducah, Kentucky, but I've just woken up and I'm liable for life imprisonment! God help me if I go outside—I've got to wear pants in Phoenix, Arizona, my shirt in Toomsboro, Georgia, and my shoes with the shoelaces tied in Bangor, Maine. In my youth, a man was fined for his yellow shorts in Yonkers, New York, but the court of appeals overruled it, "This ordinance goes too far." I can't arrive in my wheelbarrow in Topeka, Kansas, or my baby carriage in Roderfield, West Virginia, I can't roll barrels in Pensacola, Florida, or hoops in Triadelphia, West Virginia, I can't throw confetti in Borger, Texas, and I don't want to, Mr. Mayor! The railway tracks: I can't pour pickle water on them in Central Falls, Rhode Island, or soap in Magnolia, Mississippi, or salt in Andalusia, Alabama, or I get ten years minimum in the state penitentiary. I can't laugh hilariously in Helena, Montana, or frown or scowl in Pocatello, Idaho, "These reflect unfavorably upon the reputation of Pocatello and are hereby declared illegal," and I can't gargle in Baton Rouge, Louisiana, or sneeze in Asheville, North Carolina, or spit into the wind in Sault Sainte Marie, Michigan. *Ptui*, I say, and I'll paraphrase John Stuart Mill, "There are reasons for remonstrating with me or reasoning with me but not for compelling me!"

The authorities! Damn them, I say, but I can't damn them in Youngstown, Ohio, I can't throw rotten eggs at them in Rawson, Ohio, or onions in Princeton, Texas, or coal (if it's three inches wide) in Harlan, Kentucky, and I can't put a skunk in their desks in Lansing, Michigan. I give up: I can't even scream in Cos Cob, Connecticut, or go out and get drunk in Monmouth, Oregon, or commit suicide in Newark, New Jersey—if I do I'm liable for six months imprisonment, except, as the state supreme court said, "The offense is rarely charged." Well, thank you, Mr. Justice! Your mercy is not strained, sir! But when will you bigwigs listen to Lao Tse?

If I keep from meddling with people, they take care of themselves,
If I keep from commanding people, they behave themselves,
If I keep from preaching at people, they improve themselves,
If I keep from imposing on people, they become themselves,

in other words, lemme go! Hey, hey, LBJ, Tricky and Jerry, Jimmy and Gipper—would we be worse off without you?

"If our destruction comes, it will be because [of] men who were only flesh and blood," says the press secretary, retired, to one of those authorities. No, they aren't sinister people but I say they're people, period, and the best and the brightest are as imperfect as I am at administering my one and only life. In fact, they're worse, for they haven't even met me. Now hear me, America! I learned long ago and I've learned again, I mustn't indenture myself to any authorities but me, myself, my shadow and I. So long live me! The most efficient ruler of me! Viva John Sack!

7 / I Come Marching Home, Hurrah

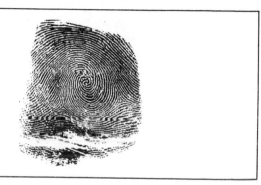

Or, The Final Solution

Now where was I? Oh, Korea, and one month later the godless communists were still on Old Mount Kojak. As for me, I was under arrest in Pusan, for (as I've been saying saying since page one)—for I'm only human and I had screwed up most consummately by sailing to Pusan on an American landing ship, an LST. Now, there're millions, *millions*, of GIs who have sailed somewhere without the whole world going into an uproar over it. But what precipitated the international incident in Pusan was that eight hundred soldiers were in that gray whale-belly, the LST, and all but your mortified author were the godless communists—the slit-eyed prisoners of the Korean War. It was all an innocent error, for I'd not have boarded the openmouthed ship if I had foreseen the story about me in thousands of daily papers as transmitted by the Associated Press,

> *Pusan, Korea, April 16—American military police gulped and looked again when they saw a pale-faced private walk off the prison ship today from Cheju Island. Then they arrested him. PFC John Sack—*

No, I'd have missed the ship willingly if I had divined that the AP would telephone the four-star commander of the Far East Command, in Tokyo, "No comment," the general's aide said.

Now what happened was—oh, go look up the official report in *Harper's*, March, 1955. The one important item is, I didn't implement the long day's nightmare of Sergeant McHugh, our tooth-powder officer in America, by being as criminally inefficient as The Late Company B and losing the Korean War. Or even losing $600,000 like the seabee in *South Pacific* ("Six hundred—! By

God, I'm going to chew that guy") who didn't stray into a landing ship but the wrong rubber raft in Empress Augusta Bay. I was an, er, embarrassment, that's all, but one wouldn't know this to hear my sonorous sergeant in the Land of the Morning Calm. A human howling baboon, on my release in Pusan he turned to a car-stopping color and (his face an about-to-burst balloon) he screamed and he *screamed* at me, "Sad Sack! You fucking freaking fuckup! How in the fucking fuck did you—"

He seemed to have cancer of the choler cells, and I began alarmedly, "I can explain it, Sergeant Scott!"

"No you can't! Not with your fucking head a fucking foot up your fucking ass! You fucking—"

Oh! A mist of hot little choler-drops hit me—his mouth was a few inches distant from mine. He wanted to bite me, to throttle me, to *short thrust! hold!* to twist a cold bayonet in my rumbling guts, to murder me—I mean it, I see the significance of bare-bone teeth even if I've evolved a hundred thousand generations from the ape. In my childhood, I know I felt imperiled if my red-faced father (a hammer in his white-fingered fist)—if the man hammered on some dramatic dent in his old jalopy while shouting at me, "God dammit, I didn't do it! You did it! You!" And *wham* went the hard-headed hammer, "You!" One day his Hudson was bumped with no real malice aforethought by a thick-trunked maple tree, and, a power saw like a sawmill in his gritted fist, he apologized to the offended gods of efficiency by just toppling it, a hole of hot summer sun supplanting it: an *irreverent* act, and I was upset enough to recount it thirty years later. "It reminded me of a Wintu story," I told someone. "The white people come and the tree says, please, don't hurt me. But still the—"

"You are the tree," the man suggested.

"—the white people kill it," I continued. "What?"

"You are the tree," the man suggested.

"I am the maple tree?"

"You are the tree," the man suggested.

At those words, the cells in my skin seemed to stand up like stubble, and I thought (as I had thirty years ago) of the loud power saw on my soft torso—*oh,* and I started sobbing, "Don't hurt me, Daddy!" And truly, the intrusion of any living thing (of grass in the gravel paths, of leaves in the water gutters, of shrubs in the garbage areas) was an abomination to my efficient father— as it was to my sergeant there in Korea, who, not toppling me, merely shipped me as far as he could without drumming me from the Far East Command. In one day, I was demoted to a mailroom boy on the eastern edge of Tokyo, a go-chip's throw from the icy Pacific Ocean. My duty there wasn't to lick the stamps single-tonguedly but to distribute them to a glum-looking group of Japanese, who did the licking themselves. " 切手," the Japanese would tell me. " を下さいませんか."

"Do you want postage stamps?" I would ask.

"切手を下さいませんか," the Japanese would tell me.

I wasn't happy there. I was just lost in loneliness there. A mist, as skin-chilling as a wet bedsheet, crept from the sea through the wood-warped windows, curling the purple postage stamps into the shape of old caterpillars and my own backbone into a limp parenthesis. A foghorn sounded outside, and the seagulls were a chorus of blackboard chalk—oh, I was cast on a cold ocean island like Ovid,

I am wasting words, for the sea sprays on my very lips as I speak them. Oh wretched me,

for the new deadly sin of not being dead, of being alive with the mind, muscle, and willpower to upset an applecart, sometimes, of being a *blot* in the perfect design—words of Jacques Ellul. "Man's intervention is a source of error, for he is tempted to make unpredictable choices," the French philosopher says. We have re-created creation, and our new world is one where we ourselves are an intolerable intrusion.

Intolerable. A man needn't be a four-star general to do so much damage that the seabee's $600,000 is practically petty cash. In recent times, a sailor in California was filling, filling, the ballast tank of a submarine till it was so full-bellied full that the $50,000,000 submarine sank, and a second fellow in California was only flying a kite, officer, when it intertwined with a high-tension wire to create a $30,000,000 fire. A couple of red-face awards: a box of candy-coated decimal points to a man in Vancouver, Canada, who dropped one in his computations for a $16,000,000 bridge, which, oh my fair lady, collapsed, and a box of honey-dipped hyphens to a couple of federal employees in Washington and Cape Canaveral, Florida. The first put the hyphen in *fruit-trees* in the tariff act, and we lost $10,000,000 by not collecting on fruit, trees, and the second left out the hyphen in (ABS((T(3,1)-T(2,1))/DENOM),GT.ERMAX), or something such, on the computer cards of a spaceship to Venus, and the $10,000,000 spaceship missed by two hundred million miles. The man who should take the cake, though—a cake without candles, please—is Mr. Hargett of Athens, Alabama, who carried a lone little candle into the old atomic reactor there. The damages due to Hargett (a blot, a stain, a flaw in the total pattern, as the commissioner said of Winston Smith in 1984) and his little holocaust were $100,000,000.

And you're angry at *me*, Sergeant Scott? How sore would you be at the perpetrator of a $375,000,000 error? If you've forgotten, one of our high-priced ships to the moon exploded like a roman candle when it was five sixths of the distance there. To plug up their sudden bucket, the astronauts used an old cotton sock and, to garter it, a roll of white adhesive tape like a Band-Aid. But their water was ice (and the hot dogs were cold dogs) as they put-put-putted down to a world where the Jains in Jain, India, the Jews at the Wailing Wall in Jerusalem, and the Pope in Vatican City ("We share the universal trepidation") prayed for the frosted astronauts of Apollo Thirteen. Alas, the stakhanovism of its ten thousand creators (the man who did ten thousand solderings, the man who did ten thousand computations, the man who filed thirty thousand drawings without error) were of no avail against the one stumblebum in Florida. A mechanic, he hadn't turned the heater off in the oxygen tank, and the temperature of a thousand destroyed the Teflon electrical insulation. "Mechanization," Giedion said, "comes to a halt before living substance," and two weeks later the spaceship became the Hindenburg II.

The bill for that man's inefficiency was a cool $375,000,000, but he wasn't the dunce number one of the twentieth century. Do you remember the Texan's misconception that his choppers, bombers, and battleships could win a war against a soldier in shower shoes? Why, that eeny-meeny error cost us $100,000,-

ooo,ooo and fifty thousand dead in Vietnam. So don't shout at me, Sergeant Scott!

Oɴᴇ day in Tokyo, my yellow personnel record or my form twenty fell in my own stamp-stick-ummed hands, and I (after hiding in the gentlemen's room of the mist-ridden mailroom) erased a certain one of its X marks before showing it to Personnel. "Oh, you're due for discharge now," the sergeant said, and I was released expeditiously from the Kools, the tooth-powder cans, the parachute packs, the tanks, the commie-class ships, and the 切手s, returning in no-starch clothes to Ike's Island and, God, a whole nother army! My best friend in Tokyo was discharged to a small assembly line—a line where at two-second intervals he painted the eyebrows on children's dolls, and a second friend colored the cactuses in *Wild West Comics*. At midnight, a third friend counted up headlines (*h*, one, *e*, one, *a*, one, *d*, one, *l*, one-half, *i*, one-half, *n*, one, *e*, one) and a fourth friend did an encyclopedia for the A&P by cribbing from the *Encyclopaedia Britannica*. Myself, I stowed my mud-colored uni-form in my mother and father's attic, and I dressed in a red-and-white uniform (and red-and-white tasseled hat) to enter on what would seem a not-too-onerous job at R. H. White's Department Store in Boston: I would be Santa Claus.

Yes, there was a Mr. Sack, Virginia, a boy whose nose was a cherry in his innocent hope to recapture some of the "ho-ho-ho"s of his ante-bellum career. On my first day, an alarm clock awak-ened me, and I was enthusiastic as I stomped to the store in the carbon-colored snow and as I punched in (*clunk*, the time clock croaked) to put on a pillow, powder my nose, put on a beard of absorbent cotton, and, of course, change out of my gray flannel pants to *les pantalons rouges* of Santa Claus. In my white-trimmed red, I was shown to the old man's throne—or rather, to one of two thrones occupied by two of three cherry-cheeked men, the others being a lean-limbed poet (the composer of

The wide, white fields of Africa
Surge and hum

and such sentiments) and a fat, florid, and sad-spirited driver of ten-ton trailer trucks, a man on whose lower jaw (or, at night, in whose locked little box) was a beard of Tibetan yak fur—for my own beard of cotton wasn't authentic, he used to say enigmatically. In this setting of one store, two thrones, and three disparate old Santas, it followed from the immutable rules of arithmetic that the jolly, jolly sounds of laughter had to proceed from me from nine-thirty to ten-thirty, eleven to twelve, twelve-thirty to one-thirty, two to three, three-thirty to four-thirty, and (ooh, my diaphragm like an old trampoline) five to six o'clock today. At those times, my station would be a red-and-green throne (as comfortable as an electric chair) and I was there at nine-thirty, precisely, as my first little girl in a pinafore ran in. Her father said, "There he is, Jennifer!"

"Ohhh," I chortled, "I remember you! You're Jennifer!"

"Yes, Santa Claus! Yes, I was here last year," Jennifer said, and she smiled her own cherry-cheeked smile.

"I remember," I chortled. "How old are you, Jennifer! You were—"

"Five," Jennifer said.

"—four last year, weren't you? And your father was off in Korea!" No, I didn't know him—he was right there with his Korean Service Ribbon.

"Yes, Santa Claus! And he's home now!"

"I know! And they gave him a Silver Star, I'm told!"

"Yes, Santa Claus! A medal!"

"Ohhh," I chortled, "I'm happy for you, Jennifer! Now what do you want for Christmas?"

"Well, Santa Claus," Jennifer said, jumping up on my red left knee. "I want—"

"*Oh Santa Claus,*" I now heard a woman interrupt us.

"—some betsy-wetsy dresses, Santa Claus," Jennifer said.

"*Oh Santa Claus,*" I heard again.

"Uh, Jennifer? For your betsy-wetsy doll?" I asked.

"*Oh Santa Claus,*" I heard. "*Yoo hoo! Yoo hoo! The little girl is on your wrong knee!*"

"Yes, Santa Claus! The doll you gave me," Jennifer said.

"*Oh Santa Claus*—"

I looked over Jennifer's shoulder. The complainant was a bony-bodied woman who, I'd been told, would be by my throne on permanent duty. A photographer, her mission would be to put profit into the operation by (*click*) by selling the mommies and daddies a one-dollar photograph of their pride and joy and Santa Claus. As her camera was to my *left*, my own mission was to seat everyone on my *right*—on my right knee, so that their wondering eyes and not their occipitals would be in the little memento. To let Jennifer seat herself on my left patella was as fatal to total efficiency as to let some soldier do forward march on his right metatarsus, and my mission (in this season of *fa lalalala lalalala*) wasn't to let life evolve but to screw every child a quarter turn to the left and to wheedle a little smile out of him her without saying, "Say cheese." And *click*, to summon the next little toddler, please. At R. H. White's, I too worked an assembly line, a predeterminate process with no more spontaneity than in Detroit—at whose assembly lines, in the old days, anyway, the men couldn't talk (the men couldn't *smile*) and, in fact, were often handcuffed to the sheet-metal presses. In my holly-walled room, it was expressly as stated by Henry Ford,

> *We expect the men to do what they're told. We couldn't for a moment allow men to have their own way. Without the most rigid discipline we would have the utmost confusion,*

as happened in *Wheels* if anyone dropped a four-inch bolt in the automobile assembly line. It led to bedlam in *Wheels*: the line would stop, the bells would clang, the sirens would wail, and Ford or some company was out six thousand dollars. Well, I was the four-inch bolt at the Santa Claus Factory in Boston.

"*Oh Santa Claus*," I now heard the woman say. "*I don't see her pretty little eyes.*"

"Uh, Jennifer," I said, and I shifted her to the proper knee, "I won't forget you at Christmas. Do you still live—"

"*All right, Santa Claus! I'm done!*"

"—on Beacon Street in Brookline?" Oh, this could be a creative occupation, everyone: the address was on a parcel in her father's arms.

"*I'm done, Santa Claus! It's time for the next little girl!*"
"Yes, Santa Claus! On Beacon Street," Jennifer cried.
"Fifteen Fifty, if I remember," I said.
"Yes, Santa Claus! In the big building," Jennifer cried.
"*I'm done, Santa—*"
Aaagh! I can't take it, I thought! I'd have liked to have yanked off all my absorbent cotton and to have hacked it into earplugs— or into cotton bolls to shove in the old scold's throat as I shouted, "I want to do it my way, mother!" Oh Christ on a Christmas tree, I thought! Is one never out of the army and the left-face, right-face, stone-faced life? I had enlisted as Santa to repossess my long-lost soul, the very entity that, it turned out, was an impediment to this photographer's studio. I was being abridged like a beggar in *The Threepenny Opera* ("In ten minutes," says Peachum, "I can make such a wreck of a man that a *dog* would weep") or, for that matter, a live *bikari* in India who must forfeit an arm or a leg, perhaps, to his chosen occupation. Like him, I'd have to amputate parts of me (my love of children in pinafores, pantaloons, and Pampers) to fit in as Father Christmas—I'd have to diminish myself *and* to diminish myself to the vanishing point to fit to a T.

Santa Claus! Humbug, I thought! To impersonate him in this century was to be Chaplin in *Modern Times,* and I (who soon suffered from an infected eardrum, too, the one in my right ear) lay a finger aside of my nose and I quit on X-day-minus-ten. But alas, there wasn't a job in America without the prerequisite (according to Jung) of my own total disintegration. In Boston, I was practically back in the army as ("Lift your spears! And shake your spears!") an extra in the Metropolitan Opera, and my duties in New York City, a sightseeing guide, were to be so second-rate that a sightseer needed to spend another dollar for a *Guide to New York City.* In Miami, I was the chaperone to the "Miss"es of Austria, Belgium, Denmark, England, France, Germany, Greece, Holland, Hong Kong, Iceland, Israel, Italy, Jordan, Lebanon, Luxembourg, Morocco, Norway, South Africa, Sweden, Switzerland, and Tunisia—oh, I suppose I can't complain, but as a disc jockey in Port-au-Prince, Haiti, my chitter-chatter had to restrict itself to whatever would sell the residue of dead dinosaurs at the

Texaco service station. "Yeah! And that was *Rum and Coca-Cola!* As for me," I'd continue, "I'll have some Texaco gasoline! Gulp! Good!"

I mean God! I even tried *writing* once, as a state senate reporter for United Press. At every vote, I'd run through the marble-walled halls to our squat little teletype: to throw the interrupt switch, to stop every teletype in three hundred miles, to tap on the *bell, bell, bell,* and *bulletin* keys, and to start writing in time to the *tatatatatatata* of that importunate apparatus. Now, Trollope had put out his pocket watch to write a thousand words every hour, but Sack at that teletype had to write a letter, comma, or period every 1818 ten-thousandths of every imperative second. And *lalala-tatatata* was the woody woodpecker's song at United Press! Oh, I had almost become a half-man, half-machine, a galley slave at that 1818 tempo, a metronome, an escapement, and if some rainy day the news in the upper chamber were *Bulletin, The state senate voted to hang the state senate reporter for United Press,* I swear I'd have *tatata*-tapped it out without tears—there wasn't time for any. "Aaagh! The hell with it!" I said once again, I wrote *thirty, thirty, thirty* to the beards, spears, and the teletypes of the gray-flannel army, and I got some seersucker combat clothes (the only cotton that's cool, man, cool) to return as a war correspondent to the 1960's combat zone: to Vietnam.

Nᴏᴛ crashing once, a chopper with a banana's shape took me to the "boonies" there—the temperature was a hundred there, or a hundred more than it was in Korea, and the total absence of snow interfered with my déjà vu. The rice paddies that, in Korea, had climbed up the hill like contour lines lay in Vietnam in the open country like a hot-off-the-iron waffle and, no longer L-shaped, the homes didn't look to the southeast but to the south, for a man has to marry a gentle woman and to live looking south, the saying goes in Vietnam. The smell in Vietnam was the same sewer smell of Korea, and our hooches (we still spoke in Japanese)—our *uchis* were the same caveman's caves with the candles in C-ration cans. The shelves were of old ammunition crates, and the nonstop sound was of Radio Lima Kilo,

Mrs. O'Malley! Out in the valley!
She suffered—

no, that was that other war, and in the sixties the nonstop sound was *Mrs. Robinson*. And again, it was through the six-inch slits that we squinted at concertina wire and the lair of the godless communists. *But*—these were the sixties now, and the commies didn't have to lounge around like the silhouettes in a shooting gallery for a GI to get their coordinates and to call in the 105's, the 155's, and the 175's on their black-haired heads. No, we were efficient now!

We had radar to see their thinnest limbs in the camouflage of the mahogany trees. We had devices (as timber rattlesnakes do) to sense their fires, and we had sensors to smell their urine, too. If any unwary communist stepped on a pellet of monkey manure— *pop*, it wasn't monkey manure but a plastic facsimile that the ladies in tear-shaped glasses built at a 140-acre factory in Phoenix, Arizona ("What is it?" "They don't say, and I don't care"). If stepped on, the brown-colored ball of explosives jolted a thing with a green antenna (green, to look like an innocent fern) that, in turn, transmitted a radio wave to a plane that, is everyone with me? transmitted a radio wave to the two best computers in Asia in the underground room at the air force base in Nakhon Phanom, Thailand. And *there* a red dot appeared on a plastic map as a colonel sat at a silver microphone, saying, "Now calling all B-52's!" Or something like that, "Now calling all B-52's! Now there is an enemy infantryman at fern number niner niner! Bombs away!"

Efficiency! A foot in some monkey manure, and a concatenation of automatic responses ended at one dead enemy infantryman, dispatched by the ghost of Rube Goldberg. In *theory*, for the communists (the one bad bulb in the Christmas tree, the one unpredictable link in the chain, the one element with the defect of not being doornail-dead)—the commies didn't choose to step in the monkey manure in Vietnam. No, they chose to say peeyoo and to step around it—the pellets didn't pop, the ferns didn't transmit, and the red dots didn't appear like a case of scarlet fever on the map in Nakhon Phanom, Thailand. For there was in those people a free and unfettered volition, in the language of Dostoevsky. "And," Dostoevsky continued, "it is never considered, and its omission sends all of our systems to the devil himself."

No, nothing worked in Vietnam. On one eerie, rainy, windy night, a GI and his radar machine (his moon-faced machine) were on the perimeter and I whispered, "Got anything?"

"I got movement," the radarman whispered.

"The Charlies?" I whispered.

"Maybe," the radarman whispered. "Or maybe in the monsoon, the banana trees."

Nor did the sensors work, for the communists didn't light fires or even urinate—except in some buckets which, a month later, we were still bombing. In time, it occurred to our generals that the difference between the wars in Korea and Vietnam was that no one knew where the communists were in Vietnam. Oh, there was in Saigon a computer with the names, addresses (and telephone numbers, perhaps) of every communist soldier, but, as that computer had no provisions for the *ngãs*, *ngangs*, or other diacritical marks of Vietnamese, its ten-pound printout was like a directory with no perceptible differences between a Mr. King and a Mr. Kong. Now, historically the infantry's mission is to find, to fix, and to destroy the enemies of the United States. But since we didn't even find the little devils, it didn't take an Attila to understand that we couldn't accomplish our mission until we had burned, bombed, or atom-bombed the whole confounded country from the Cape to China—a tactic whose serious disadvantage was the presence there of one million tons of Vietnamese.

The old lady selling us Coca-Cola. The old man tapping the dripping rubber trees. The children telling us, "You want mamasan? You want mamasan? GI, my mamasan virgin!" Now, these indigenous personnel of Vietnam (or these indignant personnel, as we had termed them in Korea) had the same susceptibility to the passions as anyone else of the two-legged genus. It was from passion (and not common sense) that the Vietnamese all wore black although it was hotter than in Arabia and that their national hat had the shape of Fujiyama—the Koreans at least had a hat shaped after a mountain outside of Taegu, Korea. But most detrimental to a burn, bomb, or atom-bomb strategy was the Vietnamese's attachment to their straw-roofed homes—to witness it, one would suppose that the Vietnamese lived in Tara, in *Gone With the Wind*. "Our house, our house," the Vietnamese sang,

> *Our ancestors built it,*
> *We must preserve it,*
> *For ten thousand years,*

or twice as long as the pyramids. In contempt of all military necessity, it was their irrational passion to live right on top of their ancestors and (it was cannibalism, practically) to eat their ancestors too in their reincarnations as thriving rice. And with *nuoc mam* or fish-flesh sauce.

In the forties, the French sought to get these homebodies out to the rubber plantations—fairylands, the French propaganda said—by promising lots of *nuoc mam* and Saturdays and Sundays off. But these people stayed put, and now we Americans sought to inveigle them to the concentration camps (to the tight barbed wires and the wooden homes with the stenciled *grenades grenades grenades*) out of our harm's way. Our thousands of red-and-black leaflets fell like a plague of flies, frogs, or locusts on these problem people. In black was a little cartoon of a bomber, a bomb explosion, and a man, woman, and child lying in front of their fire-ridden home, in red was the blood coming out of their eyes, ears, noses, and mouths, and the text to this two-color illustration was "You can expect death from the sky." But the *abc*'s weren't decipherable to these people, who, in fact, appropriated the red-and-black papers to put their catfish in and who stayed there in their first-little-piggy houses. So how could the army accomplish its mission to Win the War? No other option obtained but to incorporate all the Vietnamese in the burn, bomb, or atom-bomb concept and to eliminate them as a stumbling stone on the road to efficiency. To destroy them so as to save them, unquote.

Now, this wasn't racism. The trouble wasn't that the Vietnamese were yellow-colored people (we came close to adoring the

Siamese) but that they were people, period, and to abolish them was the only solution in Vietnam. One afternoon, a four-star general (the commander of the whole penny arcade) was up in his gray-green helicopter with a man whose shirt stated that he was war correspondent for *The New York Times*. It was his third year in Vietnam, so he had seen hundreds (as many as seven hundred in one little village) of lifeless civilians—of old men, women, and children whose face was a rotten tomato or whose skin was in scales like on old black kettles. And today as they chop-chopped over the craters, he said to the four-star general, "Are you worried about the civilian casualties, sir?"

"Yes," the general said. "But," he continued, no doubt thinking of Mao's old dictum that a guerrilla amidst the civilians should be a fish within water—"it does deprive the communists of the population, doesn't it?"

The war correspondent wrote this in his red black-market notebook. But one didn't need to be in Vietnam to appreciate what the generals (and the men behind the guns: the grunts) understood: that the war wasn't against the communists but the whole population, *all* the Vietnamese, as subversive of total efficiency as Ho Chi Minh. One only needed a newspaper, and one learned we were killing six, *at least*, civilians for any one communist soldier. A nominee for our presidency said the whole war was a massacre, and the state department explained that the communists couldn't be dislodged if their constituency (to wit: everyone in the nation) existed, unquote, from *Foreign Affairs*. The assistant secretary of defense said we were out to destroy the villages, defoliate the forests, and cover all of Vietnam with asphalt—a prospect that at last afforded me some déjà vu. It was the very same fantasy that my father had had (and the men who constructed the Futuramas had had) for all the United States of America. To pave paradise, and put up a parking lot.

IT was apocalypse now for the Vietnamese. For those twenty million misfits, it was death from the sky in the conformations of dumb bombs, smart bombs, fire bombs, napalm bombs, guava bombs with a hundred thousand bebes, and the new flechette bombs with a thousand nails—oh, talk about overkill, we had just needed three for Jesus Christ! Often, these were the innocent errors of such mortified bombadiers as Captain Brumfield, who didn't switch one of his switches on and was fined $700 (or $5 each) for the civilians he killed in Neah Luong, Cambodia. But more often, these were the mortal blows of the men who sang,

> Bomb the schools
> And bomb the churches,
> Bomb—

at the officers clubs, banging the beer glasses on the mahogany bars to the beat of *Yankee Doodle Dandy*. Of course, to have to bomb schools, churches, and hospitals didn't do the air force officers proud, and the extravagance of their lyrics ridiculed the unpleasant thought that the napalm was, in fact, falling on schools, churches, hospitals, and orphanages too. At their bars, it was through travesty that the officers demonstrated that no one was criminal, really, for one would say, "Get any women and children today?"

"Yeah, but I let a pregnant woman get away!"

"Ha ha ha!"

And they would laugh till they cried—so reported the war correspondent for *The New Yorker*. Myself, I was once, only once, in a super sabre bomber (we missed a little brown village by twenty meters) but I got enough *mal d'atmosphère* to stay after this on the terra firma, where, it appeared, the GIs (who could contemplate one half century of life, limb, and the other pleasures if only there were no Vietnamese)—the GIs were as incontinent as the air force officers. To the chagrin of English, the cannoneers called it *harassment* if they lobbed the 105, 155, or 175-millimeter shells at a random road in Vietnam, and the tankers called it *reconnaissance* if they leveled a 50-caliber machine gun (its bullets as big as hot dogs) at a little village—reconnaissance, for if there were communists there it incited them to shoot at *us*. Nor were the infantrymen the less homicidal on account of their smaller bullets. In the moss-covered water wells, the GIs would drown the Vietnamese or throw them out of the gray-green helicopters or offer them, *the children*, a chocolate cookie with a mickey of plastic explosive inside. A friend in Vietnam (his eyes averted, his first bullet missing, therefore) killed a total of nine ancient farmers, and a second friend of mine turned a machine gun on three little girls as they washed an old water buffalo. "The captain said, Cut them down. I guess," the soldier told me, a tiny twitch of disapproval registering on his upper lip, "I guess he was oneing up Alpha company's body count." A third, a sweet-smiling sergeant, went to his sunless canvas tent, saw a couple of laundry boys on a cot, sitting, looking at dirty pictures of people making love, and saying things such as "Fucky fucky." And putting a bullet into his rifle, *click, clack,* the sergeant reported, "I'm gonna do some hunting."

"I hope you'll do your hunting out yonder," a soldier said.

"I can do my hunting right here," the sergeant said. And *(bang)* after killing the laundry boys, he was all wet-eyed innocence as he asked me, "Isn't that what we're meant to do? Kill Vietnamese?"

And wasn't it? Of course, to have to commit genocide in the same quarter century as the holocaust set a load of cognitive dissonance upon the GIs, who resolved it rather retroactively by identifying all of the dead bullet-ridden or shell-splinter-ridden or bomb-broken bodies as communist soldiers—well, the argument went, if a man wasn't communist what was he doing being dead? The unlimited applicability of this assumption turned the whole country to something out of Goya. Oh, the horror of it! "Did our children cry? Oh yes," someone told a war correspondent writing for *The Washington Monthly,*

and I cried too. I just stayed in my cave, and I didn't see the sun for two years. And what did I think about? Oh, please don't let the planes come. Oh, please don't let the planes come. Oh, please don't let—

The elephants left Vietnam, the nervous rhinoceroses left Vietnam, and the tigers crept in to forage among the corpses of one million indigenous ex-personnel. In their villages, the bare-bellied bodies of men, women, and children lay in the red-tinted mud at angles of raggedy anns, and (as the rigor mortis set in) their arms became as erect as old tilted tombstones. The ants wandered out of their eyeballs, too.

It turned a man's stomach around but it didn't astonish me. For having been to Korea (to say nothing of: to America) my conclusions were that we couldn't tolerate the one temperamental element in our environment, and to terminate it with extreme prejudice (as the circumlocution went in Vietnam) was the deadly prerequisite of the triumph of total efficiency in Vietnam. Or anywhere else, for the fact is that people (the ones of *The Late Company B*, the ones at that propeller plant in Indianapolis and rudder plant in Teterboro and hangar in Kansas City, the pilots in Charlotte, North Carolina, the parachute passer-outer in Korea, the generals in Korea, the secretary of the whole bloody army, and I myself in Pusan)—is that people alone are the crick in everyone's neck in this century, and, as we're asked (and answered) by Jacques Ellul, "Is the elimination of man so unavoidably necessary? Certainly!" The murder of all mankind is our ultimate imperative.

In other words: efficiency kills us, and I'm not the first to say so. In ancient times, Aesop was telling us of a man who scrubbed on his coal-black slave until he was dead—though he still wasn't what the man wanted: white—and we also heard from Chuang Tsu, in China, of the men who did an efficient thing to No Form (a man who looked like the character in *Dick Tracy*, No Face) by boring holes in his eyeless, earless, noseless, mouthless head,

> One a day for seven days,
> And when they did the seventh opening,
> Their friend was dead.

More recently, we were treated to the mad doctors whose efforts to institute efficiency had as their consummations, death, such as the one of Mary Wollstonecraft Shelley's. His brain child ("It was already one; the rain pattered dismally against the panes, when, by the glimmer of the half-extinguished light, the dull yellow eye of the creature opened")—his creature rose in the ill-lighted laboratory to stumble off to Geneva to strangle the mad doctor's brother. And Stevenson—Stevenson had his mad doctor whose alter ego was not above clubbing his walking cane ("A storm of blows, under which the bones were audibly shattered") and killing an old member of parliament, among others. And especially there were the mad doctors (an asylum of old, sallow, sickly-looking, grim, gray, ugly-looking, emaciated—unquote—wretches) in the prophetic stories of America's Hawthorne.

A few of his demented men in black (as against white of the twentieth century) were Dr. Aylmer, Dr. Felton, and Dr. Rappacini. In spite of their intentions, each of their efficient experiments ended in the death of their wife, mother, or daughter. In *The Birthmark*, Aylmer's wife had a birthmark—a hand-shaped dot on her cheek—as her one imperfection, and Aylmer brooded and brooded upon it. "No," Aylmer told her, "you came so nearly perfect that this slightest defect shocks me." And going to his gas-smothered laboratory full of retorts, crucibles, furnaces, and electrical apparatuses, he returned to that inadequate woman with a water-colored drink. "It cannot fail," Aylmer assured her. "Drink, lovely creature." As she drank, the hand-shaped dot on her cheek disappeared, and Aylmer cried, "It is successful!" "Aylmer, Aylmer," his wife replied, "I am dying."

Alas! The hand was the bond by which an angelic spirit kept in a mortal frame. As the last crimson tint of the birthmark—that sole token of human imperfection—faded, the parting breath of the now perfect woman passed into the atmosphere,

said Hawthorne, who indicted his mad doctor for unintentional homicide instead of first-degree anything.

And another one. Felton, the title lunatic of Hawthorne's *Septimius Felton*, was just experimenting (he was just treating rheumatism) by introducing a few red flowers of *sanguinea sanguinissima* or super-super-bloodroot in his mother's patent medicine—his foster mother's, really, his Aunt Keziah's. "It does not look quite right. It does not smell quite right. Ah! Ai! Oh!" Keziah said. "It was not quite right," and

These, except for some unintelligible whisperings, were the last utterances of Aunt Keziah.

Now, Rappacini, in *Rappacini's Daughter*, had grown a garden of poisonous plants (to be dispensed as medicine, naturally) that he himself looked on as evil spirits, as deadly snakes, as savage beasts. The very butterflies died—as, eventually, did the mad doctor's daughter, saying, "My father, wherefore didst thou inflict this?" On behalf of efficiency, dear, he ought to have answered her.

In the twentieth century, the descendant of all these sociopaths is Dr. Strangelove. But after three hundred years of their trials and errors, errors, we do not allow these characters a presumption of innocent inadvertence—no, now they're premeditated murderers, just as the heartless computer was ("You're not going to like this, Dave") in 2001. In *The Physicists*, by Dürrenmatt, the assassins are no lesser lights than Newton, Einstein, and Möbius, the German mathematician. By the final act, Newton has strangled someone with a curtain cord and Einstein has strangled someone with a table-lamp cord, and Möbius says, "I've strangled Monika Stettler."

"Strangled?"

"But with the curtain cord this time."

"Möbius! How could you do it?"

"I'm sorry," Möbius says.

In *The Lesson*, Ionesco's professor inculcates efficiency on a candidate for the total doctor's degree. He asks her, as my own arithmetic teacher did, "How much are one and one?"

"Two."

"Oh, but that's very good," the professor says. He asks her the totals of two and one, three and one, four and one, five and one, six and one, seven and one—

"Eight."

"Excellent! Seven and one?"

"Eight."

"Magnificent! I congratulate you," the professor says. In her language lesson, though, she is unable to say the word *knife* in French, Monacan, Andorran, Spanish, Portuguese, Basque, Italian, Sardinian, Sardanapalian, Latin, Esperanto, or Jai Alai. "Knife," the professor shouts, doing a sort of scalper's dance around her. "Knife! Knife! Knife!"

"No, my ears hurt—"

"Knife! Knife! Knife!"

"Oh, my head aches—"

"Knife! Knife! Ahhh," the professor shouts as he murders her (his fortieth murder today) with the convenient kitchen knife. "Ahhh, that'll teach you!" If this seems absurd, remember the man who taught the word *knife* in Tagalog (the word *sundang*, and the use of the knife itself) to the stone-agers of the Philippines, who soon were killing, cooking, and eating their pets: the deer, pigeons, parrots, and, I suppose, by now each other.

As for me, my own contribution to this literature was in the late sixties. A friend in Vietnam (a man who *liked* the Vietnamese) killed at least twenty-two at the irrigation ditch in Mylai, in Quangngai, in Vietnam, and my little contribution was to suggest that he wasn't exceptional for the American army and for America. After all, at least eighty percent of Quangngai had been burned, bombed, or otherwise terminated before he had touched the toes of his combat boots to Asia. To off another twenty-two of its six hundred thousand inhabitants was no deviation in American policy ("It is typical," the colonel wrote in his after-action report, "of operations in this country from one end to the other") or in a GI's own inclinations—it didn't demand a deviant rifleman, and I didn't think I was being original to write on my yellow pad one day,

He had killed in Vietnam as one more participant on a mission that was as American as mom's cherry pie. We were all William Calley,

or as soldiers wrote on their helmets in Vietnam, "Calley dies for our sins." Oh, for the talent of Hawthorne, for I don't think I got that across to Mr. and Mrs. America, "Unproven," *The New Republic,* "Preposterous," *Time,* "I disagree," *The New Haven Reg-*

ister, "It all disgusts me," *The Washington Post*, "Tripe," *The Roanoke Times*.

Oh reader! I'm hoarse and I'm heartsick, too, to be the bearer of one lone voice in the wilderness and (as I did fifty years ago in my little crib) to be calling to cotton-stoppered ears. Oh merciful reader, hello, hello—do you still don't understand, and do you still think it can't happen here? To be sure—as of the seven o'clock news, we hadn't wasted the inefficient elements here at any great irrigation ditch. We hadn't stabbed them, as happened in recent times to one quarter million people in Indonesia, or hammered a ten-penny nail in their foreheads, as happened to one quarter million people in Burundi, or put any zyklon in their shower stalls, as happened to six million people in Germany. Or (the easiest way)—or sat in our rattan chairs as they starved, as happened to three million people in Cambodia and three million more in Nigeria. We hadn't created the fictional world of tomorrow—we hadn't blue-jaunted them as in Bester or cut off their cardioplates as in Ellison ("And his heart stopped and he was dead, that's all") or disintegrated them as in *Logan's Run* or reduced them to Triscuits as in *Soylent Green*.

But nevertheless, the inner contradictions of our society allow for no other resolution. A man, a mouse, a living thing is the one undependable part of our circuitry—is the bête noire in our empire of total efficiency, and (as the commissioner said to Mr. Smith in 1984) it must be wiped out as our public enemy number one. In twenty years, according to Asimov, we may have started to "rid the earth" of its two billion people of too little income to feed themselves, or according to Arendt we may have commenced to "exterminate" the one, two, three, or four billion people (the lady is not specific) of too low intelligence quotients. Or the sword may fall on the older folks like me, who (not having died in my twenties when a mortar shell hit my hooch in Korea or in my thirties when a recoilless-rifle shell hit my *maison* in Vietnam) am to be threescore-and-ten in the year 2000, the year of that shambling beast in Bethlehem. In any event, according to C. S. Lewis,

The methods may (at first) differ. But many a mild-eyed scientist means the same as the Nazis of Germany, for somehow the irreversibly inefficient will be the Jews of the coming century.

Already, according to Reich, we are dealing death to our own constituents. A sort of carbon monoxide comes out of our endeavors until we are choking on it

> And somehow trying,
> But still unable, to know just what it was
> That went so completely wrong, or why it is
> We are dying,

Strand. Are dying of asbestosis at asbestos factories, silicosis at glass factories, stannosis at tin-can factories, pneumomonosis in coal mines, byssinosis in cotton mills, and berylliosis ("My legs! My arms! My head! Jesus," a worker reported, "I'm being pulled apart") at factories for my father's wan fluorescent lights. At gasoline factories, the H_2S is like steel spikes in our foreheads ("I'd swear somebody stabbed me") and at raincoat factories the CS_2 is like lysergic acid—at one, we kept jumping out of a window until the management put a lattice in. En route home, the NO_2 is like nicotine, and at home we're dying of tetrachloroethylene in our water, diethylpyrocarbonate in our wine, dieldrin in our own mother's milk.

Our necrosis, though, is not accidental but is the sine qua non of this efficient environment. A coral, cactus, entity of the most static sort is passionate to preserve itself, a coral by its polypeptides, a cactus by its oxalic acid: a couple of knockout drops for its enemies, and our own environment conspires to rid itself of its one menace: us. Its hostility to us is nothing new, for our death sentence dates to the century when a man's eyes, ears, and nose were practically amputated by Galileo as impertinent to his solid geometry, as inadmissible in his efficient earth. The premise of our geometric world was the extinction of man, or, in the words of Dostoevsky, "Two and two are four, after all, is the beginning of Death."

We have hanged ourselves on our own gallows, as the engineer did in The Bell Tower, by Melville. The tower there was the noblest in Italy and the chef-d'oeuvre of Bannadonna, a man so intolerant of men's inefficiency that, in casting the bell itself, he had killed a man who committed a far-from-fatal error. And now the bell was done, and at one o'clock in the afternoon it would sound from its campanile. A bit before the appointed hour, an automaton that was the great creation of Bannadonna,

a new serf, more useful than the ox, swifter than the dolphin, stronger than the lion, more cunning than the ape,

etcetera,

yet, in patience, another ass,

an automaton aroused itself to a semblance of two-footed life: it issued out of its sentry box, it rolled on its well-oiled route, and it brought down a mace on Bannadonna's bell. And *thud*, the sound was a dull and almost inaudible one—for Bannadonna was still engrossed in a small imperfection there, and his irrevocable automaton (in the words of Melville) had not smitten the bell itself but the intervening brain of Bannadonna.

So the creator was killed by the creature, and so pride went before the fall,

and so art announced (as in *Faust* it had also announced) that we can never survive the relentless quest of efficiency: never.

Oh, we can too, the new Bannadonnas say—the effect of foot-loose efficiency is not our death but a healthy life. And yes, the pestilences of the pre-seventeenth centuries—the plagues of plague, leprosy, typhus, tuberculosis, sweating sickness, and even measles (the big killer of children in our grandfather's day)—are no longer with us. To attribute this to efficiency is illogical, though, and is not even *post ergo propter*, as each of these practically disappeared prior to the medicine for it. And yes, we are not just destroying life but are now creating it, congratulating ourselves on what *worms* accomplish by not even stopping to think—as we're reminded by Roszak. It is, he continues,

a measure of our alienation that we do not regard that man as a fool who grimly devises laboratory procedures for [the] magnificent gift of his most natural desire, and Mumford, on peeping in on these unessential laboratories, said he wouldn't suspect that life on the planet already exists and, in fact, exists in the ground he has stood upon and the air he has breathed. And yes, we are assured that we will achieve immortality in one and a half centuries, but I answer applesauce.

Au contraire. We are necrophiliacs, says Fromm—the arch not the architect, the creature not the creator, will be the immortal one if our imperative prevails. For implicit in total efficiency is total extermination, and the sole survivor of five thousand years of our so-called civilization will be either us or it. "The struggle," according to Rollo May, "is for the human being in a world in which everything ends in Vietnam."

8 / The Sorcerer's Apprentice

Or, The Counterproductive Culture

Coming home, I was hired as a $30-daily extra (a red-horned patron at the Satyr Club) in *The President's Analyst*, in Hollywood. In Detroit, a friend from the 'Nam put the cigarette lighters in Fords ("Man, jail ain't never been this bad," an auto worker says in *Working*) and a second friend put the bumpers in sulfuric acid—the acid splashed in his eye, though, and he was fired. An ex-disc-jockey, I say hurrah for WDEE, in Detroit, for spinning an off-color copy of *Take This Job and Shove It,*

> *I can't wait to see their faces*
> *When I get the nerve to say,*
> *Take this job and—*

shelve it, for three mutinous hours, and a third friend marched to a mushroom-soup assembly line in Pittsburgh. At the hot retort, he kept his eagle's eye (and his own magnifying glass) on a red thermometer, to assure himself that the twenty thousand cans were at 250 degrees—*exactly*. One degree less and the soup consumers would die, and one degree more and (*bang*, twenty thousand times) the walls of the old retort would be a mural of mushroom soup, an *objet* of pop-pop-art of onion powder, garlic powder, salt, sugar, starch, dipotassium phosphate, monosodium glutamate, mushrooms, and the invisible signature of Warhol. It had *happened*, and it would again if my red-eyed, low-lidded, crow-footed friend didn't hold to a life whose lower and upper limits were 249 and 251.

My friends and I: we were bent out of shape by society's pliers, said Dylan, we were banged by its silver hammer, said McCartney, we were beset by the iron age—the dark age, the death age, the *kali yuga*, said the ancient scriptures of India. In the golden age, we had lived to a ripe hundred thousand years, but in this efficient *kali yuga* we were depraved, unquote,

> *Our kings will be churlish-spirited, violent-tempered, and ever addicted to wickedness, inflicting death on men, women, children, and cows, their appetites insatiable. The earth will be venerated just for its minerals till we approach our utter annihilation,*

the *Vishnu Purana*. Not optimistic, the *Purana* predicted a *kali yuga* continuing to the year 428,899—to midnight of Tuesday, February 17, I suppose New Delhi Time. In the late 1960's, though, a generation rebelled and, to its rescue, a whole procession of pirs, sris, lamas, swamis, roshis, rishis, yogis, gurus (in other words: authorities) arrived on our shores to deliver it expeditiously from the *kali yuga's* chains—and I sampled them too one day, I was dubious but I'd try anything. In white, black, and salt-and-pepper beards as long as God's, these gurus urged me to meditate on some mantra: on some magic words in Sanskrit, to participate in their general exodus. It was, these gurus agreed, the One Best Way.

The trouble was, the gurus couldn't agree on the One Best Mantra of the seventy million listed in the *Mantra Shastra*. One guru recommended श्रीश्रीश्री for me (and ह्रीह्रीह्री for Paul and ऐंऐंऐं for John and ह्रीह्रीह्री for George and ऐंऐंऐं for Ringo: they're confidential but I found out), but another recommended ॐ नमः शिवाय as its five syllables acted on my five elements: my earth, water, air, fire, and ether. "It's very scientific," he said while seated on his throne, three white stripes on his brow, a blood-red dot on his third eye. He gave me some ginger tea, but another guru recommended ੴ ਸਤਿ ਨਾਮੁ ਸ੍ਰੀ ਵਾਹਿਗੁਰੁ : eight syllables, as *eight* is two little wheels, a wheel represents machines, and a machine represents the iron age: the *kali yuga*. "And eight represents infinity," the guru said.

"In what way, sir?" I asked him.

"Sideways," he said while slumped in a Barcalounger. "And

you've twenty-six vertebrae, and two and six are eight. And twenty-six bones in your foundation: feet, and two and six are eight again," he continued like my old arithmetic teacher. "And your sperm: it swims around the egg eight times."

"It does, sir?" I asked him.

"I read it in *Life*," the guru declared, giving me tea of ginger, cinnamon, cardamon, jasmine, and clover: that and an eight-pieced pear. "It's very scientific."

"Thank you, sir," I said, and I toddled off to a guru with yellow stripes on his brow: vertical ones.

"No, eight aren't enough," the guru insisted, giving me tea and sweet potatoes sautéed in *ghee*: in buffalo butter that he had offered, too, to a marble doll of Krishna, who ignored it. And opening it, he quoted from the *Kalishantarana Upanishad*, "The thirty-two syllables of हरे कृष्ण हरे कृष्ण कृष्ण कृष्ण हरे हरे । हरे राम हरे राम राम राम हरे हरे । are the only way to counteract the *kali yuga*'s contaminations. The only way," the guru repeated.

"But sir," I said, "I was told this morning that if I said ॐ नमः शिवाय seventy million times, I'd have said the equivalent of one hundred and sixty million हरे कृष्ण हरे कृष्ण कृष्ण कृष्ण हरे हरे । हरे राम हरे राम राम राम हरे हरे ।'s."

"No, that's rubbish— ॐ नमः शिवाय is just eighty-four percent as efficient as हरे कृष्ण हरे कृष्ण कृष्ण कृष्ण हरे हरे । हरे राम हरे राम राम राम हरे हरे । according to the *Bhakti Rasamrita Sindhu*. And," the guru declared, "it isn't enough to repeat it: you must go out and chant it."

"How come?" I asked.

"It's very scientific. See, we're in the *kali yuga* with its noises, automobiles, airplanes, and you must overpower it."

"I must outshout it," I contributed, and I tottered off to a guru without any red, white, or yellow cosmetics.

"Any word will do," the guru assured me. "Coca-Cola! Coca-Cola!"

Really, I was confused! I felt I had various sergeants shouting at me, "Left face!" "No, right face!" "No, dope, about face!" In this extremity, I fled that night to a guru whose mantra—सो ऽ हम्, pronounced *so'ham*—was, he declared, the *maha mantra* or major mantra of India. "To not know it is slavery, and to know it," he declared, "is freedom," an orange robe, an orange vest, and an orange cap (it looked like a skier's cap) on his cross-legged form. And chewing a roasted clove, he sang an old song in Sanskrit,

> Oh, contemplate the words so'ham,
> Oh, contemplate the words so'ham,

his eyes closed in ecstasy like Sinatra,

> Breathe in the second syllable
> And breathe the first one out
> And they reverse. And they become so'ham
> And end the earth's entanglements,
> Oh Brahmananda.

His anthem over, the guru declared, "The words so'ham mean, I am God. Now, Christ said, The kingdom of God is within you, and Krishna said, Oh Arjuna, God is within you now, and I say say so'ham." He himself, he rose in his pink motel room at three o'clock every day to say so'ham, to shower and say so'ham, to have a modest meal (a cup of hot water: hold the tea) and say so'ham: a total of three thousand so'hams before sunup. "Try it," the guru urged.

All right, I tried it. I wasn't alone: I was one of a thousand hippies, trippies, people in tie-dies, people in ties, chrissakes, and yes: and some movie stars (the counter culture, it was called, the opposite to our society) in the guru's circus tent by the Pacific Ocean. So'ham, so'ham, so'ham, we told ourselves until, a long hour later, we chanted in Sanskrit, "Oh Swami Muktananda," the guru's name was Swami Muktananda, "at your feet we surrender ourselves," and, in column fours, we marched to his white-tuffeted seat to more or less grovel while we offered him an apple or pear, orange or lemon, or coconut from a fruit stand outside. The guru received an avocado from Marsha Mason and roses from Jill Clayburgh, Jill telling him, "You deserve it, Baba."

"So'ham, so'ham, so'ham," the guru thanked her.

Myself, I felt nothing ventured, nothing gained: I handed him a banana and he, in turn, swatted me (as he had swatted the one thousand others: with a green peacock's tail) as though a fly had alighted on my tip-top chakra: *swat, swat,* my private punkah wallah, *swat,* my substitute for the laying on of his hands, apparently. His face was coconut-colored and his countenance was one of a pond, unruffled, exempt from the age's anxieties. To look at, he was content to sit swatting me for the whole *kali yuga*—he was as happy as Santa Claus and I thought, All that from saying *so'ham?* Why wasn't *I* all that from saying *so'ham?*

"Baba, I want to ask about *so'ham.* Thank you," I said, accepting a piece of coconut-covered candy. "In the 1920's," I began, "a zoologist took a chicken egg from the chicken coop. It hatched: the chicken was by itself but it said cluck cluck cluck. In the 1960's," I continued, "a zoologist put Nembutal into an infant chicken and he amputated its inner ears—it was deaf but it also said cluck cluck cluck. I wonder, Baba, why don't I know intuitively to say *so'ham* when the chickens knew to say cluck cluck cluck? Thank you," I said, biting the coconut-covered candy.

The guru smiled. "But see, you do know intuitively," he told me. "You were saying *so'ham* in your mother's womb. You were saying, I am God."

"I was saying it, Baba?" I asked him.

"In your navel."

"In Sanskrit, Baba?" I asked him.

"No. But coming out of the great gate," he continued as his interpreter (his mother's reincarnation, reportedly) winced, "was a great trauma, according to the *Garbhopanishad,* and you stopped saying *so'ham* and you started saying *ko'ham,* instead."

"Is that equal to *waaa* in English?" I asked him.

"Yes. It doesn't mean, I am God. It means, Who am I?"

I paused. An intimation of wisdom inhered in his ontogenetics, which, in fact, reminded me of my own genesis and of Traherne's "How wise was I in infancy,"

> I then saw in the clearest light,
> But corrupt custom is a second night.

I sat and chewed the coconut-covered candy (and the peanut butter inside) meditatively.

"You were saying *waaa*. But asleep," the guru continued, "you still were saying *so'ham*."

"I was, Baba?" I asked him.

"You were snoring it—*so'ham, so'ham, so'ham*," he snored, his eyelids down. "And 21,600 times every day, you are still saying *so'ham*. Are breathing it—*so'ham, so'ham, so'ham*," he breathed.

"But Baba," I said, "if I'm really breathing it 21,600 times, what is the use of *saying* it?"

"To know you're breathing it."

"Then what is the use of *knowing* it, Baba?"

"To become free."

"But Baba!" I pleaded with him. "I am not happy saying *so'ham!* In fact, I hate saying *so'ham!* I feel, I'm a boy saying do-re-mi or a GI saying hut-two-three or, worse, my father saying ברוּךְ אתה ה ! It isn't inside me! It feels imposed!"

"Do you know what to do?"

"No, Baba, I don't!"

"Continue saying *so'ham*."

Well, I tried! At home, I sat and said *so'ham* until in my ears there were cobwebs and in my eyes, cement, but I also thought of King Janaka of India, who said *so'ham, so'ham, so'ham*, until he heard someone do a mantra not in the *Mantra Shastra*. It meant, "My wooden water bowl."

"Be quiet," the king commanded. "I'm meditating that I am God. And you're interrupting me with your wooden water bowl."

"But this really is my wooden water bowl."

"So who says it *isn't* your wooden water bowl?"

"And who says that you're not God?"

"You're right," the king conceded, and he stopped saying *so'ham* but I was still sitting efficiently, saying *so'ham* till my fingernails fell on my oriental rug. All right, I'll agree that if barn swallows are God then people are too, but God shouldn't want to repeat it 21,600 times like a crazy patient of Coué's, "Every day and every way, I'm God." Once would be quite enough if God really believed it, am I right? Myself, I'd got about as much from *so'ham* as I'd get from cluck cluck cluck—like the girl in *A Chorus Line*, I'd dug to the bottom of my soul and I'd tried, Baba, I'd tried but I'd felt nothing. I was still caught in the *kali yuga's* clutches.

As millions did, I even went to Asia again: to India, an orchid-covered mountain in India, and was imparted a mantra that (a lama in yellow told me) would vibrate at 250,000 hertz. As evidence, he cited experiments in Calcutta, but another mantra (a guru in orange told me) would vibrate better: at 320,000 hertz. "Sir, I don't understand," I said.

"It has eight syllables. And rotated through the five lotuses is eight times five is forty, correct?"

"Um," I said.

"And that times the 1000-lotused petal—"

"Um, the 1000-petaled lotus?" I said.

"Is forty thousand times eight is 320,000, correct?"

"No," I said. "You multiplied by eight earlier on."

"In the inner cycle. But this is the outer cycle now."

"Um," I said, but I'd had enough of the two-times-twos (the least likely exits from the *kali yuga*, if you're asking me) and I just said भूल जावो or the hell with them, fleeing to Egypt. And there, a guru of sorts assured me that solid geometry, of all discredited disciplines, is the one best route of escape from the *kali yuga*'s anguish. The Great Pyramid at Giza, he had calculated, has a 921,453-millimeter perimeter and a 146,515-millimeter altitude: the same ratio (with an error of one ten-thousandth) as the earth's circumference and the earth's radius. It—pay attention, please: the Pyramid—is a lens on the earth's *élan vital*, he had concluded, and an elixir to one who sleeps in its geometric center, in its sanctum sanctorum: in its burial room. In that particular place, to sleep is to go through the looking glass out of the *kali yuga*'s jurisdiction, according to this intense (no, that isn't it: *maniacal*) man, an American, his eyes a couple of hot charcoals, his beard a bristled black. "I'll sleep there tonight," he told me in Egypt. "What about you?"

"Whatever works," I answered.

If nothing else, I knew I'd wind up in *The Guinness Book of Records*. In fifty centuries, no one—not even the pharaoh, who (if he was ever there) wasn't asleep, he was dead—no one had ever slept in that burial room. Oh, tourists would come and go. Or fall on the floor saying, "Help!" Or die—a woman died in that month of, well, some doctors called it a heart attack, and the adventurous author of *One Flew Over the Cuckoo's Nest*, Ken Kesey, was sick unto death, unquote. In August, 1799, Napoleon, on his Egyptian campaign, where (as the legend has it) a soldier shot off the Sphinx's nose—Napoleon entered the burial room and, on exiting, wasn't dead but as pale as a man just guillotined. "*Mon général,*" someone said. "What happened there?"

"I will never say," Napoleon said.

But later, he was asked again on St. Helena. "*Mon général.* What happened in the Great Pyramid?"

"All right," Napoleon said. "I will say. No," Napoleon reconsidered. "I will never say, for you will never believe me." And died, I had read in a two-pound book.

Although, if you don't count bats, we would (or *wouldn't*, it wasn't legal, after all) be the first creatures to sleep in this haunted house, we wouldn't be the first to sit there throughout the night, a feat brought off in the 1930's by a British reporter. A torch—a British flashlight—and a thermos of tea beside him, he sat from sunset to sunrise by the stone sarcophagus till he quote stumbled out. "Monstrous," I am still quoting him—"Monstrous elemental creations, horrors of the underworld, forms of grotesque, insane, uncouth, and fiendish aspect afflicted me with unimaginable repulsion. Never again," the British reporter wrote. "Never again." Similarly, a Canadian reporter said he saw hideous forms in his wide-awake night in the Pyramid, "If they found me dead in the morning, it wouldn't matter."

We weren't downhearted. No, and that afternoon the resolute guru and I drove to the desert, to the area where like an old volcano (coated by its own ashes) the Pyramid was. And stopping our car and stepping out, we were overrun by the Arabs there, "You want caftan?" "You want camel ride?" "You want Cleopatra's Needle?" "You want Washington Monument?" Christ, I was just about buggered as I was dragged onto a camel's hump for a Polaroid, "You want photograph?" In his blue caftan, the chief of the guides approached us. A fifty-year-old, in his youth he had hopped up the Pyramid in five minutes flat, and, in fond recollection, he still called himself the Champion, and the guru greeted him.

"I'm Dr. Flanagan."

"I know about you," the Champion said.

"And this is Mr. Sack."

"I know about you," the Champion said.

"And—"

"You want to sleep in the Pyramid," the Champion said.

An agent for Interpol? "We want to sleep there," the guru confessed.

"You can't," the Champion said. "No one permit it."

"No one?"

"No one, I *told* you," the Champion said. "Not even President Sadat."

"No one, hmm."

"No one except for the Champion!"

"*Okay*," the guru exclaimed.

We climbed up a little pyramid out of everyone's earshot. It was late afternoon—as the sun caught fire, as it snubbed itself out in the yellow sand, the Champion told us, "Business is business, understand?"

"I understand," the guru repeated. We were three kingbirds on the pyramid's point.

"All men want money," the Champion said.

"I understand."

"A camel, do you know what's eating? Corn," the Champion said.

"Corn."

"Clover," the Champion said.

"Clover."

"Halfa halfa," the Champion said.

"Alfalfa."

"And everything's higher," the Champion said. "Is five piasters before, is ten piasters now."

"Terrible."

"I pay people eighty dollars," the Champion said. "Understand?"

"I understand."

Oh Lord! Were we or weren't we the worst philistines to ever embarrass one of the world's seven wonders? I turned to sublimer things: to Cairo, to the sounds of the sunset prayers, and, to the west, to the fiery ellipse itself. "The sun, everyone," I whispered. "Beautiful," the guru conceded. "Are traveler's checks okay?" "Egyptian money," the Champion said.

We climbed off the little pyramid, and, *cut*, by midnight we were inside the forbidden land: in a tunnel with the fluorescent fixtures of a subway stop on the IRT, a tunnel so low, one meter plus, as well as so steep, fifty percent, that we stooped like the seven dwarfs in their diamond mine. I was positioned as Dopey: at the rear, while ahead were the wild-eyed guru and the Champion and, in a sweater of hot orange, burnt orange, just orange, yellow, chartreuse, olive, cranberry, ashes of roses, shocking pink, flesh, lavender, aquamarine, deep aquamarine, peacock, *repeat*— in a sexy striped sweater was the guru's lover, a Hollywood star: Eve Bruce of *The Love Machine*. I tell you: the world is small after all, as the dolls at Disneyland say, for I had once dated her too: a six-foot-barefoot bosomy blonde. To consort with a giantess was a turn-on to Baudelaire,

> *To feel at leisure her stupendous shapes,*
> *Crawl on the cliffs of her enormous knees,*
> *And—*

but I, Dopey the Dwarf, hadn't known where to begin or let alone consummate matters, and I'd had dinner with her in Malibu and kissed her on her stupendous shoulder, bye. No matter: she had graciously slept in her own little plastic pyramid, reporting to me, "I felt this energy—*tss*, I had this total orgasm."

"It was enjoyable?" I asked.

"It was incredible!" Eve answered.

I had been happy for her. And now I stayed tuned in this massive pyramid as Eve exclaimed, "*Oh*," ahead of her the night watchman: a fifty-year-old, a man who was playing the punkah wallah by flapping his white pajama shirt at her passionately. To cool her off?

"Are you okay?" I asked her.

"I'm okay," Eve answered. "*Oh!*"

At midnight, we entered the burial room. It was five meters by ten meters by six meters high. It was solid stone, and at the other end was a stone sarcophagus—empty, if one ignored the puddle of odorous urine in lieu of a pharaoh. "Be afraid nothing," the Champion said as he and the watchman departed and as they flicked the fluorescents out. We lit a little candle: the wall reflected its yellow light, and one hundred meters away we heard the gate getting locked: clang.

"We're here!" Eve cried, I mean really cried. "He kept trying to feel me!"

"*Who?*" I and the guru gasped.

"He kept telling me, They're beautiful. And kept telling me, They're hot—"

"*He didn't!*"

"—and I will cool them. And kept reaching in and fanning them. And trying to kiss me."

"*Where?*"

"Out there. On the gangplank. Oh," Eve said incredulously, "the Arabs are something else!" And laughing about it, she covered the cold stone floor with a bed blanket from the Nile Hilton. On the wall, the shadows danced from the bottles of bottled water but, I observed, there were no big brown bats (a blessing, for Eve was born premature when a bat swooped down on her mother) and no forms of fiendish aspect as were reported by the Britisher and Canadian. "So let's get on," Eve suggested. "On to higher things."

We lay down—we were, remember, in that mausoleum to try to somnambulate out of our troublesome century. But holy mother of Isis, we hadn't thought it meant trying to sleep in a room which reverberated like an orchestra overture to three people with the Pharaoh's Curse. "I heard something," Eve reported.

"*Boom,*" the room answered her.

"I heard something, I'm sure," Eve repeated.

"Our stomachs, I wish they'd stop," the guru announced.

"*Boom,*" the room answered.

"*Giggle,*" Eve giggled.

"*Boom.*"

Be prepared. An ex-eagle scout, I was equipped to catch some z's in that pyramid even if we should burst into the *Hallelujah Chorus*. For starters, I had inflated the air mattress that if I'd had in Tepoztlán, Mexico, I'd have fallen asleep in a pyramid long ago. A friend down in Tepoztlán had built a model pyramid in his living room by using a cheap protractor to set its slopes at 51 degrees, 51 minutes, and I had offered to sleep there. It was quiet there. The floor of the room, though (although, auspiciously, the locale of the very first mushroom trip for Timothy Leary)— the floor was of back-breaking stone, and I was there thirty minutes and I said screw it. No such misfortune tonight with my Air Lift Mattress! And lying on it, putting an eye mask on, and pulling a pillow over my ringing ears, I—well, I was still awake. No other way, I sat up and swallowed a chloral hydrate with a water chaser.

And fell asleep. And dreamt of—I'm not sure but I think Daphne Davis, the ex-editor of *Rags*. In the dream, we were getting onto a Volkswagen bus. At the door was a man taking names, but Daphne was using another name—Sally, let's say.

"Name," the man said to Daphne.

"Sally," and I woke up.

Oh, anything for a Joseph to interpret this! I'm getting ahead of our story but I'd visit, later, the white-walled office of an Egyptian psychoanalyst, Dr. Akil Youssef, and I'd sit in a white wooden chair not a couch as Youssef would ask me, "Do you remember the second name?"

"I don't remember it."

"Was it a common name? Or you know, exotic?"

"A common name, I think."

"A common name."

"I *think*."

"A bit easternized or—"

"No."

"—or westernized, would you say?"

"It wasn't an Arabic name."

"You know," Youssef would say, Youssef now showing sweat on his upper lip, he hadn't an air conditioner and it would be one hundred there, "if you aren't used to Arabic you would sort of associate it with sleeping out in the desert in—"

"It wasn't an Arabic name," I'd say with regret.

All that was later: now it was five o'clock in our hall of the mountain king and I was just waking up. "What's that?" I heard Eve say.

"It sounded like a diesel train!" I heard the guru answer.

"It wasn't anyone's stomach!" I heard Eve say.

"I didn't hear it, I was asleep," I said.

"We didn't sleep at all!" I heard Eve say. "We didn't sleep at all!" I heard Eve say. "We didn't sleep—"

Oh, great ghost of Cheops! Stop it, my skin was a solid stone in the Hall of Fame! For five thousand years, the finger of fate was turning as though it were stirring a witch's pot—it turned till it pointed right at me. "I can't believe it," I said. "I'm the only person in history who's slept in the Pyramid!"

"That's right," Eve said admiringly.

I stretched. At five o'clock, I didn't feel I was infused with the earth's *élan vital*—no, I felt precisely like me, I was still stuck in the *kali yuga* despite my night in a room whose proportions were in the ratio of two times pi. Well, I can't say I was astonished.

"I'm afraid," the guru declared, "the Pyramid is no instantaneous enlightenment machine."

"No," Eve agreed.

"A monkey would come out a monkey. Arab, would come out an Arab—an Arab guide."

"It doesn't turn me on," Eve agreed. "I'm not even in the mood for sex."

"In here? In the men's room of Grand Central Station?"

"It smells like it," Eve agreed.

At six o'clock, the fluorescents went on. And rolling up the bed blanket, mattress, and pillow, we exited through the tiny tunnel, the Champion leading us Quasimodos outside. As the day dawned in Cairo, the moon was still pinning the night to the Pyramid and our guru declared, "Well, goodbye, Great Pyramid."

After that day, he gave up solid geometry and, I heard, turned to the bottle: a little bottle of cape cobra venom, diluted in jasmine tea, as his own antidote to the aspirin age. A disaster: he almost overdosed and Eve, who swore off the stuff, turned to a guru (a white-bearded one: an Indian maharishi) to learn to fly the whole chicken coop: to fly to the sky without the encumbrances of the iron age's propellers. "In one month I'll levitate," Eve said, departing. "And then whee!"

I confess I was dubious. To teach a six-foot-barefoot woman to fly: the guru could do it, I knew it, but could he teach her to land without cracking up? Long ago, Icarus learned that a man cannot generate the παρν²s to maintain altitude and

> Oh, father, father, said he
> And tumbled into the sea,

according to Ovid. Icarus, I was aware, was a myth, though later the ballet dancer who was Icarus in *Daedalus and Icarus* did indeed tumble into the Roman emperor's box (Nero was splattered with the dead dancer's blood) in Rome. Another myth was the father of King Lear, King Bladud, who managed to fly and die in England in the ninth century, while the first actual man to fly, and almost to kill himself, was Dr. Abul Qasim Abbas Bin Firnas of Córdoba, Spain, who threw himself off an "eminence" in the same century. And

> In the feathers of a vulture
> He flew faster than a phoenix,

a poet wrote in Arabic, in whose perfect meter it didn't seem out of *Hiawatha*, but after circling over Córdoba he broke his back upon landing.

And that was with vulture feathers, and Eve wouldn't even be with chicken ones. In the sixteenth century, a white-habited abbot in Scotland had some chicken feathers when he jumped from the parapets of Stirling Castle. His destination was Paris, but the invasion of a half-human half-hen in a bird's jurisdiction was an affront to the gowk, gormaw, and gled—the cuckoo, cormorant, and kite—according to a not-too-serious poet,

The gowk, the gormaw, and the gled
Beft him with buffets till he bled,
Thick was the clud of kays and craws
Of merlins, mittanes, and of maws,

and the abbot agreed that his ill success (he had dropped to the ground like a dead duck, cracking his thigh bone) was due to his injudicious use of the chicken feathers. "My wings were the feathers of dunghill fowls, and, by a certain sympathy," he said, "were attracted to the dunghill, whereas had my wings been of *eagles—*" In my own youth (in my own fourth month) a man in two six-foot wings had the stubbornness to try, try, in spite of all precedents, by throwing himself off a bridge a mile from my $49.95 crib in Manhattan. The wings were of—I don't know, pigeon feathers, perhaps, and

An old hoop-skirt or two, as well as
Some wire, and several old umbrellas,

as in *Darius Green and His Flying Machine*. Alas, a bolt that broke at his distal phalanx dashed his ambition of reaching the Polo Grounds, the home of the New York Giants, who were playing the Braves that day, and the man settled like Darius Green

In a wonderful whirl of tangled strings,
Broken braces and broken springs,
Broken tail and broken wings,
Shooting-stars, and various things,

into the Harlem River.

Eve, at least, had a foam-rubber mattress to land on, I learned, and her guru's official aviator's manual, the *Rig Veda* of India,

Oh, celebrate the sportive storm gods!
The thunder roars like a mother cow
Roaring for her calf. The rain
Inundates everything,

a marginal day for her solo, in my own opinion. *I can fly*, she and her squadron meditated, till she had revved herself to V-sub-one, roaring, "Oh! Ohh! Ohhh! It sounded," Eve admitted to me by long-distance telephone, "as if I were having an orgasm, honestly." "Um, did you ever fly?" I asked. "No, but I heard some others fly." "You *heard* them fly?" I asked. "I heard them land. I heard their thuds behind me." "Um, were they hurt?" I asked. "No, they had the foam-rubber mattresses." "Um," I said.

I had other friends than Eve who attempted to fly, literally, from the *kali yuga's* realms. A man I knew repeated, repeated, the eleven-syllable mantra that (a guru assured him) was the Sanskritic equivalent of "Contact!" A woman I knew contorted herself like a plane's propeller at a guru's instructions, "And come up, please, to kneel on all your fours, relax, please, and *whip* your spine twenty-seven times. Up and down! Up and down! It's like a roller coaster, whee! And now," the guru began after the one-hour warmup, "come to lie on the floor, please, and be aware of a subtle pulsing throughout you, and now ride that pulsing into the sky." But alas, that woman by now was asleep, and I even knew a man who swallowed a poisonous plant: a jimsonweed, to get quite literally high but got dizzy, instead. And two other women I knew went south of the Rio to search out a flight instructor—a *brujo*, a male witch, a sorcerer—in three different villages of Ixtlan, having heard of these sorcerers' competence in *Journey to Ixtlan*, the doctoral dissertation by Carlos Castaneda.

I met those women in Bogotá, Colombia. One was Maryanne Raphael, the first wife of Lennox Raphael, the author of *Che*, the first play in Manhattan to put on sexual intercourse ("Graphic," *The New York Times*), and the other was Brenda Smiley, the sexy bikini girl in *Scuba Duba* ("Sexy," *The New York Times*). The two assured me that sorcerers choose to congregate in Catholic churches on Sundays, adding, "We're going too! Come along!"

"Why not?" I agreed.

It was a cool clear day in Bogotá. Maryanne wore black, Brenda a see-through shirt and a see-through skirt with a pattern of white butterflies on pastel pink. "Oh, I don't want to look sexy," she said preposterously as we walked to Carrera Séptima, the counterpart of Fifth Avenue. We passed people trying to sell us Parker pens, photos, lottery tickets, emeralds or "emeralds" in white tissue paper (scratching them on the windows to show they're emeralds, the old women back of the windows shouting shoo) and we passed beggar boys. To every one, Maryanne handed a peso although she had one last dollar in Bogotá. "Oh Maryanne," Brenda said. "Keep walking!"

"Brenda, I'm just giving him a penny!"

"Oh Maryanne! You're going broke!"

We entered the Third Order of the Franciscans. In that white church were—aw, no sorcerers, though there was a priest in a long green *ruana* to give communion to Brenda (Brenda putting her tongue out as her middle finger tapped her sunglasses back) and to Maryanne, who walked to her pew thinking thank you, Jesus, and looked around for a sorcerer, walking right into a spiral staircase. "*Ow*," she screamed in that sacred place, and she was soon surrounded by the worried parishioners, most of them shouting in Spanish, "Get her some ice!" We hurried out to an ice-cream cart, and a Colombian woman cried, "Ice cream, please!"

"What flavor, *señora*?"

"It doesn't matter!"

The vendor gave her a strawberry popsicle—a *helado de los ángeles extra fina*, but Maryanne was now broke and a popsicle was beyond her modest centavos. A nice woman buying it, Maryanne said *muchas gracias* and, the popsicle pressed to a bump bigger than a wristbone, walked to the first little beggar—a boy with an awful disease, impetigo, perhaps—in whose twisted hands she impulsively put the strawberry popsicle. At her hotel, she collapsed in the elevator, cracking the glass on the sign RESTAURANTE COLONIAL, and in her room sought to compose herself in the lotus and lion postures. The two didn't work, and she departed the following morning on Braniff, for she still hadn't found a sorcerer to initiate her in a do-it-yourself way of flying home.

BRENDA did better, though. She learned of a real sorcerer, a man whose name was Norberto who was silent, sullen, and rather surly (his lips were twisted as if they were holding a dozen roofing nails) who was contracted to a Brazilian businessman. A tragic tale: the Brazilian, a shampoo manufacturer, was in his apartment a few years earlier when a man in a mask broke in and kidnapped his son and, not even asking ransom, left a note stating, "*Seu filho foi seqüestrado*," "Your son has been kidnapped." And nothing more—and the Brazilian, a wavy-haired man, had hired the close-mouthed sorcerer to accomplish what the police department couldn't: to fly to his long-lost son to recover him.

At four in the morning, accordingly, we—the sorcerer in a heavy white robe and a hat, also white, shaped like a flowerpot upside down, and two off-duty women sorcerers, two para-psychologists, two anthropologists, two documentary cameramen, a reporter for *Rolling Stone* ("I feel like a doll on display here," the sorcerer pouted) and, of course, the Brazilian in his pinstriped suit and Brenda and I—were taking a half-dozen taxis to a secret rendezvous north of Bogotá. In the pouring rain, the *autopistas* were paved in the gold reflections of sodium-vapor lamps, and the potholes were so full of rain water that the taxi driver didn't see one and almost overturned. In two hours, we reached a site straight out of *Brigadoon*—a valley that's full of fairyfolk, surely, and, as the rain became morning mist, we climbed to the red rocks over the sacred lake of Guatavita, the "moneybox" for the sixteenth-century indians and the origin of El Dorado.

A cameraman turned on an Arri, an anthropologist turned on a Sony, a reporter took out a Bic as the sorcerer put his magical staff on the rocks around him. And sitting down (and not yet flying) he started to scowl relentlessly at a snapshot of the kid-napped boy—a very together-looking boy of boy scout age—a snapshot that the Brazilian had brought in his black attaché case. The photo was propped on someone's shoe on the rust-colored rocks, and the sorcerer scowled at the boy through a pint-shaped bottle of—I'm not sure. The labels were off, but it seemed to be Aguardiente, a clear licorice-tasting liquor, and as the sorcerer scowled he shook the Aguardiente in a shake-before-using way and his left index finger pointed to it. "I need to know where the boy was," the sorcerer said.

"He was home," the Brazilian whispered. "In the dining room, and he was watching the TV. It was 8:15 and the man burst in."

"Where?"

"In Rio, Brazil."

"Where is it?"

"It's near the sea."

"In the vicinity, is there an underground town or underground village or underground building, sort of?"

"Well, they're building a subway now. But they weren't then."

"Is there an underground cave?"

"Yes. Definitely yes," the Brazilian whispered. "Is the boy there?"

"*Un momento,*" the sorcerer said, and he stared through his flat crystal ball of Aguardiente. And setting this on the rust-colored rocks, he started to clap while curling his fingers into a note-well configuration. Far below us, a boat was slicing a mile-long line in the sacred lake as the sorcerer said, "He's far away. And far away there's a mountain—there's where the child is. He is not dead yet, but they're thinking about it and *you're* the one who can save him. You've committed sins—"

"Do you mean in another life?"

"No," the sorcerer said.

"Do you mean in another life?"

"No," the sorcerer said. "In this life, and now you're paying for it. You must do a conscious act of contrition now. The sun, the wind, the water—all of nature knows where the child is, and man being part of nature knows too. If the sun, the wind, the water can see him, you can see him too."

Bravo! Beautiful poetry, I say, but the sorcerer stayed seated and as of press time he still hadn't flown to the lovely-looking boy. His ceremony over, he sprinkled the Aguardiente to the four compass points, took off the flowerpot hat to scratch himself, took off a sandal to fix its thong, replaced it, and chewed on the coca leaves in his *mochila* or shoulder bag as he communed with the sacred lake—the taxis started, and Brenda and I had breakfast of something made out of horses' hoofs as we drove back to Bogotá, discouraged. Damn, I thought, is there really a sorcerer (*presto,* the man might say, and the missing child is seen soaring over the sacred lake in a hang glider, singing, as Tommy does, *I'm coming, I'm coming)*—is there a flight instructor in all of Latin America? Is there a Don Juan or Don Genaro?

His body shivered. The tail of his costume vibrated and he took off. He went over the trees, and I heard him say, "Why don't you come and fly with me?" I felt I wanted to—

oh, is there more than a crock of *abono de toros* in Carlos Castaneda? In Bogotá, I inquired at Cipar, the Colombian Institute of Parapsychology, and learned that the world's greatest sorcerer was at eight thousand feet in the Andes in a holy indian village that no Caucasian—no, nor indians if they weren't wearing white—was allowed in, the tiny village of Ceucumque, Colombia. To reach it, I was told that a jeep in four-wheel drive didn't do, a man must climb up the cliffs himself—well, at least without pitons. The world's greatest sorcerer was eighty years old, he had a thing against *gringos* and he spoke nothing but Aruac, I was told.

All right, reader. *Ad astra per aspera,* and I flew north in a small propeller plane, hired a taxi, a jeep, a mule—that's it, *amigo,* and I leapt like a mad mountain goat on the stones in the icy rivers at eight thousand feet,

A youth who bore 'mid snow and ice
A banner with the strange device,

Excelsior, I say. And down another dizzy cliff (the rocks tumbling under me) and over another river and up another slippery hill and—ah, Ceucumque, my El Dorado, stopping, of course, a few feet below it and sitting beneath a vase-shaped plant, a source of a sorcerer's white fiber. In fifteen minutes, the world's greatest sorcerer came from the holy village in his sun-browned feet (his very toenails were brown, somehow) to see who sat in the shade of his century plant. He seemed as old as the mountains around me—his face was a mummy's face, and his gray beard was as venerable as Ho Chi Minh's. Without hesitation, I rose saying, *"Teti azzimezzari,"* which is good morning, sir, and is just about all of my Aruac.

He ignored me. And sitting down on a boulder, he addressed himself to my interpreter (there was an interpreter with me)—an indian dentist from a distant town. "Coca," the sorcerer said in Aruac and put some leaves in his yellow-discolored mouth, "is supposed to be poison, people say. But look at me, I eat coca leaves and I'm eighty years old. And grandma's a hundred and thirty."

"I've heard about you, sir," I said, "and I've come many kilometers to visit you."

"Oh, visitors, visitors," the old sorcerer said. "And, *click*, and they take photographs and say, I'll send you the photographs, sir. And they never do—they're liars, and I don't want to be fooled anymore. I don't want visitors."

"But sir, I've come five thousand kilometers to—"

"I don't want photographs, no."

"Do you want anything, sir?"

At last the old sorcerer looked at me. And baring his left shoulder, he showed me where he had hurt himself falling off a mule that year. He said in Aruac, "*Na yuni vitaminas,*" and the dentist interpreted this, "It hurts and I want some vitamin pills."

"I'll get you the vitamin pills, sir. And then—"

"I'll do whatever you ask me," the world's greatest sorcerer said. "Perhaps."

"*Vavava duni,*" I told him. Or thank you, sir—all right, that was it, the rest of my Aruac.

And down the mountain again. The air was clean as a cirrus-filled sky, and the only sounds were the running rivers as I went scrambling to the one pharmacy—a one-room store on whose splinter-ridden shelves were Anacin, Dristan, Laxol, and Vicks Vaporub. But not even Bugs Bunny Vitamins, so I went again to the airport again and Bogotá to cable my own nutritionist in Hollywood, Dr. Whitaker. My message was ANDES INDIAN SORCERER AGE APPROXIMATELY EIGHTY FELL OFF A MULE BROKE COLLARBONE HE WANTS VITAMIN PILLS DO YOU RECOMMEND ABCD OR E QUERY PLEASE CABLE SACK. And good old Doc Whitaker! A day later, his answer came, a cable telling me 1 SIBERIAN GINSENG 2 BETAIN HYDROCHLORIDE 3 MAGNESIUM 4 CALCIUM 5 NATURAL FOODS THREE TIMES A DAY LOVE WHITAKER.

Lotsa luck. I'll explain in a twenty-volume edition how to get ginseng in Bogotá, Colombia—in the meantime, suffice it that even calcium comes in amalgams of ten other questionable chemicals known as Calcio-Nil. But where there's a will there's, etcetera, and I put ten pounds of vitamin pills (and yes, even ginseng in silver-coated drops) into a mountaineer's backpack to go again to the solar system's greatest sorcerer, whose name was Juancho, incidentally (I think I've shown great restraint in not calling him Don Juancho). Over hill, over dale—*caramba,* and I sat again at the century plant to pass salted crackers to a black-haired hog as I waited breathlessly for the old sorcerer. He came and I spread my treasures before him.

"Oh, I'll become young again," the sorcerer cried, "and I'll make love with all the Aruac women!"

"And sir, you've got to eat natural foods," I said.

"If there aren't natural foods in Ceucumque," the sorcerer joked, "I'll get them somewhere else." And standing up, he motioned me to come with him—it was sorcery time.

0_F course, the village of Ceucumque was off limits for me, a *gringo*—also for my interpreter, who in his yellow boots and his yellow striped pants (and his black porkpie hat) was not wearing white, so we adjourned to a farmhouse near us. At the sorcerer's orders, we shuttered up the white windows and lit a kerosene lantern that we had cleaned in the kitchen's stone sink and had trimmed with a razor blade ripped from my Gillette Trac II. It was five o'clock: the sundown hour, and the afternoon rain was a hundred voodoo drums on the galvanized steel roof. The sorcerer sat on a cot in the bedroom saying, "All right, what do you want me to do?"

"To fly," I replied, for I still aspired to apprentice myself and to exit the *kali yuga* aerodynamically. "I want you to fly to my girlfriend in Hollywood."

"All right," the sorcerer said. "I'll need a teacup, first—" I fetched him a teacup from the pitch-black kitchen. "A teacup that's full of water, please—" I stumbled into the blackness again to put water in. "A couple of fresh lemons—" I ran through the drenching rain to buy some lemons nearby. "A bottle of Aguardiente—"

"Aguardiente? There isn't any," I said.

"I'll need the Aguardiente," the sorcerer said.

Despair! "Well, I have some antiseptic alcohol," the dentist-interpreter said.

"Aguardiente's better. But alcohol will do. And," the sorcerer said, at last completing his difficult requisition list, "a photograph of the girl in Hollywood."

"I have it," I told him. Paxxie, my faraway friend, was a Hollywood star (she was the kumquat in W.C. *Fields and Me*) and zippered into my backpack was a much-loved copy of Paxxie's composite. On it Paxxie was buying orange juice at a supermarket, smiling, and, on the other side, she was dressed like a sorcerer in a heavy white robe but was kicking at the cameraman's camera. In some bafflement the sorcerer stared at it.

"What is she doing here?"

"She is doing karate, sir."

"A sport?"

"She is doing a sport, sir."

The sorcerer set the composite aside. He dipped his fingertips in the interpreter's bottle and he scattered the antiseptic alcohol to the four compass points. He sliced a lemon open and he squeezed the lemon juice into the water-filled teacup. He carried the kerosene lantern to the plaster mantel opposite him. And sitting down on the cot again, he took out of his *mochila* a little glass ball—a puree we called it at camp, playing marbles—he dipped the puree into the teacup to cleanse it and squinted at the kerosene lantern through it. The flame was a tiny pilot light in the sorcerer's circular eye—oh, this was becoming spooky, I promise you. And then while the rain continued like a wild voodoo ritual, he floated from the cot and passed through the roof, bound for California.

For the life of me, I couldn't see it—I'd swear that he was still sitting there (and was *talking* to me, for heaven's sake) but in one half hour he would assure me that yes, indeed, he had flown to Hollywood in another body—in a separate reality. "I see her," the sorcerer said now.

"You see her!"

"She is traveling now," the sorcerer said.

"She is traveling now! But traveling where?"

"East," the sorcerer said.

"She is traveling east!"

"She is traveling east. To the west," the sorcerer said.

"Oh, she is traveling west!"

"No, she is already west and is traveling east," the sorcerer said. "To the west."

"I don't understand," I confessed. "Is she traveling to the sunrise or to the sunset, please?"

For ten long minutes, the sorcerer peered at the flat tongue of flame through the small crystal ball. The only light was the yellow lantern light (in its shadows he looked like a pirate with a glass eye) and the only sound was the rain on the tin-pan roof. At last the old sorcerer asked me, "Your house in Hollywood. Is the man still alive who built it?"

"No. It was built by a man who's dead now."

"It was built by Stravinsky for Dylan Thomas," I now hoped the sorcerer would say. He'd have been a hundred percent correct, for I lived in that very guesthouse, but he asked instead, "Do you live with a woman there?"

"No. But last year I lived with a woman there."

"A red-headed black Peruvian pop singing star," I now hoped the sorcerer would say. Ah, Robertha, I missed you—she was starring then at the Hilton in San Juan, Puerto Rico. But the sorcerer asked, "Is she dead now?"

"No. She's very alive."

"I'm not being silly," the sorcerer said. "If—"

"Oh, I don't think you're silly, sir!"

"If you ever lived with a woman who's dead it's a negative influence," the sorcerer said, "and I must erase it. Eradicate it."

I thought a few moments more. "I once lived for a week with a woman who's dead."

"She died later on?"

"Of course. She died very horribly."

"She was eaten alive by a shark while swimming from New York City to London," I still thought the sorcerer would say. It was the truth, dammit—her name was Britt Sullivan and her catastrophe made the front page of *The New York Times*. But the sorcerer asked me, "Did she die suddenly? Or did—"

"She died suddenly."

"Ah." And putting the puree in his *mochila* again, the sorcerer rose in our usual worldly reality. He commenced to open the shutters, saying, "The work is finished now."

"Is finished? Is finished, sir? But isn't there anything else you see? Is my girlfriend in Hollywood? Is she feeling good? Is she feeling bad? Is she getting work? Is she traveling east? Is she traveling west? Is she—"

"*Aguardiente*," the sorcerer howled.

I didn't hire him as my flight instructor. No, I went on foot, mule, jeep, and a disintegrating taxi to the airport again and by mechanical means: by Braniff, to Hollywood, to learn that at five o'clock in the Andes (or three o'clock in Hollywood) Paxxie had not been traveling north, east, south, nor west but catnapping up in the sleeping loft of her immobile home. In fairness, a little later her telephone rang and she rolled three feet to the east to answer it. "You have a commercial call on Monday," her agent said. "At two o'clock at Don Brown Films. Go get it."

"Thank you, George," she had replied. And hung up and fell asleep, rolling three feet to the west to do so.

Myself, I'd had it with gurus of every beard: the white, the black, the salt-and-pepper-colored: a lot of covert authorities, a firm of efficiency experts, a pack of sheep-shirted wolves, a coven of wild witch doctors as counterproductive as Dr. Loizeaux, the man who supplanted my sweet serenity with the *kali yuga*'s agonies at Fifth Avenue Hospital. As one who was dragged, upside down, into the age of anxiety, my way of escape wouldn't be to be dragged again (a fillet of a living being) to those other exercises in Asia, Africa, and the Andes. No, what's wrong with the System is that it's a system, period: an iron collar, an iron maiden, even if it's imposed upon me by God's greatest messengers, and I'm more efficient without it. God, send us no more saviors, please, said D. H. Lawrence,

> When wilt thou teach the people,
> God, to save themselves,

to put not their trust in the advocates of One Best Way Or the Other?

Myself, I say leggo of us. I promise, if I'm promoted to guru-general and if I'm attired in red, red robes like the Rose Bowl Queen, if I'm perched on my local pyramid, the Matterhorn, at Disneyland, and even if I've *alighted* there, I promise I'll cry out like Zarathustra, "Beware me! Beware me!"

"But why, Great Guru?"

"Because! I'm not your guru!" I'll cry to the crowd below me. "You are, yourselves!"

"But Great Guru! You can fly and we can't!"

"*You can too*," I'll cry, "and without geometry, too! The boomerang formula," I'll say, somehow, my tongue in an overhand knot, "is $\Omega \propto \dfrac{v}{i}$, according to a Dutch mathematician, but the Australian aborigines don't know a Ω from the Taj Mahal. The frisbee formula is $P \propto sin\ i$ according to Euler and $P \propto sin^2\ i$ according to Newton but you yourselves know that a flat flip flies straight. The formula for a Zulu's spear," I'll continue in French, "is *le poids du fléau est nul*, according to a French anthropologist, but I'll run away faster from a Zulu. And who ever heard of a kite that flies into the wind, please?"

"Great Guru? Who?"

"No one down at McDonnell Douglas," I'll continue. "But one was built by a man in a blue-green sarong: by Yasok Bin Umat Bin Abu Bakar at the Beach of Passionate Love in Malaysia. The man can't even divide but he prayed, instead,

Hey, three princesses! The oldest is Princess Hang Kilau, the middle is Princess Sedang Rakna, the youngest is Princess Bijak Laksana! Hey, please lift my kite up!

And then," I'll continue, my hands unclasped, "as everyone shouted *hairan* or that's impossible, it really flew into the wind at the National Kite-Flying Contest in Kuala Lumpur. And then there was Mr. Schultz," I'll continue.

"Mr. Schultz, Great Guru?"

"A speedometer salesman from Chicago. At his motel in Detroit, he made a paper airplane from the *Detroit Free Press* and mailed it to New York City: to the Great International Paper Airplane Contest. But there were twelve thousand others," I'll continue. "Paper planes from people at Boeing, Martin, McDonnell, who understood that in paper planes the

$$\lambda_1 = \frac{2}{\pi} \int_0^\pi \frac{y}{c} \frac{1}{1-\cos\theta} \, d\theta,$$ whew, and who engineered them to the silliest millimeter, and the winner was—"

"It was Mr. Schultz?"

"Let's hear it for Mr. Schultz!" I'll cry. "Give me an S! Give me a C! Give me—"

"But Great Guru! We ourselves, we still can't fly!"

"You can! You can!" I'll cry, I'll cry. "Just listen to Chiang!"

"To who, Great Guru?"

"The old bird in *Jonathan Livingston Seagull!* He said there's nowhere you cannot fly! All you've got to remember is," I'll conclude, and I'll spread my arms apart to depart like a California condor, "is you're already there, is you're already there, is—" *Flap!*

9 / Fingerprint

Or, Which Way Out?

"THE moon in June," I wrote in the 1970's, commencing my authorized autobiography. "And little slivers of moonlight in the Hudson River." No, I thought, there weren't mills on the Palisades or slivers there in the Hudson—my fingers flipped, my eraser erased the inappropriate metaphor and I wrote, "And little eels of moonlight in the Hudson River. On the left bank," I wrote, intent on the one best way to impress (on myself, especially) that the great imperative: *efficiency*, is itself inefficient, that we are most efficient if left alone, inviolate. We are efficient, everyone. We! Are! Efficient!

I woke up at four o'clock, sometimes, a phrase at my itching fingers, to scribble it on my yellow pad. And erase it, till there was a layer of carbon-colored dust on these sentences till it was, *whoo*, was blown away. My letters leaned to the right: coconut trees in the westerlies, victims of violent tempests, of endless afflatuses, of irresistible impulses, my *I*'s almost toppling onto the sea-green lines. I wrote with a pencil, *please*, for I didn't filter my *p*'s and *q*'s through the key, key lever, and key lever interposer of an IBM, hop, hop, hopping ahead like a toad, unable to lure myself back to cancel one little sliver. Of all the embodiments of autocratic efficiency, the epitome (if I say so) is the one that's insensible to one's second thoughts: is that thing of the Medes, the *machine*, and my preference was to flit hither, thither, on a yellow pad, as free as a happy hummingbird.

I know: I'm told that I'm *homo faber*, a man who makes machines, a man whose ascent is measured in ergs generated by his little finger's flick. I know what happened in history as reenacted in 2001: in the pleistocene period, an ape adopted a sun-bleached bone to kill or KO a second ape to the music of *Thus Spake Zarathustra*. Dum dum dum: *dum dum:* the first machine, and the ape celebrated by tossing this to the heavens, where (as three million years of man diminished to one stunning second) the bone dissolved to a bone-shaped spaceship in 2001 anno domini. Oh, that sublime second—to incorporate everything from the cavemen's clubs to *Columbia,* though to credit the last thirty thousand centuries to our insatiate appetite for a more efficient machine (instead of to just having fun, say: Huizinga's opinion) is actually counterfeit history. To begin with, there were no cavemen's clubs (well: we haven't discovered a club or a club-drawing anywhere) in their innocent epoch, and in ancient times—well, let's start in Egypt, please.

So: it was without machines, *without wheels,* that the Egyptians got the two and one half million stones to that resonant pyramid at Giza. No, Virginia, the nice people in Orion didn't send the ancient astronauts with the anti-gravity gadget that is proposed on *In Search of Ancient Astronauts.* Sure, I heard on that documentary that if the Egyptians had "the extraordinary rate" of ten stones every day, the pharaoh wouldn't have a pyramid until he had been embalmed for six hundred years—well, I heard it and ran outside to the neighboring home of the executive producer of *In Search of Ancient Astronauts.* So help me God, I seized that man and I shouted, "Listen to me! It says in Herodotus it took a hundred thousand men to move those stones! It took eight men on every stone, so one hundred thousand divided by eight is 12,500 crews! And their goddam names are in red ocher ink in the goddam pyramid! The North Crew! The South Crew! The Vigorous Crew," I shouted at that thunderstruck executive producer. "And *furthermore,* to move those stones was a ten-day trip, so 12,500 crews divided by ten is 1,250 stones every day or 10,000 stones every week or 500,000 stones every year or all 2,500,000 stones in only five years, *and,*" I shouted, and I have witnesses, dammit, "it says in Herodotus it took twenty years to build the Great Pyramid. The only mystery, motherfucker, is why it took so goddam long!"

"Don't blame me, I'm just the executive producer," the man replied.

So much for Egypt, as, in historical order, we go to the steam machines of Greece: the *(chirp)* the twittering birds and the Tritons blowing on wreathed horns. Or lift up the apple called kappa: it connected (according to Hero) to the stopper delta, and the angry dragon omega—oh, wonder of wonders—hissed. If they cared, the Greeks had the wherewithal to run railways (the Greeks had a *doll* on some wooden wheels on some wooden rails) but had preferred to endure inefficiency than to permit a "monstrosity" in: Walter. Archytas, who invented the screw, the pulley, and (incidentally) the baby rattle, was reprimanded by Plato for having disgraced geometry

by obliging her to use matter, which is the object of servile trades,

and Archimedes, who catapulted a 1,250-pound stone or a 10-pound stone (the ancient authorities vary) at the ships of Rome and who shook out the sailors like salt—Archimedes, the hero, perhaps, of a new documentary on the *Son of the Ancient Astronauts*, was abashed to have dragged geometry down to the sea level, and in his thirteen books he didn't write of his crass machines but of spirals, spheroids, and such unessential riddles as the one whose answer is 846,192,410,280 white cows and 574,579,-625,058 black cows.

And time marched on: in Rome, there were a few machines but Vespasian employed the unemployed, instead, to transport stones up the Capitoline Hill. And then, for a thousand years there were no new machines but the windmills, which, even so, were often outlawed on the principle that the wind didn't belong to someone's serf. In the middle ages, a saint insisted the word *machine* comes from the Latin *maechor:* to commit adultery,

for man's mind is, as it were, adulterated, since it is created for spiritual things and not for material things,

and men not machines (and not even pious ancient astronauts) took the whole thirteenth century for the cathedrals of Rouen and Reims. Nor did this arrant inefficiency deface any of Europe—no, a *stool* of the fifteenth century is still twenty thousand dollars at

Parke-Bernet. Fine wines came out of France without the spectrometers, spectroscopes, and chromatographs of the one hundred chemists at Gallo, and fine violins out of Italy without the oscilloscopes (to contemplate maple at 440 hertz) at Suzuki Violins.

Or did they? Or did Italy's violins owe to the implements of Orion's ancient astronauts? Stradivarius, after all, was half illiterate: he wrote *li bacio le mane* instead of *le bacio le mani* and he once wrote that he had sent violin, omitting the *the*. At ninety, his fingers did an incessant tremolo while he wrote on a violin label, in Italian, "I am ninety years o—" *accidente*, his quill slipped, he got another label, he pasted it onto label number one and he wrote, "I am ninety years old!" Now honestly, can we believe that a violin built by this dotard at ninety years old is still being played by Yehudi Menuhin? No—Stradivarius, we will hear on some documentary, undoubtedly, looked up one afternoon to discover a steel-suited crew of ancient astronauts with a sort of Point Four Plan.

"*Buon giorno, Signor Stradivari.*"

"*Buon giorno, signori! Chi siete?*"

"*Siamo antichi astronauti. Vogliamo assistervi, signor.*"

"*Prego.*"

"*Ecco, abbiamo un oscilloscopio—*"

My God! We are such devotees of that inorganic thing, the *machine*, that we cannot conceive of people without it. Without it, we insist that the ancients were the same utter incompetents that we conceive that we ourselves would be, and picturing pointed ears on our engineers we insert them in yesteryear, anachronistically. Oh, ye of little faith in this species, listen to me! *Ga gaga grkk*, Orion language for bug off, for not till the seventeenth century did the engineers (from the planet earth) begin to assure us that anything we could do, they—their machines—could do better, introducing a plowing machine, a weaving machine, an adding machine, and, I'm not fooling, an automobile: a steam-driven miniature at the time of King Louis. "No, thank you," our answer was—in England the king outlawed the ribbon and lace machines, in Danzig the *rada* hanged a man (a public menace, the *rada* declared) who had invented a ribbon machine, and, at last, when the lace machine came to England, the Luddites sang,

> And night by night when all is still
> And the moon is hid behind the hill,
> We forward march to do our will
> With hatchet, pike, and gun,

and wielded them on the cursed machines, unquote, at Cart-wright's Mill. "They imagined," Byron declared, "that the industrious poor were of greater consequence than the improvement in the implements of trade," addressing a quite unreceptive audience: the House of Lords.

And what about now? In the twentieth century, should we use a prohibitionist's hatchet on analyzers, batteries, capacitors, detectors, electrodes (or let alone, wheels) as Vonnegut does in *Player Piano?* "My answer is: I wouldn't weep," said Candhi, but I'm not against machines if we aren't reduced to one of their worm-wheels: if we aren't their slaves, said Ellis, if we aren't their servants, said Galbraith, if we aren't their tools, said Thoreau, "Lo, men have become the tools of their tools," if we aren't emasculated, said D. H. Lawrence: if we aren't milled to fit to their narrow tolerances. If they aren't our Gods,

> We have Gods, for our strong nerve
> Falters before [what] we own.
> Which shall be master? Which shall serve?
> Which wears the fetters? Which the crown?

said Henry Adams.

The test is simple: will a machine defer to our own inherent efficiency? For instance: I'm not against mousetraps and I've even beaten a path to Pennsylvania, to the manufacturer of the mouse-traps with the little metal plates for the Swiss cheese. Now, these aren't irreproachable: the staples come out, the customers say: Indiana, "Ooh," Pennsylvania, "Ouch," Delaware, "Damn," Ohio, "Now, I know how the mouse feels." To make a better mouse's mickey, the manufacturer is considering acrilonitride butadine styrene (the stuff of the Steelers helmets) instead of ponderosa pine: fine, but I must insist that he quit at 99-hundredths efficiency in deference to our own inalienable rights. See, there can't be a perfect mousetrap as long as you, dear reader, or I are alive on the planet earth, or we might steal the Swiss cheese.

"Or we might pilfer," I wrote,
but I erased it and wrote, instead, on my yellow pad, my one
hundredth yellow pad, "Or we might steal the Swiss cheese." By
now, I felt I had heated the sulfur-colored pads to their ignition
point: *poof*, to the final incineration of the men who mistrusted
my own organic efficiency: of Dr. Loizeaux and Dr. Holt, of Miss
Rofinot and Miss Crockett, of Sergeant McHugh and Sergeant
Scott, of the meddlesome presidents of the United States. Their
ashes, black as my pencil points, rested in peace (or torment,
perhaps) in my dark desk drawer, no longer lugging me round and
round like a ring-nosed pig. So why, *why*, did I feel I was still
enslaved to the same great dictator, please, of those troubled
years? For still, I felt wrapped in a binder twine and I couldn't end
my story without confronting it.

I sat, cerebrating, my sand-colored pad (as barren as the Sa-
hara) on my sagging lap. In school, I had sometimes thought,
Well, why should there be a Universe? Why shouldn't there be
nothing, instead, and why should there even be Space? A puzzle,
because (it was half apparent to me) to eliminate everything was
to eliminate me and my Jesuitical question, too. Frankly, I'd been
stumped: as empty-headed as I was now, writing, erasing, *whoo*,
on my pad, searching for my real slave driver, till it just burst
upon me: I was enslaved (as, *my God*, my tortured father was)
by my yellow pad and my bone-black scratches. My little *abc*'s
were encephalograms of my twitching intellect, preserved like the
nature director's specimens: like the little black bats in their yellow formaldehyde, and I too was an intellect-beaten beast. The
mind-forged manacles (said Blake) actually are a man's most absolute authorities, and not the Loizeauxs and Louis XIVs. Said
Goldsmith,

> How small of all that hearts endure
> That part which kings can cause or cure,

and how *inefficient* to try to escape from the Louises and not
escape from the may, might, musts, and the could, would, shoulds

—the crumbs, according to Cummings, in our own gingerbread heads.

Our intellects. Our cookie cans in

> *which the six subjunctive crumbs*
> *twitch like mutilated thumbs;*

he wrote in a poem about someone whose name was Effie: Efficiency? Our pots of potato soup in which the moldered croutons are the old commands of doctors, teachers, sergeants, of Mommy, of Daddy, and our urns with the orange ashes (orange, as they still smolder) of millions of Simon Legrees. For worse than a southern slave, to Thoreau, is the man who's enslaved to himself: a man like myself, writing, erasing, *whoo*, to document to my own autocratic intellect that it could abdicate and I wouldn't decompose to a sort of blackstrap molasses. The man who most mistrusted my inner efficiency was me, and I was staining my yellow pads to convert myself to a bird or a bee, comparatively,

> *Reasoning [as] he treads,*
> *Man yet mistakes his way,*
> *Whilst things whom instinct leads*
> *Are rarely known to stray,*

from *The Doves*, by Cowper, and I was quoting, quoting, to convince myself of those whispered words of wisdom: let it be. My irresistible impulse as I sat writing my left-to-right-listing letters was to get myself to stop writing them and to silence the may, might, musts in my little cookie can. It was judo: to exert my invincible intellect to depose my invincible intellect: my sleepless sergeant, spitting at me, "Ta ya left! Ta ya left! Ta ya left, right, left!"

I had come close. By now, I knew in that canister what I'd known in those chromosomes under the immemorial moon in June, when according to Traherne

> *I on the earth did reign,*
> *Within, without me all was pure—*
> *I must become a child again,*

or better, an embryo, like the men of the pre-seventeenth centuries. I knew that my blessed efficiency—or yours, devoted reader—isn't the doing of any high-hatted authority, within or without ourselves, but is as inherent as, *pitter, patter,* our heartbeats or the instincts that tell us infallibly to eat, eliminate, sleep. It's really the One Best Way, and I knew that to trust in this without *thinking* is to escape (by the only outlet: ourselves) from the "efficiency" that is our one imperative. But me, I preached this but I didn't practice it. I still didn't rip my ineffectual pad to yellow confetti to toss to the clouds, soaring like so many swallowtails in the glorious sun—no, I still didn't listen to Wordsworth, "Up, up, my friend, and quit your books!" A bitter-ender, I was and I'm still indoors and I'm still recording my brain waves, debating (with the aid of my *Webster's*) whether to tell myself to discontinue, desist, or, Jesus, stop it. *Jesus,* I'm thinking. *Stop it! Stop it!*

In fact—